CrewAI

The Developer's Guide to Multi-Agent Systems and Advanced AI Workflows

©
***Written by
Camila Jones***

CrewAI
The Developer's Guide to Multi-Agent Systems and Advanced AI Workflows

© 2024 Camila Jones
All rights reserved.

No part of this publication may be reproduced, distributed, or transmitted in any form or by any means, including photocopying, recording, or other electronic or mechanical methods, without the prior written permission of the publisher, except in the case of brief quotations embodied in critical reviews and certain other noncommercial uses permitted by copyright law.

Disclaimer:
The information in this book is provided "as is" without any warranties or guarantees, express or implied. While every effort has been made to ensure the accuracy of the information provided, neither the author nor the publisher will be held responsible for any errors or omissions or for any damages arising from the use of the information in this book.

Acknowledgments:
I would like to thank all those who contributed to the creation of this book.

Table of Contents

Preface   5
Chapter 1: Introduction   8
    1.1 What is CrewAI?   8
    1.2 Why Multi-Agent Systems?   12
    1.3 The Role of CrewAI in Advanced AI Workflows   16
    1.4 Key Benefits of Multi-Agent Systems   21
    1.5 Overview of the Book   25
Chapter 2: Setting Up Your Development Environment   30
    2.1 Required Tools and Technologies   30
       34
    2.2 Installing and Configuring CrewAI   34
    2.3 Environment Setup Validation   41
    2.4 Troubleshooting Common Issues   48
Chapter 3: What Are Agents in Multi-Agent Systems?   55
    3.1 Defining Agents and Their Characteristics   55
    3.2 Core Principles of Multi-Agent Design   59
    3.3 Applications of Multi-Agent Systems in Real Life   64
    3.4 Concept-to-Code: Creating a Simple Agent   67
Chapter 4: CrewAI Architecture   74
    4.1 Overview of CrewAI's Modular Design   74
    4.2 Communication Protocols in CrewAI   78
    4.3 Orchestration and Decision-Making in Multi-Agent Systems   84
    4.4 Concept-to-Code: Building Agent Communication Pipelines   91
Chapter 5: Designing and Building Agents   97
    5.1 Structuring Agent Behavior   97
    5.2 Creating Specialized Agents for Specific Tasks   104
    5.3 Agent-to-Agent Communication: Protocols and Patterns   110
    5.4 Handling Errors and Failures in Agent Interactions   116
    5.5 Concept-to-Code: Building a Functional Agent System   122
Chapter 6: Collaboration and Coordination   129
    6.1 Strategies for Agent Collaboration   129
    6.2 Centralized vs. Decentralized Coordination   135

    6.3 Conflict Resolution and Consensus Mechanisms   141
    6.4 Algorithms for Distributed Decision-Making   147
    6.5 Concept-to-Code: Collaborative Task Allocation   152
Chapter 7: Building Advanced AI Workflows with CrewAI   158
    7.2 Leveraging Machine Learning in Multi-Agent Workflows   163
    7.3 Real-Time Communication and Data Sharing in Workflows   168
    7.4 Project: Multi-Agent Workflow for a Logistics System   173
Chapter 8: Scaling Multi-Agent Systems   179
    8.1 Challenges in Scaling Multi-Agent Systems   179
    8.2 Distributed Deployment Strategies   184
    8.3 Load Balancing and Dynamic Agent Allocation   191
    8.4 Optimizing Performance and Resource Utilization   197
    8.5 Concept-to-Code: Scaling a Fleet of Agents   203
Chapter 9: Debugging and Monitoring Multi-Agent Systems 209
    9.1 Tools and Techniques for Debugging CrewAI Applications   209
    9.2 Setting Up Real-Time Monitoring and Logging   216
    9.3 Ensuring System Stability and Reliability   222
    9.4 Example: Debugging a Faulty Agent Interaction   229
Chapter 10: Security and Ethical Considerations   236
    10.1 Security Challenges in Multi-Agent Systems   236
    10.2 Securing Communication Between Agents   242
    10.3 Designing Resilient Systems to Handle Attacks   249
    10.4 Ethical Design of Agent Behaviors   254
    10.5 Mitigating Risks of Unintended Outcomes   260
Chapter 11: Integrating Machine Learning with CrewAI   267
    11.1 Using Machine Learning for Agent Optimization   267
    11.2 Reinforcement Learning in Multi-Agent Systems   275
    11.3 Combining CrewAI with Pretrained Models   282
    11.4 Project: Reinforcement Learning in Multi-Agent Environments
    291
Chapter 12: Real-World Applications and Case Studies   300
    12.1 Automation and Robotics   300
    12.2 Distributed Problem Solving   307
    12.3 AI-Powered Marketplaces and Trading Systems   315
    12.4 Collaborative Research and Innovation Systems   325
    12.5 Case Study: CrewAI in Smart City Management   333

Chapter 13. Advanced Topics 340
13.1 Multi-Agent Systems in Cloud and Edge Environments 340
13.2 Integrating IoT with CrewAI for Smart Systems 349
13.3 AI + Multi-Agent Systems Synergies 357
13.4 Concept-to-Code: Emerging Research in Multi-Agent Systems 365

Chapter 14: Hands-On Projects 375
14.1 Project 1: Building a Collaborative AI Fleet 375
14.2 Project 2: Workflow Automation for a Customer Support System 376
14.3 Project 3: Real-Time Task Allocation in Logistics 378
14.4 Project 4: Simulating Competitive and Cooperative Agent Behaviors 380
14.5 Project 5: Integrating AI Agents with External APIs 382

Chapter 15: Developer Challenges 384
15.1 Beginner Challenges 384
15.2 Intermediate Challenges 386
15.3 Advanced Challenges 387
15.4 Real-World Problem-Solving Scenarios 388
15.5 Solutions and Explanations 389

Conclusion 401
Summary of Key Learnings 401
16.2 Future of CrewAI and Multi-Agent Systems 405
16.3 Resources for Further Learning 411

Preface

Imagine a fleet of autonomous delivery drones collaborating seamlessly to deliver packages across a bustling city, adapting to traffic, weather, and obstacles in real time. Picture a smart city where traffic lights adjust dynamically to ease congestion, powered by intelligent agents that communicate and make decisions faster than any human could. Envision a disaster response system where robotic agents coordinate to locate survivors, deliver medical supplies, and reroute resources in the aftermath of a calamity. These are not distant dreams—they are real-world applications made possible by multi-agent systems (MAS), and at the heart of this revolution lies CrewAI.

This book, CrewAI: The Developer's Guide to Multi-Agent Systems and Advanced AI Workflows, is your gateway to understanding, building, and mastering MAS. Whether you're a developer taking your first steps into this fascinating field or an experienced engineer looking to explore advanced applications, this guide is designed for you.

Why Multi-Agent Systems?
Traditional AI systems excel at handling isolated tasks, but what happens when the problems are too large, too dynamic, or too complex for a single system? This is where multi-agent systems shine. With their ability to operate autonomously, communicate effectively, and collaborate intelligently, MAS are transforming industries:
- E-commerce: Agents optimize supply chains and recommend products in real-time.
- Healthcare: Intelligent systems monitor patients, coordinate resources, and provide life-saving insights.
- Smart Cities: Distributed systems manage energy, water, and traffic, creating sustainable urban ecosystems.

However, the challenges of designing these systems—ensuring coordination, avoiding conflicts, and optimizing performance—

require a specialized skill set. This book equips you with the tools, techniques, and frameworks to meet these challenges head-on.

What You Will Discover
The journey begins with a deep dive into the fundamentals: what agents are, how they work, and why they matter. We'll explore the CrewAI framework, a powerful tool designed to simplify the development of multi-agent systems, and guide you through setting up your environment with clear, step-by-step instructions. From there, we venture into the practical world of agent design and coordination. How do agents communicate effectively? How can they resolve conflicts and reach consensus? You'll learn these concepts and more, illustrated through real-world scenarios like autonomous fleets and logistics optimization.

Hands-On Learning and Real-World Stories
This book doesn't just teach you concepts—it brings them to life. Each chapter is packed with hands-on projects and examples inspired by real-world challenges:
- Collaborative AI Fleets: Build a system where drones work together to deliver packages efficiently.
- Smart Customer Support: Automate workflows with agents that respond to queries, escalate issues, and follow up with customers.
- Disaster Management: Simulate multi-agent coordination in life-and-death scenarios, from locating survivors to allocating resources.

These examples aren't just theoretical—they're actionable blueprints you can adapt and implement in your projects.

Beyond the Basics
As you progress, we delve into advanced topics that push the boundaries of what MAS can achieve. Learn how to integrate machine learning with CrewAI, using reinforcement learning to train agents that adapt and improve over time. Explore the

possibilities of combining MAS with IoT for smart systems or blockchain for secure, decentralized interactions.

We also address critical topics like security and ethics, ensuring the systems you build are not only efficient but also safe, fair, and transparent. With CrewAI, you'll not only create functional MAS but also systems that users trust and depend on.

Why This Book?
In a world where AI is reshaping industries at an unprecedented pace, developers have the unique opportunity to lead this transformation. This book is written for developers, by developers, with a clear focus on practical applications and actionable insights. Our goal is to empower you to not only understand MAS but to build systems that solve real problems and create meaningful impact.

By the end of this journey, you'll have the knowledge and skills to design multi-agent systems for any domain, from logistics and robotics to smart cities and beyond. More importantly, you'll be equipped to innovate, experiment, and shape the future of this exciting field.

Are You Ready to Build the Future?
If you've ever wondered how autonomous systems collaborate, how distributed decision-making works, or how AI can tackle complex, dynamic challenges, this book is for you. CrewAI: The Developer's Guide to Multi-Agent Systems and Advanced AI Workflows is more than a guide—it's a call to action. Together, let's explore the possibilities of multi-agent systems and build the intelligent, collaborative systems of tomorrow.

Let's get started!
Y

Chapter 1: Introduction

1.1 What is CrewAI?

CrewAI is a cutting-edge framework designed to enable the development, deployment, and management of multi-agent systems. Multi-agent systems consist of multiple autonomous entities, called agents, that work collaboratively to solve problems or achieve goals that would be difficult or impossible for a single agent or traditional systems to accomplish. CrewAI provides a structured and modular environment for developers to build such systems efficiently, making it an essential tool for advancing artificial intelligence workflows.

Multi-agent systems are increasingly important in industries such as logistics, robotics, automation, and decision-making processes where distributed intelligence is needed. CrewAI simplifies the challenges associated with designing, orchestrating, and scaling these systems by providing ready-to-use tools, frameworks, and protocols. Let's delve deeper into the framework's essence, features, and capabilities.

CrewAI is best described as a specialized toolkit for creating multi-agent systems that emphasize collaboration, scalability, and efficiency. The framework abstracts much of the complexity of multi-agent communication and coordination, enabling developers to focus on building intelligent agents rather than wrestling with low-level details.

Here are the key characteristics that define CrewAI:
1. Agent-Centric Architecture:
    - CrewAI revolves around the concept of "agents." Each agent is a modular, autonomous unit capable of perceiving its environment, making decisions, and executing tasks.
    - These agents can act independently or as part of a team to achieve shared objectives.

2. Decentralized Collaboration:
    - CrewAI supports decentralized systems where agents communicate and collaborate directly, reducing reliance on a central controller.
    - This makes the system more fault-tolerant and scalable, especially in distributed environments.
3. Inter-Agent Communication:
    - The framework includes robust communication protocols, allowing agents to share information, negotiate, and coordinate tasks seamlessly.
    - Developers can choose between peer-to-peer, message-passing, or client-server models, depending on their application needs.
4. Built for Complex Problem-Solving:
    - CrewAI is ideal for environments that require distributed intelligence, such as supply chain optimization, swarm robotics, or collaborative machine learning.
    - The framework ensures agents can work both competitively and cooperatively, depending on the task requirements.
5. Focus on Modularity:
    - CrewAI is designed with modularity in mind, allowing developers to easily add or remove agents and functionalities without disrupting the entire system.
    - This modularity accelerates development and simplifies troubleshooting.

CrewAI's features and capabilities make it a standout choice for developing multi-agent systems. These functionalities are designed to simplify development while ensuring systems are powerful, scalable, and adaptable.

1. Agent Lifecycle Management:
    - CrewAI handles the entire lifecycle of agents, from creation and initialization to termination.

- Developers can define unique roles, tasks, and goals for each agent, which the framework executes effectively.
2. Robust Communication Protocols:
    - Communication is the backbone of any multi-agent system, and CrewAI excels in this domain.
    - It supports:
        - Synchronous and Asynchronous Communication: Ensuring flexibility in agent interactions.
        - Secure Channels: Protecting data exchanged between agents.
        - Scalable Protocols: Supporting systems with thousands of agents.
3. Task Allocation and Scheduling:
    - CrewAI includes built-in algorithms for assigning tasks to agents based on their capabilities, availability, and current workload.
    - Examples include:
        - Task prioritization based on deadlines.
        - Dynamic reassignment of tasks if an agent fails or becomes unavailable.
4. Decision-Making Frameworks:
    - Agents in CrewAI are equipped with decision-making frameworks that allow them to operate autonomously.
    - The framework supports:
        - Rule-Based Systems: For deterministic decision-making.
        - Learning-Based Systems: Using reinforcement learning or pre-trained models to adapt over time.
5. Scalability and Performance Optimization:
    - CrewAI is built to handle large-scale deployments, ensuring that systems can operate efficiently even when scaled to hundreds or thousands of agents.

- Features like load balancing and dynamic resource allocation help maintain performance under heavy workloads.
6. Plug-and-Play Integration:
    - CrewAI can be integrated with existing AI and data processing frameworks, such as TensorFlow, PyTorch, and various APIs.
    - This makes it versatile for developers looking to enhance their systems with machine learning or external data sources.
7. Debugging and Monitoring Tools:
    - The framework includes tools for real-time monitoring of agent performance, communication, and decision-making.
    - These tools help developers identify bottlenecks or errors quickly, ensuring smooth operation.
8. Support for Real-World Applications:
    - CrewAI is designed to handle diverse real-world scenarios, including:
        - Logistics and supply chain management.
        - Swarm robotics for search and rescue operations.
        - Distributed financial systems for market analysis and trading.
9. Extensibility and Customization:
    - Developers can extend CrewAI's functionality by writing custom modules, creating specialized agents, or integrating domain-specific logic.
    - The open architecture allows for rapid adaptation to unique project requirements.
10. Fault Tolerance and Resilience:
    - CrewAI includes mechanisms to ensure that agent failures or communication breakdowns do not compromise the entire system.
    - Features like agent replacement, retry mechanisms, and fallback plans ensure robust operation.

Why CrewAI Matters
In today's fast-evolving world of artificial intelligence, multi-agent systems are solving increasingly complex problems. CrewAI provides a bridge for developers, empowering them to create systems where agents work together harmoniously and effectively. Its capabilities make it suitable for applications across industries, from automating repetitive tasks to designing systems capable of sophisticated decision-making.

CrewAI is not just a framework; it is a complete ecosystem for building intelligent, scalable, and adaptable systems. Its modularity, communication protocols, and scalability position it as a leader in the field of multi-agent systems, making it an invaluable tool for developers aiming to build the future of AI collaboration.

1.2 Why Multi-Agent Systems?

Multi-agent systems (MAS) are a modern approach to solving complex problems that exceed the capabilities of traditional AI systems. Unlike monolithic AI systems, which rely on a single entity to perform all tasks, multi-agent systems consist of multiple autonomous entities (agents) that work together to achieve shared goals. This collaborative approach overcomes many challenges inherent in traditional AI while offering unique benefits like decentralized decision-making and scalability.

This section explores the challenges of traditional AI systems and highlights the advantages of decentralized decision-making, shedding light on why multi-agent systems have become a critical tool in advanced AI workflows.

Traditional AI systems often operate as monolithic structures where a single centralized program or model handles all computations and decision-making. While this approach works well for straightforward tasks, it becomes problematic when

dealing with complex, dynamic, or large-scale problems. Below are the key challenges faced by traditional AI systems:
1. Limited Scalability
    - Traditional AI systems struggle to scale efficiently when faced with large, distributed datasets or operations.
    - Example: A centralized AI system managing a city's traffic control may become a bottleneck as the number of vehicles and intersections increases.
2. Single Point of Failure
    - In centralized systems, all processes depend on a single entity. If this central system fails, the entire operation collapses.
    - Example: If a centralized AI controller for warehouse robots crashes, the entire logistics process is disrupted.
3. Computational Bottlenecks
    - Monolithic systems often require immense computational power to process data and make decisions, leading to delays and inefficiencies.
    - Example: Centralized AI processing for a large e-commerce platform may take longer to analyze real-time customer data, affecting user experience.
4. Inflexibility in Dynamic Environments
    - Centralized AI systems are often rigid and struggle to adapt to rapidly changing environments.
    - Example: A single-agent AI system controlling a drone fleet may fail to respond quickly to unexpected weather changes or obstacles.
5. Lack of Collaboration
    - Traditional AI systems are typically designed for isolated tasks and lack the ability to collaborate with other systems.
    - Example: A warehouse robot with a centralized controller cannot easily coordinate with robots from

other manufacturers without extensive customization.
6. High Maintenance Costs
    - Managing and upgrading monolithic systems often requires significant resources and downtime, as changes must be implemented across the entire system.
    - Example: Updating a centralized AI system for a manufacturing plant may require halting operations, leading to lost productivity.
7. Inability to Handle Complex, Distributed Problems
    - Centralized AI systems are ill-suited for problems requiring distributed intelligence or localized decision-making.
    - Example: In a disaster relief operation, a single AI system cannot effectively coordinate multiple drones, vehicles, and rescue teams in real time.

Multi-agent systems solve many of the challenges associated with traditional AI by leveraging decentralized decision-making. In MAS, individual agents are capable of making independent decisions based on local information, while collaborating with other agents to achieve a global objective. This decentralized approach offers numerous benefits:

1. Improved Scalability
    - Decentralized systems can easily scale by adding more agents without overwhelming the overall system.
    - Example: Adding more delivery drones to a logistics network doesn't require reconfiguring the entire system; each drone operates autonomously.
2. Robustness and Fault Tolerance
    - Decentralized systems eliminate single points of failure, ensuring that the failure of one agent doesn't disrupt the entire system.

- Example: If one autonomous car in a multi-agent traffic system malfunctions, the remaining cars continue to function without interruption.
3. Enhanced Efficiency
    - Agents in decentralized systems make decisions locally, reducing communication overhead and processing delays.
    - Example: In a smart energy grid, each household appliance can decide when to consume power based on real-time data, optimizing energy usage.
4. Flexibility in Dynamic Environments
    - Decentralized systems adapt quickly to changes in the environment, as agents can independently update their behavior.
    - Example: In a search-and-rescue operation, drones can independently adjust their search patterns based on new information about the disaster area.
5. Collaboration and Synergy
    - Agents in MAS can share information and coordinate actions, leading to more effective problem-solving.
    - Example: In a multi-robot warehouse, robots collaborate to efficiently pick, pack, and deliver items, avoiding collisions and delays.
6. Distributed Problem-Solving
    - MAS distribute computational and decision-making tasks among agents, enabling the system to tackle large-scale, complex problems.
    - Example: A fleet of autonomous vehicles can collectively optimize routes to reduce traffic congestion across a city.
7. Lower Maintenance Costs
    - Decentralized systems are modular and easier to update or maintain without disrupting the entire system.
    - Example: Updating software on one robot in a factory doesn't affect the operations of other robots.

8. Parallel Processing
    - Each agent processes its tasks independently, enabling parallel execution and faster overall performance.
    - Example: In financial trading, multiple agents can simultaneously monitor different markets and execute trades, responding faster to opportunities.
9. Greater Resilience in Distributed Systems
    - Decentralized decision-making ensures that localized problems don't escalate to system-wide failures.
    - Example: In a sensor network monitoring an agricultural field, if one sensor fails, others continue to gather and transmit data.
10. Support for Diverse Applications
    - The flexibility and scalability of MAS make them suitable for a wide range of applications, from robotics and logistics to healthcare and smart cities.
    - Example: In healthcare, multiple AI agents can independently monitor different patients while sharing critical updates with a central system.

Summary: Why Multi-Agent Systems?
Multi-agent systems represent a significant leap forward in AI design by addressing the inherent limitations of traditional AI systems. Their decentralized nature ensures scalability, resilience, and adaptability, making them ideal for solving complex, distributed problems. As industries increasingly adopt automation, multi-agent systems powered by frameworks like CrewAI will play a central role in shaping the future of intelligent systems.

1.3 The Role of CrewAI in Advanced AI Workflows

CrewAI is a revolutionary framework that enables developers to build multi-agent systems capable of automating complex workflows, optimizing processes, and facilitating effective

collaboration between autonomous agents. Its modular and scalable architecture allows it to integrate seamlessly into advanced AI workflows, solving challenges that traditional AI systems struggle to address.
This section explores CrewAI's role in automation, optimization, and collaboration, along with real-world examples that demonstrate its practical impact.

CrewAI's strength lies in its ability to streamline processes, enhance decision-making, and enable collaborative intelligence across diverse domains. Below are the key areas where CrewAI excels:

1. Automation
   CrewAI automates repetitive and resource-intensive tasks by delegating them to agents that can operate independently or as part of a team. This reduces human intervention and increases operational efficiency.
   - Example: Workflow Automation
     In an e-commerce warehouse, CrewAI can manage a fleet of robots that pick, pack, and transport goods. Each robot operates autonomously, ensuring smooth operations even during peak demand.
   - Example: Data Processing
     CrewAI agents can process vast amounts of data in parallel, enabling faster insights in fields like finance and healthcare.
2. Optimization
   CrewAI optimizes resource utilization, task allocation, and decision-making processes by employing intelligent algorithms and real-time data analysis.
   - Example: Task Allocation
     In a logistics company, CrewAI assigns delivery tasks to drones based on their battery levels, locations, and payload capacities, minimizing downtime and energy consumption.

- Example: Dynamic Routing
  In a smart city, CrewAI-powered autonomous vehicles optimize traffic flow by dynamically adjusting routes to avoid congestion.
3. Collaboration
   Collaboration is a cornerstone of CrewAI's design. Agents can share information, negotiate solutions, and coordinate actions to achieve shared goals.
   - Example: Multi-Robot Collaboration
     In a manufacturing plant, multiple robots equipped with CrewAI coordinate to assemble complex products, reducing errors and production time.
   - Example: Distributed Research
     Researchers use CrewAI agents to collaboratively analyze datasets from different sources, accelerating the discovery of insights in fields like genomics and climate science.

The versatility and efficiency of CrewAI have enabled its adoption across industries, addressing real-world challenges with innovative solutions. Here are some impactful examples:

1. Supply Chain and Logistics
   - Scenario: A global logistics company needed a solution to handle last-mile deliveries efficiently while reducing costs and carbon emissions.
   - Solution: Using CrewAI, the company deployed a fleet of drones and ground robots that collaboratively deliver packages. The system optimizes routes in real time and reallocates tasks if a robot or drone becomes unavailable.
   - Outcome: The company achieved a 25% reduction in delivery times and a significant decrease in operational costs.
2. Smart Cities
   - Scenario: A city was facing traffic congestion and inefficiencies in public transportation scheduling.

- Solution: CrewAI powered a network of autonomous vehicles and traffic management systems that communicate with each other to balance traffic loads and adjust schedules dynamically.
- Outcome: The city experienced smoother traffic flow, reduced commute times, and a 20% improvement in public transportation efficiency.

3. Healthcare
   - Scenario: A hospital needed an efficient way to manage patient care and medical equipment in high-demand scenarios like emergencies.
   - Solution: CrewAI agents were deployed to monitor patient vitals, allocate medical staff, and ensure that critical equipment was available where needed.
   - Outcome: The hospital reduced response times in emergencies and optimized the use of medical resources, leading to improved patient outcomes.

4. Industrial Automation
   - Scenario: A manufacturing plant wanted to increase production rates without compromising quality.
   - Solution: CrewAI managed a team of robots responsible for different assembly tasks. The agents collaborated to identify bottlenecks and adjust their workflows in real time.
   - Outcome: The plant increased production efficiency by 30% while maintaining strict quality control.

5. Disaster Response
   - Scenario: In a natural disaster, rescue operations often face coordination challenges due to dynamic and unpredictable conditions.
   - Solution: CrewAI powered a team of drones and ground robots to locate survivors, assess damage, and deliver supplies. Agents shared real-time data to ensure comprehensive coverage and minimal redundancy.

- Outcome: Rescuers were able to cover a larger area in less time, improving survival rates and accelerating disaster recovery.
6. Agriculture
    - Scenario: Farmers needed a more efficient way to monitor and manage crops in large fields.
    - Solution: CrewAI agents, integrated with IoT sensors, monitored soil health, weather conditions, and crop growth. Autonomous drones sprayed fertilizers or pesticides only where necessary.
    - Outcome: Farmers reduced resource wastage by 40% and increased crop yields.
7. Financial Markets
    - Scenario: Financial institutions require real-time monitoring and execution of trades across multiple markets.
    - Solution: CrewAI agents analyzed market trends, executed trades, and adjusted strategies dynamically based on incoming data.
    - Outcome: The system increased profitability by identifying opportunities faster than traditional methods.
8. Education and Training
    - Scenario: Virtual learning environments required personalized support for students.
    - Solution: CrewAI agents acted as virtual tutors, adapting to each student's learning pace and providing tailored feedback.
    - Outcome: Student engagement and learning outcomes improved significantly.

Summary: CrewAI's Role in Advanced AI Workflows

CrewAI's ability to automate tasks, optimize operations, and facilitate collaboration has made it a cornerstone for advanced AI workflows across diverse industries. From managing supply chains to enhancing healthcare and education, CrewAI addresses real-world challenges with intelligent, decentralized solutions. Its impact is evident in improved efficiency, reduced costs, and higher adaptability, positioning it as a vital tool for the future of artificial intelligence.

1.4 Key Benefits of Multi-Agent Systems

Multi-agent systems (MAS) offer a transformative approach to problem-solving and decision-making by leveraging the collective capabilities of autonomous agents. These systems are built to address challenges in dynamic, large-scale, and complex environments, providing distinct advantages over traditional centralized systems. Two primary benefits of multi-agent systems include flexibility, scalability, and fault tolerance and improved decision-making through collaboration.

Multi-agent systems are inherently designed to adapt, expand, and function reliably even in the face of failures or unexpected challenges. These traits make MAS suitable for real-world applications across industries.

1. Flexibility
    - Multi-agent systems are highly adaptable, allowing them to operate effectively in dynamic and unpredictable environments.
    - Agents within a system can modify their behaviors or roles in response to changing conditions without requiring system-wide updates.
    - Example: In disaster response, MAS can adjust their search and rescue strategies based on real-time environmental data, such as shifting search areas after a new landslide.
2. Scalability
    - MAS can easily scale up or down by adding or removing agents without disrupting the overall system.

- Unlike traditional centralized systems, where adding more functionality may require significant architectural changes, MAS handle scaling inherently due to their decentralized design.
- Example: In logistics, adding more delivery drones to a fleet managed by MAS improves capacity without needing centralized recalibration.
3. Fault Tolerance
    - The decentralized nature of MAS ensures that the failure of one or more agents does not compromise the entire system.
    - Each agent operates autonomously, so the system can reassign tasks or adjust workflows dynamically when an agent becomes unavailable.
    - Example: In a smart energy grid, if one power station fails, the system redistributes load across other stations, ensuring uninterrupted service.
4. Distributed Workloads
    - Tasks and responsibilities in MAS are divided among agents, reducing the risk of overloading any single entity.
    - Distributed workloads also enable better resource utilization across the system.
    - Example: In a multi-agent farming system, individual drones monitor specific zones of a field, ensuring no single drone is overburdened.
5. Resilience in Complex Environments
    - MAS are robust against external disruptions, such as sudden spikes in workload or environmental changes.
    - They can seamlessly adapt to new conditions without requiring human intervention or system downtime.
    - Example: In financial trading, MAS agents adapt to market fluctuations by dynamically altering strategies in response to real-time data.

Collaboration is a cornerstone of multi-agent systems, enabling agents to share knowledge, coordinate actions, and collectively solve problems more effectively than any single agent could on its own. This collaborative approach leads to better decision-making in complex and distributed environments.

1. Sharing Knowledge and Data
    - Agents in MAS communicate with each other to exchange information and insights, building a shared understanding of the environment or task.
    - This exchange improves the overall accuracy and speed of decision-making.
    - Example: In traffic management, MAS agents (e.g., smart traffic lights) share data about congestion and adjust signal timings to optimize flow across a city.
2. Decentralized Problem-Solving
    - MAS allow decisions to be made locally by individual agents or groups of agents, reducing the dependency on a central controller.
    - Decentralized problem-solving is particularly effective in time-sensitive or large-scale scenarios.
    - Example: In search-and-rescue missions, individual drones can decide which areas to scan while coordinating with others to avoid overlap.
3. Improved Efficiency Through Task Allocation
    - Collaboration enables MAS to allocate tasks efficiently among agents based on their current capabilities, locations, and availability.
    - Example: In a warehouse, MAS assigns robots to pick items closest to their location, reducing transit time and improving throughput.
4. Conflict Resolution and Consensus Building
    - Agents in MAS use algorithms to resolve conflicts and reach consensus when faced with competing objectives.

- Collaborative decision-making ensures that the system operates harmoniously without requiring manual intervention.
- Example: In fleet management, MAS agents negotiate optimal routes for vehicles to avoid congestion or resource conflicts.

5. Parallel Decision-Making
    - Collaboration in MAS enables parallel decision-making, where multiple agents simultaneously evaluate and act on different parts of a problem.
    - This reduces processing time and enhances the system's responsiveness.
    - Example: In a weather monitoring system, MAS agents analyze data from different regions in parallel, providing real-time updates faster than a centralized system could.
6. Adaptive Learning and Improvement
    - Collaborative agents can learn from each other's successes and failures, improving their decision-making capabilities over time.
    - This shared learning is particularly useful in environments where conditions evolve rapidly.
    - Example: In autonomous vehicle systems, MAS agents learn traffic patterns from each other, leading to smoother navigation over time.
7. Synergistic Outcomes
    - By working together, agents in MAS can achieve results that exceed the capabilities of individual agents operating independently.
    - Collaborative synergy enables MAS to tackle challenges that require diverse skills or perspectives.
    - Example: In robotics, a team of collaborative robots assembles complex machinery, with each robot performing a specialized task that complements the others.

Summary: Why Multi-Agent Systems Excel
The flexibility, scalability, and fault tolerance of multi-agent systems make them ideal for dynamic and large-scale applications. Coupled with their ability to improve decision-making through collaboration, MAS provide a robust and efficient framework for tackling complex challenges. From managing traffic in smart cities to optimizing supply chains and enabling disaster response, the benefits of MAS are clear and wide-ranging.

These capabilities position MAS as a cornerstone of modern AI workflows, empowering developers to create systems that are not only intelligent but also resilient, adaptive, and highly effective in real-world scenarios.

1.5 Overview of the Book

This book, CrewAI: The Developer's Guide to Multi-Agent Systems and Advanced AI Workflows, is designed to provide a comprehensive and practical understanding of CrewAI and multi-agent systems. Whether you are a beginner stepping into the world of multi-agent systems or an experienced developer seeking advanced insights, this book will guide you through the theory, implementation, and real-world applications of CrewAI.

In this section, we'll explain how the book is structured and provide tips to help you get the most out of this guide.

The book is organized into logical sections, progressing from foundational concepts to advanced topics. Each chapter builds upon the previous one, ensuring a seamless learning experience. Here's an overview of the structure:

1. Introduction
    - Provides a foundation for understanding multi-agent systems and CrewAI.
    - Explains the challenges of traditional AI systems and how CrewAI addresses them.

- Highlights the benefits of multi-agent systems, setting the stage for the rest of the book.
2. Setting Up Your Development Environment
    - Guides you through installing and configuring CrewAI and the necessary tools.
    - Ensures your environment is correctly set up with troubleshooting steps and validation tips.
3. Core Concepts of Multi-Agent Systems
    - Covers the theory behind agents, their roles, and the principles of designing multi-agent systems.
    - Introduces foundational concepts such as communication, collaboration, and task allocation.
4. Building and Designing Agents
    - Focuses on creating agents with defined behaviors and responsibilities.
    - Explains inter-agent communication protocols and error handling techniques.
    - Includes practical examples and exercises.
5. Collaboration and Decision-Making
    - Explores how agents work together to solve complex problems.
    - Introduces algorithms for conflict resolution and consensus building.
    - Demonstrates real-world scenarios of collaborative systems.
6. Scaling and Optimizing Multi-Agent Systems
    - Explains strategies for scaling multi-agent systems to handle large-scale applications.
    - Covers distributed deployment, load balancing, and performance optimization.
7. Debugging and Monitoring Multi-Agent Systems
    - Provides tools and techniques for debugging and monitoring agent performance.
    - Explains how to identify and resolve system bottlenecks.
8. Security and Ethical Considerations

- Focuses on designing secure systems and mitigating risks.
- Discusses ethical concerns in deploying autonomous systems.
9. Real-World Applications and Projects
    - Showcases real-world use cases of CrewAI, including logistics, healthcare, and smart cities.
    - Provides step-by-step project guides to implement multi-agent systems for practical problems.
10. Advanced Topics
    - Explores cutting-edge areas like reinforcement learning in MAS, IoT integration, and MAS in cloud/edge environments.
    - Prepares readers for emerging trends in multi-agent systems.
11. Hands-On Challenges
    - Offers exercises and projects to test and apply your knowledge.
    - Ranges from beginner to advanced levels, ensuring a wide appeal.
12. Conclusion
    - Summarizes the key takeaways from the book.
    - Provides guidance on next steps for further learning and professional growth.
13. Appendix
    - Includes a glossary of terms, quick references, and recommended resources for extended learning.

To maximize the value of this book, here are some tips tailored for different learning styles and levels of expertise:

1. Follow the Chapters in Sequence
    - The chapters are arranged to build progressively on concepts.
    - Beginners should start from the introduction and work through the book step-by-step, while experienced developers can jump to specific sections of interest.

2. Engage Actively with Examples and Exercises
   - This book emphasizes hands-on learning through code examples and projects.
   - Write and run the code provided in the book, and try modifying it to deepen your understanding.
   - Don't skip the challenges—they are designed to reinforce concepts.
3. Use Visual Aids to Understand Complex Concepts
   - Diagrams, flowcharts, and screenshots are included to clarify complex ideas.
   - Refer to these visuals whenever you feel stuck; they provide a clear picture of how multi-agent systems operate.
4. Experiment Beyond the Book's Content
   - While the book provides structured guidance, experimenting with your own projects will enhance your learning.
   - Use the knowledge gained to build custom multi-agent systems tailored to your specific needs.
5. Leverage the Appendix and Resources
   - The appendix contains a glossary of terms and quick-reference materials.
   - Use the recommended resources for further learning and to stay updated with the latest developments in CrewAI.
6. Troubleshoot Issues Proactively
   - Debugging is an essential skill for working with multi-agent systems.
   - Refer to the debugging and monitoring chapter for tools and techniques to resolve common issues.
7. Connect Theory with Real-World Applications
   - Each chapter includes real-world examples to illustrate the practical applications of CrewAI.
   - Relate these examples to your projects to better understand the relevance of multi-agent systems.
8. Adapt the Content to Your Goals

- If you're learning for a specific application, focus on the sections most relevant to your needs (e.g., scaling and optimization for large systems).
- Developers aiming to specialize in AI can dive deeper into advanced topics and case studies.

9. Ask Questions and Explore Further
   - For concepts that seem unclear, revisit earlier chapters or seek additional resources.
   - Use online forums, research papers, or CrewAI's documentation to deepen your understanding.

10. Stay Current with Emerging Trends
    - Multi-agent systems are rapidly evolving. The advanced topics section introduces emerging trends, but staying updated with the latest research and tools will help you stay ahead.

Summary

This book is designed to be a practical, step-by-step guide to understanding and implementing multi-agent systems using CrewAI. By following the chapters in sequence, engaging with the hands-on exercises, and applying the tips provided, you will gain a solid foundation in CrewAI and multi-agent systems, enabling you to build and deploy intelligent systems with confidence.

Chapter 2: Setting Up Your Development Environment

To begin working with CrewAI and multi-agent systems, it's essential to set up a robust development environment. This chapter will guide you through the tools, technologies, and system requirements needed to ensure a smooth start. Proper setup is crucial for avoiding technical challenges later and maximizing the efficiency of your development process.

2.1 Required Tools and Technologies

CrewAI relies on a combination of programming languages, libraries, and frameworks that work together to enable the development, testing, and deployment of multi-agent systems. This section outlines the core tools and technologies you'll need.

CrewAI is designed to integrate seamlessly with widely used programming languages and AI frameworks, making it accessible to developers from various backgrounds. Below is an overview of the key technologies:

1. Programming Languages
    - Python:
      Python is the primary language used for CrewAI development due to its simplicity, flexibility, and extensive ecosystem of libraries. Its popularity in AI and machine learning makes it an ideal choice.
        - Why Python?
            - Easy to learn and write, even for beginners.
            - Rich libraries for AI and multi-agent systems, such as NumPy, SciPy, and TensorFlow.
            - Strong community support and regular updates.

- Versions Supported: Python 3.7 or later.
    - Optional Languages:
    While Python is the primary language, other languages like Java or C++ can be used for performance-critical components if needed.
        - Java: Suitable for large-scale enterprise applications.
        - C++: Used for optimizing performance in real-time systems like robotics.
2. Libraries
    - Core Libraries for CrewAI Development:
        - NumPy: For numerical computations and data manipulation.
        - Pandas: For handling and analyzing structured data.
        - Matplotlib/Seaborn: For creating visualizations of agent behaviors or system performance.
    - AI and Machine Learning Libraries:
        - TensorFlow/PyTorch: For building intelligent agents that leverage deep learning models.
        - Scikit-learn: For implementing simple machine learning algorithms in agents.
    - Communication Libraries:
        - ZeroMQ: For enabling high-performance message passing between agents.
        - gRPC: For agent-to-agent communication in distributed systems.
    - Agent Simulation Tools:
        - Gym (from OpenAI): For testing and training agents in simulated environments.
3. Frameworks
    - CrewAI Framework:
    The central framework for developing and managing multi-agent systems.

- Includes built-in modules for agent communication, task allocation, and decision-making.
- Provides APIs for integrating with external systems.
    - Flask/Django:
    For building web interfaces or APIs that interact with CrewAI agents.
    - Docker:
    For containerizing your applications to ensure consistency across different development and production environments.
4. Development Tools
    - IDE/Code Editors:
        - PyCharm: Full-featured IDE for Python development.
        - VS Code: Lightweight editor with powerful extensions for Python and AI.
    - Version Control Systems:
        - Git: For managing your project's source code and collaborating with teams.

To run CrewAI efficiently, it's important to have hardware and software that meets the framework's needs. Below are the recommended requirements:

1. Hardware Requirements
    - Processor:
        - Minimum: Intel i5 (4 cores) or equivalent.
        - Recommended: Intel i7 (8 cores) or higher, or AMD Ryzen 7 for faster computation.
    - Memory (RAM):
        - Minimum: 8 GB (suitable for basic agent simulations and small-scale applications).
        - Recommended: 16 GB or more for running complex simulations and training agents.
    - Storage:

- Minimum: 256 GB SSD (Solid-State Drive) for faster read/write operations.
- Recommended: 512 GB SSD or more, especially if you're working with large datasets or machine learning models.
  - Graphics Processing Unit (GPU):
    - Optional but recommended for AI-related tasks.
    - Examples: NVIDIA GTX 1660 (entry-level) or RTX 3060 and above (for deep learning tasks).
2. Software Requirements
   - Operating Systems:
     - Compatible with major platforms, including:
       - Windows 10/11 (64-bit).
       - macOS 10.15 (Catalina) or later.
       - Linux (Ubuntu 20.04 LTS or equivalent preferred for server environments).
   - Python Environment:
     - Install Python 3.7 or higher.
     - Use a virtual environment manager such as virtualenv or conda to isolate dependencies.
   - CrewAI Framework:
     - Install the latest stable version from the official repository or package manager.
   - Dependencies:
     - Use pip (Python Package Installer) or conda to install required libraries.

Example:
bash

```
pip install numpy pandas matplotlib grpcio
```

- Database (Optional for Agent Data Storage):
  - Examples: SQLite (lightweight), PostgreSQL (robust and scalable).

3. Network Requirements
    - Internet Connection:
        - Required for installing dependencies, accessing documentation, and cloud-based simulations.
    - Ports:
        - Ensure necessary ports are open for agent communication, especially when using gRPC or ZeroMQ.
4. Additional Tools
    - Simulation Environment:
        - Install OpenAI Gym or similar platforms for agent training and testing.
    - Containerization:
        - Use Docker for consistent development and deployment environments.
    - Monitoring Tools:
        - Tools like Prometheus or Grafana for tracking agent performance in production.

Summary

Setting up the right development environment is the first step toward successfully working with CrewAI and multi-agent systems. With Python as the core language, essential libraries like NumPy and TensorFlow, and powerful frameworks such as CrewAI and Docker, you'll have a robust setup to develop, test, and deploy intelligent agents.

2.2 Installing and Configuring CrewAI

Installing and configuring CrewAI correctly is essential for building and running multi-agent systems smoothly. This section provides a step-by-step guide to installing CrewAI and explains how to troubleshoot common errors you may encounter during the process.

To set up CrewAI, ensure your system meets the requirements outlined in the previous section. Follow these steps for a successful installation:

Step 1: Install Python
CrewAI requires Python 3.7 or higher. Verify and install Python on your system:
1. Check if Python is installed:
    - Open a terminal (Command Prompt, Terminal, or PowerShell).

Run the command:
bash

```
python --version
```

   - If Python is installed, the version will be displayed (e.g., Python 3.8.10).
2. Install Python if not present:
    - Download the latest version of Python from the official website.
    - During installation, ensure you select the "Add Python to PATH" option.

Verify the installation:
bash

```
python --version
```

Step 2: Set Up a Virtual Environment
Using a virtual environment isolates dependencies and avoids conflicts with other Python projects.
1. Create a virtual environment:

Navigate to your project directory:
bash

```
mkdir crewai_project
cd crewai_project
```

Create the virtual environment:
bash

```
python -m venv venv
```

2. Activate the virtual environment:

On Windows:
bash

```
venv\Scripts\activate
```

On macOS/Linux:
bash

```
source venv/bin/activate
```

3. Verify the virtual environment is active:
    a. You should see (venv) before your command prompt.

Step 3: Install CrewAI
Install CrewAI and its dependencies using pip.
Install CrewAI:
bash

```
pip install crewai
```

Install additional dependencies (if required for your project):
bash

```bash
pip install numpy pandas grpcio matplotlib
```

1. Verify the installation:

Check if CrewAI is installed correctly:

```bash
pip show crewai
```

- This command will display CrewAI's version and other details.

Step 4: Test the Installation

To ensure CrewAI is installed and functional, run a basic test.

1. Create a Python script to test CrewAI:

Save the following code as test_crewai.py:

```python
from crewai import Agent

# Define a simple agent
class HelloAgent(Agent):
    def perform_task(self):
        print("Hello from CrewAI!")

# Instantiate and run the agent
if __name__ == "__main__":
    agent = HelloAgent(name="TestAgent")
    agent.perform_task()
```

Run the script:

```bash
python test_crewai.py
```

2. Expected Output:

If CrewAI is installed correctly, you should see:
csharp

Hello from CrewAI!

Step 5: Configure CrewAI (Optional)
CrewAI's default configuration works for most projects, but you can customize settings for specific use cases.
- Create a configuration file (optional):

Save the following as crewai_config.json:
json

```
{
  "logging": {
    "level": "INFO",
    "file": "crewai_logs.log"
  },
  "communication": {
    "protocol": "grpc",
    "port": 50051
  }
}
```

Load the configuration in your script:
python

```
from crewai import Config

# Load configuration
Config.load("crewai_config.json")
```

- Customize settings as needed:
    - Logging: Define log levels (DEBUG, INFO, ERROR) and output files.

- Communication: Set protocols (grpc, zeromq) and ports for inter-agent communication.

Even with a well-documented process, installation errors can occur. Below are some common issues and how to resolve them.

Issue 1: Python Not Recognized
Error Message:
kotlin
'python' is not recognized as an internal or external command.

Solution:
- Ensure Python is installed and added to your system's PATH.
- Reinstall Python and select the "Add Python to PATH" option during installation.

Verify with:
bash

python --version

Issue 2: Virtual Environment **Activation Fails**
Error Message:
csharp
venv\Scripts\activate is not recognized.

Solution:
- On Windows, ensure you're running the terminal as an administrator.

On macOS/Linux, check execution permissions:
bash

chmod +x venv/bin/activate

Issue 3: CrewAI Installation Fails
Error Message:
arduino
ERROR: Could not find a version that satisfies the requirement crewai

Solution:
- Ensure you're using Python 3.7 or higher.

Upgrade pip to the latest version:
bash

pip install --upgrade pip

Issue 4: Missing Dependencies
Error Message:
vbnet
ModuleNotFoundError: No module named 'numpy'

Solution:
Install missing dependencies manually:
bash

pip install numpy

Issue 5: Script Fails to Run
Error Message:
arduino
AttributeError: module 'crewai' has no attribute 'Agent'

Solution:
- Ensure you're running the script inside the virtual environment.

Check if CrewAI is installed:
bash

```
pip show crewai
```

Issue 6: Communication Port Already in Use
Error Message:
vbnet
Error: Port 50051 is already in use.

Solution:
Use a different port in your configuration file:
json

```
{
  "communication": {
    "protocol": "grpc",
    "port": 50052
  }
}
```

Summary
This step-by-step guide ensures you can install and configure CrewAI successfully, preparing you to build and test multi-agent systems. If you encounter any errors, refer to the troubleshooting section for quick solutions.

2.3 Environment Setup Validation

Validating your development environment is a critical step to ensure that everything is configured correctly and ready for use. This section will guide you through the process of testing the setup for functionality and provide sample scripts to confirm that CrewAI and its dependencies are working as expected.

After installing and configuring CrewAI, it is essential to verify that:
1. Python is installed and accessible.
2. The virtual environment is active.
3. All dependencies are correctly installed.
4. CrewAI is functional and able to execute basic operations.

Step 1: Verify Python Installation
1. Open a terminal (Command Prompt, Terminal, or PowerShell).

Check the Python version:
bash

```
python --version
```

- The output should display Python 3.7 or later (e.g., Python 3.9.5).

Step 2: Confirm Virtual Environment Activation
1. Activate your virtual environment:

On Windows:
bash

```
venv\Scripts\activate
```

On macOS/Linux:
bash

```
source venv/bin/activate
```

2. Ensure the virtual environment is active:
   - The terminal prompt should include (venv).

Step 3: Check Installed Packages
List the installed packages:
bash

```
pip list
```

1. Confirm that CrewAI and its dependencies (e.g., numpy, pandas, grpcio) are listed.

Step 4: Test CrewAI Installation
Run a simple test to ensure that CrewAI is installed and functional. This involves creating a basic agent and running a script to confirm it executes without errors.

Below are sample scripts to validate different aspects of your CrewAI setup.

Validation Script 1: Basic Agent Test
This script tests whether CrewAI can define and execute a basic agent.
Code:
python
```python
from crewai import Agent

# Define a simple agent
class BasicAgent(Agent):
    def perform_task(self):
        print(f"Hello, I am {self.name}. I'm ready to work!")

# Instantiate and run the agent
if __name__ == "__main__":
    agent = BasicAgent(name="TestAgent")
    agent.perform_task()
```

Steps to Test:
1. Save the script as test_basic_agent.py.

Run the script:
bash

```
python test_basic_agent.py
```

Expected Output:
css

Hello, I am TestAgent. I'm ready to work!

What This Validates:
- CrewAI is correctly installed.
- Basic agent creation and execution are functional.

Validation Script 2: Inter-Agent Communication Test
This script tests whether CrewAI supports communication between agents.
Code:
python
```python
from crewai import Agent

# Define two agents
class SenderAgent(Agent):
    def perform_task(self):
        message = {"greeting": "Hello, Receiver!"}
        self.send_message("Receiver", message)

class ReceiverAgent(Agent):
    def on_message(self, sender, message):
        print(f"Received message from {sender}: {message['greeting']}")

# Instantiate and run the agents
if __name__ == "__main__":
    sender = SenderAgent(name="Sender")
    receiver = ReceiverAgent(name="Receiver")

    # Simulate sending and receiving a message
```

```
    sender.send_message = receiver.on_message  # Mock communication
    sender.perform_task()
```

Steps to Test:
1. Save the script as test_communication.py.

Run the script:
bash

```
python test_communication.py
```

Expected Output:
csharp

```
Received message from Sender: Hello, Receiver!
```

What This Validates:
- Agents can communicate with each other.
- Message handling is functional.

Validation Script 3: Task Allocation Test
This script tests whether CrewAI can allocate tasks among multiple agents.
Code:
python

```python
from crewai import Agent

# Define a manager agent
class ManagerAgent(Agent):
    def allocate_tasks(self, agents, tasks):
        for agent, task in zip(agents, tasks):
            agent.perform_task(task)

# Define a worker agent
class WorkerAgent(Agent):
    def perform_task(self, task):
```

```
    print(f"{self.name} is performing task: {task}")

# Instantiate and allocate tasks
if __name__ == "__main__":
    manager = ManagerAgent(name="Manager")
    worker1 = WorkerAgent(name="Worker1")
    worker2 = WorkerAgent(name="Worker2")

    tasks = ["Assemble parts", "Package items"]
    manager.allocate_tasks([worker1, worker2], tasks)
```

Steps to Test:
1. Save the script as test_task_allocation.py.

Run the script:
bash

```
python test_task_allocation.py
```

Expected Output:
csharp

```
Worker1 is performing task: Assemble parts
Worker2 is performing task: Package items
```

What This Validates:
- Task allocation functionality.
- Interaction between manager and worker agents.

Validation Script 4: Logging and Configuration Test
This script tests logging and configuration in CrewAI.
Code:
python
```
from crewai import Agent, Config

# Load a sample configuration
Config.load_dict({
```

```python
    "logging": {
      "level": "DEBUG",
      "file": "test_crewai.log"
    }
})

class LoggingAgent(Agent):
  def perform_task(self):
    self.log("DEBUG", "This is a debug message.")
    self.log("INFO", "This is an info message.")

if __name__ == "__main__":
  agent = LoggingAgent(name="LoggerAgent")
  agent.perform_task()
```

Steps to Test:
1. Save the script as test_logging.py.

Run the script:
bash

```
python test_logging.py
```

2. Expected Output:
   - Log messages will be written to test_crewai.log.

Verify the log file contains:
vbnet

```
DEBUG: LoggerAgent: This is a debug message.
INFO: LoggerAgent: This is an info message.
```

What This Validates:
- Logging functionality.
- Ability to configure CrewAI using custom settings.

Summary

Environment setup validation ensures your CrewAI installation and configuration are functional. By running these sample scripts, you can confirm that the framework, its dependencies, and your development environment are ready for advanced development. If any issues arise during validation, revisit the installation or troubleshooting sections to resolve them.

2.4 Troubleshooting Common Issues

While setting up and using CrewAI, you might encounter some common issues that can disrupt your workflow. This section identifies these issues, explains their causes, and provides detailed steps to resolve them. Proper troubleshooting is crucial to ensure a smooth development experience and avoid unnecessary delays.

Below are some of the most frequently encountered errors, categorized for clarity:

1. Python-Related Issues
Error 1: Python Not Recognized
- Message: 'python' is not recognized as an internal or external command.
- Cause: Python is not added to your system's PATH environment variable during installation.
- Solution:
    1. Reinstall Python and ensure the "Add Python to PATH" option is selected during installation.
    2. Manually add Python to PATH:
        - Windows: Go to Control Panel → System → Advanced System Settings → Environment Variables. Edit the PATH variable to include the path to python.exe.

macOS/Linux: Add the following line to your .bashrc or .zshrc file:
bash

```
export PATH="$PATH:/path/to/python"
```

Verify by running:
bash

```
python --version
```

Error 2: Incorrect Python Version
- Message: SyntaxError: invalid syntax or ModuleNotFoundError: No module named 'crewai'.
- Cause: Using an outdated version of Python (lower than 3.7).
- Solution:
    a. Install the latest version of Python from the [official Python website](#).

Update pip:
bash

```
pip install --upgrade pip
```

2. Virtual Environment Issues
Error 3: Virtual Environment Activation Fails
- Message: 'venv\Scripts\activate' is not recognized or Permission denied.
- Cause: The virtual environment script is not executable or the terminal lacks required permissions.
- Solution:
    1. On Windows:
        - Run your terminal as an administrator.
        - Check file permissions in the venv\Scripts folder.
    2. On macOS/Linux:

Ensure the script is executable:
bash

```bash
chmod +x venv/bin/activate
```

3. Activate the environment using the appropriate command:

Windows:
```bash
venv\Scripts\activate
```

macOS/Linux:
```bash
source venv/bin/activate
```

Error 4: Dependencies Not Installed in Virtual Environment
- Message: ModuleNotFoundError: No module named 'numpy'.
- Cause: Dependencies were installed outside the virtual environment.
- Solution:

Ensure the virtual environment is active:
```bash
source venv/bin/activate
```

Install dependencies within the environment:
```bash
pip install numpy pandas grpcio
```

3. CrewAI Installation Issues
Error 5: CrewAI Installation Fails
- Message: ERROR: Could not find a version that satisfies the requirement crewai.

- Cause: Using an unsupported version of Python or an outdated pip.
- Solution:

Upgrade pip:
bash

```
pip install --upgrade pip
```

Ensure you are using Python 3.7 or later:
bash

```
python --version
```

Reattempt installation:
bash

```
pip install crewai
```

Error 6: CrewAI Version Compatibility
- Message: AttributeError: module 'crewai' has no attribute 'Agent'.
- Cause: Incompatible version of CrewAI or Python.
- Solution:

Uninstall the current version:
bash

```
pip uninstall crewai
```

Install the correct version:
bash

```
pip install crewai==<specific_version>
```

4. Runtime Issues
Error 7: Port Already in Use

- Message: Error: Port 50051 is already in use.
- Cause: Another process is using the default port for CrewAI communication.
- Solution:
    1. Identify the process using the port:

Windows:
bash

```
netstat -aon | findstr :50051
```

macOS/Linux:
bash

```
lsof -i :50051
```

2. Kill the process:

Windows:
bash

```
taskkill /PID <process_id> /F
```

macOS/Linux:
bash

```
kill -9 <process_id>
```

Alternatively, configure CrewAI to use a different port:
json

```
{
  "communication": {
    "protocol": "grpc",
    "port": 50052
  }
}
```

Error 8: Communication Failures Between Agents
- Message: TimeoutError: Unable to connect to agent.
- Cause: Network issues or misconfigured communication settings.
- Solution:
    1. Check firewall settings to ensure required ports are open.
    2. Verify agent names and communication protocols in your code.
    3. Use a network debugging tool to test connectivity.

5. Logging and Configuration Issues

Error 9: Logging File Not Created
- Message: FileNotFoundError: [Errno 2] No such file or directory: 'crewai_logs.log'.
- Cause: The logging configuration specifies a non-existent directory.
- Solution:

**Update the logging configuration to use a valid path:
json**

```json
{
  "logging": {
    "level": "INFO",
    "file": "./logs/crewai_logs.log"
  }
}
```

**Ensure the directory exists:
bash**

```bash
mkdir logs
```

Error 10: Configuration Not Loaded
- Message: KeyError: 'communication'.
- Cause: Missing or incorrect configuration file.

- Solution:
    1. Verify the configuration file exists and contains valid JSON.

Load the configuration explicitly in your script:
python

```
from crewai import Config
Config.load("crewai_config.json")
```

Summary

Troubleshooting is an integral part of any development process. By understanding these common issues and their resolutions, you can ensure a smooth workflow and minimize downtime. Always double-check your environment setup, configuration files, and dependencies to avoid recurring problems.

If further issues persist, consult the official CrewAI documentation or seek help from the developer community.

Chapter 3: What Are Agents in Multi-Agent Systems?

Agents are the fundamental building blocks of multi-agent systems (MAS). They are autonomous entities designed to perceive their environment, make decisions, and perform tasks either independently or collaboratively. Understanding what agents are and how they function is critical to building effective MAS. This section defines agents, explores their core features, and categorizes them into distinct types based on their behaviors and capabilities.

3.1 Defining Agents and Their Characteristics

An agent can be described as a software or hardware entity that operates within an environment, perceives changes in that environment, and takes actions to achieve specific goals. In a multi-agent system, multiple agents interact with each other and their environment to solve problems collaboratively.

Key Characteristics of Agents

To qualify as an agent in MAS, an entity must exhibit certain core features: autonomy, communication, and adaptability.

1. Autonomy
    - Autonomy refers to an agent's ability to operate independently without requiring constant human intervention or external control.
    - Agents make decisions based on their perception of the environment and their internal logic or objectives.
    - Example:
        - A delivery drone that navigates to a destination on its own is autonomous. It doesn't need step-by-step instructions once the goal is set.
    - Benefits:

- Reduces the need for centralized control, enabling scalability.
- Allows agents to function effectively in dynamic or unpredictable environments.

2. Communication
    - Communication is the ability of agents to exchange information with other agents or systems to coordinate actions, share knowledge, or achieve common goals.
    - Communication can occur through predefined protocols, such as message-passing or broadcasting.
    - Example:
        - In a fleet of autonomous vehicles, each vehicle communicates its position and speed to other vehicles to avoid collisions.
    - Types of Communication:
        - Direct Communication: Sending messages directly to specific agents.
        - Indirect Communication: Sharing information through a shared medium or environment (e.g., writing to a shared database).

3. Adaptability
    - Adaptability refers to an agent's ability to modify its behavior or strategy in response to changes in the environment or its objectives.
    - Adaptive agents learn from their experiences or updates in the environment, making them more efficient over time.
    - Example:
        - A robotic vacuum cleaner adapts its cleaning pattern based on obstacles detected in real time.
    - Techniques for Adaptability:

- Rule-based systems: Predefined rules for specific situations.
- Learning-based systems: Machine learning techniques, such as reinforcement learning.

Agents in a multi-agent system can be categorized based on how they perceive their environment, make decisions, and execute actions. The three primary types are reactive agents, proactive agents, and hybrid agents.

1. Reactive Agents
   - Reactive agents respond to changes in their environment in real time without maintaining a history or planning future actions. They operate on a simple perception-action model: they sense an event and immediately take an action.
   - Characteristics:
     - Lack memory or long-term goals.
     - Operate based on predefined rules or conditions.
     - Highly efficient in predictable or static environments.
   - Example:
     - A thermostat adjusts the temperature based on the current room temperature without storing historical data or predicting future conditions.
   - Advantages:
     - Simple and computationally efficient.
     - Suitable for tasks that require immediate responses.
   - Disadvantages:
     - Limited ability to handle complex or dynamic environments.
     - Lack of foresight and learning capabilities.

2. Proactive Agents
   - Proactive agents are goal-driven and capable of planning and making decisions to achieve specific objectives. They can anticipate future events and act accordingly.
   - Characteristics:

- Maintain internal states, such as memory or knowledge bases.
- Use planning algorithms to achieve long-term goals.
- Operate effectively in dynamic and uncertain environments.
  - Example:
    - An autonomous vehicle plans its route based on real-time traffic data and its ultimate destination.
  - Advantages:
    - Can handle complex decision-making tasks.
    - Effective in dynamic and unpredictable environments.
  - Disadvantages:
    - Require more computational resources than reactive agents.
    - Complexity increases with the scope of their goals.

3. Hybrid Agents
   - Hybrid agents combine the characteristics of reactive and proactive agents, enabling them to respond quickly to changes while also planning and pursuing long-term objectives.
   - Characteristics:
     - Use a layered architecture, where the reactive layer handles immediate actions and the proactive layer focuses on planning and goals.
     - Balance efficiency and complexity, making them versatile.
   - Example:
     - A robotic assistant in a smart home reacts to a fire alarm by directing occupants to safety (reactive behavior) while simultaneously notifying emergency services and planning an evacuation route (proactive behavior).
   - Advantages:
     - Flexible and adaptable to a wide range of scenarios.

- - Can operate effectively in both static and dynamic environments.
- Disadvantages:
  - More complex to design and implement.
  - Require careful coordination between reactive and proactive components.

Summary

Agents in multi-agent systems are defined by their autonomy, communication, and adaptability, making them well-suited for tasks that require intelligence, collaboration, and responsiveness. The classification of agents into reactive, proactive, and hybrid types provides developers with a clear framework to design systems tailored to specific applications.

- Reactive agents excel in simplicity and speed, making them ideal for straightforward tasks.
- Proactive agents shine in goal-driven environments, handling complex decision-making processes.
- Hybrid agents offer the best of both worlds, balancing immediate responsiveness with strategic planning.

Understanding these characteristics and classifications lays the foundation for designing efficient, scalable, and intelligent multi-agent systems.

3.2 Core Principles of Multi-Agent Design

Designing multi-agent systems (MAS) requires adhering to certain core principles to ensure that the system operates efficiently, is scalable, and can handle failures gracefully. These principles—modularity, scalability, and resilience—serve as the foundation for building robust and adaptive multi-agent systems. Understanding and applying these principles allows developers to create systems that are flexible, efficient, and capable of addressing real-world challenges.

1. Modularity

Modularity refers to designing a system as a collection of discrete, self-contained components (agents) that can operate independently but interact to achieve a common goal. Each module (agent) has a specific role or responsibility, simplifying the design and maintenance of the overall system.

Core Aspects of Modularity:
- Independent Functionality:
  Each agent operates autonomously, performing tasks without relying on the internal processes of other agents.
  - Example: In a warehouse, one agent handles inventory tracking while another manages robot movements. If one agent fails, the others continue functioning independently.
- Clear Interfaces:
  Modularity requires well-defined communication interfaces, ensuring agents can interact without exposing their internal workings.
  - Example: Agents in a traffic management system exchange position data without sharing their internal decision-making algorithms.
- Ease of Integration and Replacement:
  Modular design allows agents to be added, updated, or replaced without disrupting the entire system.
  - Example: A factory automation system can integrate a new type of robot agent to handle packaging tasks without modifying the existing assembly-line agents.

Benefits of Modularity:
- Simplifies system design by breaking it into smaller, manageable parts.
- Enhances flexibility, enabling developers to adapt the system to new requirements.
- Reduces maintenance complexity, as changes to one agent do not affect the entire system.

2. Scalability

Scalability is the ability of a system to handle an increasing number of agents, tasks, or data without a significant drop in performance. In MAS, scalability ensures that the system can grow as demands evolve.

Core Aspects of Scalability:
- Horizontal Scalability:
  Adding more agents to the system to handle additional tasks or workloads.
    - Example: In a ride-sharing application, new driver agents can join the network as the number of customers increases.
- Dynamic Resource Allocation:
  Efficiently allocating tasks and resources to agents based on their current workload and capabilities.
    - Example: In cloud computing, MAS assigns tasks to servers dynamically based on their availability and processing power.
- Minimal Centralization:
  Avoiding centralized control ensures that adding more agents does not overwhelm a single point in the system.
    - Example: A peer-to-peer file-sharing network grows efficiently as more users (agents) join, without relying on a central server.

Design Strategies for Scalability:
- Use distributed algorithms to enable agents to make decisions locally.
- Implement communication protocols that scale efficiently, such as broadcasting or selective messaging.
- Design agents to be lightweight and optimized for specific tasks to reduce computational overhead.

Benefits of Scalability:
- Accommodates growth in the number of agents or workload.
- Maintains performance even as the system expands.
- Ensures the system remains cost-effective by scaling only as needed.

3. Resilience

Resilience is the ability of a system to continue functioning effectively despite failures, unexpected disruptions, or adverse conditions. In MAS, resilience ensures that the failure of one or more agents does not compromise the entire system.

Core Aspects of Resilience:
- Fault Tolerance:
  The system can detect and recover from agent failures or communication breakdowns.
  - Example: In a drone delivery system, if one drone malfunctions, its tasks are reassigned to other drones.
- Decentralized Control:
  Distributed decision-making ensures that no single agent failure halts the system's operation.
  - Example: In a multi-robot search-and-rescue operation, each robot operates independently while collaborating with others.
- Redundancy and Backup:
  Critical agents or resources are replicated to provide backup in case of failure.
  - Example: In a data center managed by MAS, multiple servers host the same data to ensure availability during outages.

Design Strategies for Resilience:
- Implement monitoring mechanisms to detect failures and trigger recovery actions.
- Design agents with fallback behaviors to handle situations where they lose communication with peers.
- Use robust communication protocols that handle packet loss or delays gracefully.

Benefits of Resilience:
- Minimizes the impact of agent failures or disruptions.
- Increases system reliability, especially in mission-critical applications.

- Enhances trust in the system's ability to operate under unpredictable conditions.

Applying These Principles in Real-World Scenarios
1. E-Commerce Logistics
    - Modularity: Separate agents handle inventory, delivery routing, and customer support.
    - Scalability: Add more delivery agents during peak seasons without modifying the system.
    - Resilience: Reassign deliveries from malfunctioning robots to operational ones.
2. Smart Cities
    - Modularity: Traffic lights and autonomous vehicles operate as independent agents.
    - Scalability: Add more sensors and vehicles as the city grows.
    - Resilience: In case of a sensor failure, nearby sensors fill the gap to maintain traffic flow.
3. Healthcare Systems
    - Modularity: Agents monitor patients, manage appointments, and handle diagnostics.
    - Scalability: Add new monitoring agents as the number of patients increases.
    - Resilience: If one diagnostic agent fails, the system reroutes tasks to another.

Summary

The core principles of modularity, scalability, and resilience are essential for designing effective multi-agent systems. These principles ensure that the system is flexible, can grow to meet increased demands, and remains reliable even in the face of failures. By adhering to these concepts, developers can create systems that are not only robust and efficient but also adaptable to a wide range of real-world applications.

3.3 Applications of Multi-Agent Systems in Real Life

Multi-agent systems (MAS) have found extensive applications across industries, where their ability to solve complex, distributed problems shines. By leveraging autonomous, collaborative agents, MAS provide robust solutions in areas such as robotics, logistics, and smart systems. This section explores real-life applications of MAS, highlighting their impact and efficiency in these domains.

1. Robotics

Multi-agent systems have revolutionized robotics by enabling teams of robots to work together, share information, and accomplish tasks collaboratively. This approach is particularly useful in environments that require distributed intelligence and adaptability.

- Industrial Robotics
    MAS are widely used in manufacturing plants to coordinate robotic arms and assembly line robots. Each robot performs a specific task (e.g., welding, assembling, or painting) while collaborating with others to ensure a smooth production flow.
    - Example: In an automotive manufacturing plant, robotic arms equipped with MAS coordinate to assemble car components in parallel, optimizing time and reducing errors.
- Swarm Robotics
    Inspired by natural swarms (e.g., ants or bees), MAS in swarm robotics enable a group of robots to work together without centralized control. Each robot follows simple rules, but collectively they achieve complex objectives such as exploration, search, and rescue.
    - Example: In search-and-rescue operations, a swarm of drones equipped with MAS can cover large areas, communicate findings, and locate survivors in disaster-stricken zones.

- Healthcare Robotics
  In healthcare, MAS is applied to robotic assistants that collaborate to provide patient care, deliver medications, and even assist in surgeries.
  - Example: In hospitals, delivery robots work as a team to distribute medical supplies and food to patients, reducing the workload on medical staff.

2. Logistics

The logistics industry relies heavily on MAS to optimize supply chains, manage fleets, and coordinate delivery operations. The decentralized nature of MAS ensures scalability and fault tolerance, making them ideal for large-scale, dynamic systems.

- Warehouse Automation
  MAS is widely used in automated warehouses where robots handle tasks like picking, packing, and transporting goods. Each robot operates autonomously but collaborates with others to maximize efficiency.
  - Example: Amazon's robotic warehouses use MAS to manage thousands of robots that retrieve items, deliver them to packing stations, and return to their charging docks, optimizing the entire fulfillment process.
- Fleet Management
  MAS helps coordinate fleets of vehicles, including delivery trucks, drones, and cargo ships, to ensure timely and efficient delivery of goods.
  - Example: In last-mile delivery, MAS assigns tasks to drones based on their battery levels, payload capacities, and proximity to delivery points, reducing operational costs and delivery times.
- Supply Chain Optimization
  MAS can monitor and optimize supply chains by coordinating suppliers, distributors, and retailers. Agents communicate in real time to adjust production schedules, track shipments, and respond to demand fluctuations.

- Example: A retail chain uses MAS to manage inventory levels across multiple stores, automatically placing orders and rerouting deliveries based on real-time sales data.

3. Smart Systems

MAS play a vital role in the development of smart systems that require distributed intelligence, such as smart cities, energy grids, and transportation networks.

- Smart Cities
  In smart cities, MAS coordinate various subsystems, including traffic management, waste collection, and public safety, to improve urban living conditions.
    - Example: MAS-powered traffic lights communicate with each other and with autonomous vehicles to optimize traffic flow, reduce congestion, and minimize travel times.
- Smart Energy Grids
  MAS are used in smart grids to balance energy supply and demand, manage distributed energy resources (e.g., solar panels), and ensure efficient energy distribution.
    - Example: In a smart grid, MAS agents at different power stations and homes adjust energy production and consumption in real time to avoid blackouts and reduce energy waste.
- Intelligent Building Management
  MAS enable the management of smart buildings by coordinating heating, ventilation, lighting, and security systems. Each agent controls a specific subsystem while collaborating to optimize energy efficiency and occupant comfort.
    - Example: In a smart office, MAS agents adjust lighting

3.4 Concept-to-Code: Creating a Simple Agent

In this section, we will explore how to create a simple agent using CrewAI. By walking through a hands-on example, you will gain a practical understanding of how to define, configure, and execute an agent within a multi-agent system. This step-by-step approach ensures that even beginners can follow along and build their first agent successfully.

A basic agent is an autonomous entity capable of performing a specific task independently. In this example, we will create an agent named GreeterAgent that performs a simple task: greeting users with a message. This example covers all the foundational steps to help you understand the workflow of building and running agents in CrewAI.

Step 1: Setting Up the Environment
Before starting, ensure you have completed the following prerequisites:
1. Install Python: Use Python 3.7 or later.

Set up a virtual environment:
bash

```
python -m venv venv
source venv/bin/activate  # On macOS/Linux
venv\Scripts\activate    # On Windows
```

Install CrewAI:
bash

```
pip install crewai
```

Step 2: Creating the GreeterAgent
Define the Agent Class
Agents in CrewAI are created by extending the base Agent class

and implementing their behavior in the perform_task method. In this example, the agent will greet the user when its task is executed.

Code:
python

```
from crewai import Agent

# Define a simple agent class
class GreeterAgent(Agent):
    def perform_task(self):
        # Task: Print a greeting message
        print(f"Hello! I am {self.name}. How can I assist you today?")
```

1. Explanation:
    - The GreeterAgent class inherits from Agent, which provides essential functionalities for CrewAI agents.
    - The perform_task method contains the logic for the agent's behavior—in this case, printing a greeting message.
    - The self.name attribute refers to the agent's name, which will be set during initialization.

Step 3: Instantiating and Running the Agent
Instantiate and Execute the Agent
The agent must be instantiated and then triggered to perform its task. This is done by calling the perform_task method on the agent instance.

Code:
python

```
if __name__ == "__main__":
    # Create an instance of GreeterAgent
    greeter = GreeterAgent(name="GreeterAgent")

    # Execute the agent's task
```

```
greeter.perform_task()
```
   2. Explanation:
        - The if __name__ == "__main__": block ensures that the script runs only when executed directly, not when imported as a module.
        - The GreeterAgent is initialized with the name "GreeterAgent".
        - The perform_task method is called to execute the agent's logic.

Step 4: Running the Script
1. Save the Script
   Save the above code in a file named greeter_agent.py.

Execute the Script

Open a terminal, navigate to the directory containing the script, and run:

bash

```
python greeter_agent.py
```

Expected Output
css

```
Hello! I am GreeterAgent. How can I assist you today?
```

   2. What This Validates:
        - The CrewAI framework is correctly installed.
        - The basic agent is functional and executes its task as intended.

Step 5: Enhancing the Agent
To make the example more interactive, let's extend the agent to accept user input and respond dynamically.
Interactive GreeterAgent
Modify the perform_task method to ask the user's name and respond with a personalized greeting.
Code:

python

```python
from crewai import Agent

# Define an interactive agent class
class GreeterAgent(Agent):
    def perform_task(self):
        # Ask for the user's name
        user_name = input("What is your name? ")
        # Respond with a personalized greeting
        print(f"Hello, {user_name}! I am {self.name}. How can I assist you today?")

if __name__ == "__main__":
    # Create an instance of GreeterAgent
    greeter = GreeterAgent(name="GreeterAgent")

    # Execute the agent's task
    greeter.perform_task()
```

Run the Script
Execute the modified script as before:
bash

```
python greeter_agent.py
```

Expected Interaction:
css

What is your name? John
Hello, John! I am GreeterAgent. How can I assist you today?

1. What This Demonstrates:
    - Agents can interact dynamically with users.
    - Input/output operations can be integrated into an agent's behavior.

Key Concepts Covered
1. Agent Definition:
    - Agents are created by extending the Agent class and implementing the perform_task method.
2. Autonomous Execution:
    - Agents operate independently, executing their tasks without external control.
3. Interactivity:
    - Agents can interact with users or other systems to provide customized responses.

Extensions and Next Steps
Task Variation
Extend the agent to perform different tasks based on user input. For example:
python

```python
if user_input == "weather":
    print("I can provide weather updates!")
elif user_input == "news":
    print("I can share the latest news.")
```

1. Communication Between Agents
   Introduce multiple agents that communicate with each other using message-passing mechanisms.
2. Integration with Real-World APIs
   Enhance the agent by integrating external APIs, such as fetching weather data or news headlines.

Summary
In this section, we built a simple agent using CrewAI, explored its structure, and executed its task. By extending the basic agent, we demonstrated how to make agents interactive and adaptable. This foundational example serves as the building block for more

complex multi-agent systems, where agents collaborate, share information, and execute distributed tasks.

Chapter 4: CrewAI Architecture

4.1 Overview of CrewAI's Modular Design

CrewAI's architecture is designed to provide a robust and flexible framework for building multi-agent systems. It emphasizes modularity, enabling developers to create systems composed of independent yet interoperable components. This modular approach allows for scalability, maintainability, and adaptability, making CrewAI suitable for a wide range of applications, from small-scale projects to large, complex systems.

This section explores CrewAI's modular design, focusing on its key components: agents, the communication layer, and decision-making logic.

The architecture of CrewAI is built around three fundamental components that work in harmony to create a functional multi-agent system:

1. Agents

Agents are the core building blocks of any CrewAI system. Each agent is an autonomous entity designed to perform specific tasks, interact with its environment, and collaborate with other agents.

Characteristics of Agents in CrewAI:
- Autonomy: Agents operate independently, making decisions based on their objectives and the information available.
- Specialization: Each agent can be tailored for a specific role or function, such as data processing, task execution, or coordination.
- Modularity: Agents are self-contained, making it easy to add, update, or remove them without affecting the overall system.

Agent Lifecycle:
- Initialization: The agent is instantiated with its name, role, and initial state.

- Task Execution: The agent performs its designated tasks, often defined in the perform_task method.
- Communication: The agent exchanges messages with other agents or external systems as needed.
- Termination: The agent completes its tasks and shuts down gracefully.

Example:
- In a warehouse automation system:
  - Picker Agent: Retrieves items from shelves.
  - Transporter Agent: Moves items to the packing station.
  - Coordinator Agent: Assigns tasks to picker and transporter agents.

2. Communication Layer

The communication layer in CrewAI facilitates the exchange of information between agents and external systems. It is designed to support various communication protocols, ensuring flexibility and compatibility with diverse application requirements.

Core Features:
- Message Passing:
  - Agents communicate through structured messages that can contain data, instructions, or status updates.
  - Example: A picker agent sends a message to a transporter agent indicating that an item is ready for pickup.
- Protocols Supported:
  - gRPC: For high-performance, scalable communication.
  - ZeroMQ: For lightweight message passing in distributed systems.
  - HTTP/REST: For integration with web services or APIs.
- Synchronous and Asynchronous Communication:
  - Synchronous: The sender waits for a response before proceeding.

- Asynchronous: The sender continues its tasks without waiting for a reply, enabling parallel execution.

Message Flow:
- Direct Messaging: Messages are sent directly between specific agents.
- Broadcast Messaging: Messages are sent to all agents within a group or system.
- Request-Response Pattern: One agent sends a request, and another responds with the required data or action confirmation.

Example:
- In a smart energy grid:
  - Agents at power stations communicate with home energy agents to balance supply and demand in real time.

3. Decision-Making Logic

Decision-making logic is at the heart of an agent's autonomy. It enables agents to analyze data, evaluate options, and choose actions that align with their goals. CrewAI supports both simple and advanced decision-making models, depending on the complexity of the application.

Core Components of Decision-Making Logic:
- Rule-Based Systems:
  - Agents make decisions based on predefined rules or conditions.
  - Example: A thermostat agent adjusts the temperature if it detects a change beyond a specific threshold.
- Algorithmic Approaches:
  - Algorithms are used to evaluate options and select the best course of action.
  - Example: A delivery agent uses a shortest-path algorithm to determine the optimal route.
- Learning-Based Systems:

- Agents use machine learning models, such as reinforcement learning, to adapt their behavior over time.
- Example: A trading agent adjusts its strategy based on market trends and historical performance.

Coordination and Collaboration:
- Agents work together to achieve shared goals, often requiring negotiation, conflict resolution, or consensus-building mechanisms.
- Example:
  - In a disaster response scenario, a team of drones negotiates task assignments to ensure all affected areas are covered.

How These Components Work Together

The modular design of CrewAI allows its components—agents, communication layer, and decision-making logic—to function independently yet collaboratively, creating a seamless system.

Workflow:
1. Agents Execute Tasks:
   - Each agent performs its assigned tasks, guided by its decision-making logic.
2. Communication Ensures Coordination:
   - Agents share information, request resources, and report status updates using the communication layer.
3. Decision-Making Drives Actions:
   - Decision-making logic ensures that agents act intelligently, optimizing their performance based on the current environment and system goals.

Example Use Case:
- Smart Traffic Management:
  1. Agents:
     - Traffic light agents control individual intersections.
     - Vehicle agents represent autonomous cars.
  2. Communication Layer:

- Traffic light agents communicate with vehicle agents to prioritize emergency vehicles.
3. Decision-Making Logic:
    - Traffic light agents adjust signal timings dynamically based on traffic flow data.

Benefits of CrewAI's Modular Design
1. Scalability:
    - New agents can be added to the system without disrupting existing functionality.
2. Flexibility:
    - The modular design allows components to be replaced or upgraded independently.
3. Resilience:
    - The failure of one agent does not compromise the entire system, as other agents can adapt to maintain functionality.
4. Ease of Development:
    - Developers can focus on individual components, simplifying the design and debugging process.

Summary

CrewAI's modular architecture, centered around agents, the communication layer, and decision-making logic, provides a powerful framework for building scalable, flexible, and resilient multi-agent systems. By understanding how these components interact, developers can design systems that are adaptable to a wide range of applications, from industrial automation to smart cities and beyond.

4.2 Communication Protocols in CrewAI

Effective communication is the backbone of any multi-agent system (MAS). In CrewAI, communication protocols define how agents exchange information to collaborate, coordinate, and make decisions. This section covers the types of communication protocols supported by CrewAI, focusing on peer-to-peer and client-server models, and provides a detailed explanation of how to implement communication pipelines.

CrewAI supports two primary communication models: peer-to-peer and client-server. Each model is suited to specific scenarios, offering flexibility and scalability in designing multi-agent systems.

1. Peer-to-Peer Communication

In the peer-to-peer (P2P) model, agents communicate directly with each other without relying on a central server. Each agent acts as both a sender and a receiver, enabling distributed and decentralized systems.

Characteristics:
- Direct communication between agents.
- No central point of failure, making it resilient and fault-tolerant.
- Suitable for decentralized systems where agents operate independently but need to share information.

Advantages:
- Scalability: New agents can join the system without overwhelming a central server.
- Fault Tolerance: If one agent fails, others can continue communicating.
- Efficiency: Reduces latency by bypassing intermediate servers.

Disadvantages:
- Complexity: Implementing P2P communication requires robust protocols for agent discovery and message routing.
- Security: Direct connections can be vulnerable without proper encryption.

Example:
- In a swarm robotics system, drones use P2P communication to share positional data and avoid collisions.

2. Client-Server Communication

In the client-server model, agents (clients) communicate through a central server. The server acts as an intermediary, handling message routing, coordination, and sometimes decision-making.

Characteristics:
- Centralized communication hub.
- Simplified message routing and management.
- Suitable for systems where agents need centralized control or coordination.

Advantages:
- Simplified Design: The server handles communication, reducing complexity for individual agents.
- Centralized Management: Easier to monitor and control agent interactions.
- Security: The server can enforce authentication and encryption.

Disadvantages:
- Single Point of Failure: If the server fails, communication between agents is disrupted.
- Scalability Limitations: High traffic can overwhelm the server, affecting performance.

Example:
- In a smart energy grid, home energy agents communicate with a central server that coordinates energy distribution and monitors consumption patterns.

Communication pipelines in CrewAI are the mechanisms that enable agents to exchange messages seamlessly. Implementing these pipelines involves defining the communication protocol, configuring agent endpoints, and enabling message passing.

1. Peer-to-Peer Communication Pipeline

In a P2P communication pipeline, each agent has a unique identifier and endpoint. Messages are exchanged directly between agents using a lightweight protocol like ZeroMQ.

Steps to Implement:
1. Define Agent Endpoints:

- Assign a unique endpoint (e.g., IP address and port) to each agent.
- Example:
  - Agent A: tcp://127.0.0.1:5001
  - Agent B: tcp://127.0.0.1:5002

2. Initialize Communication:
   - Use a library like ZeroMQ for message passing.

Code:
python

```python
import zmq

# Initialize ZeroMQ context
context = zmq.Context()

# Create a socket for sending messages
sender = context.socket(zmq.PUSH)
sender.connect("tcp://127.0.0.1:5002")

# Create a socket for receiving messages
receiver = context.socket(zmq.PULL)
receiver.bind("tcp://127.0.0.1:5001")
```

3. Send and Receive Messages:

Sending:
python

```python
message = {"greeting": "Hello from Agent A"}
sender.send_json(message)
```

Receiving:
python

```python
received_message = receiver.recv_json()
print(f"Received: {received_message}")
```

4. **Run Agents:**
   - Start both agents, and they will exchange messages directly.

Use Case:
- A team of autonomous vehicles sharing positional data to avoid collisions.

2. Client-Server Communication Pipeline

In a client-server model, a central server mediates communication between agents. The server listens for incoming messages, processes them, and forwards responses.

Steps to Implement:
1. Set Up the Server:
   - Use a library like gRPC or Flask for server implementation.

Code (Server):
python

```python
from flask import Flask, request, jsonify

app = Flask(__name__)

# Handle incoming messages
@app.route("/message", methods=["POST"])
def handle_message():
    data = request.json
    print(f"Received: {data}")
    response = {"response": f"Hello, {data['sender']}"}
    return jsonify(response)

if __name__ == "__main__":
    app.run(port=5000)
```

2. Configure Clients:
   - Agents act as clients, sending messages to the server and waiting for responses.

Code (Client):
python

```python
import requests

message = {"sender": "Agent A", "message": "Hello, Server!"}
response = requests.post("http://127.0.0.1:5000/message", json=message)
print(f"Server Response: {response.json()}")
```

3. Run the System:
    - Start the server, then execute client agents to communicate through it.

Use Case:
- In a supply chain system, a central server coordinates inventory updates from multiple warehouses.

Key Considerations When Choosing a Protocol
1. System Requirements:
    - Use P2P for decentralized, resilient systems.
    - Use client-server for centralized management and monitoring.
2. Scalability:
    - P2P scales well with many agents but can be complex to implement.
    - Client-server is easier to scale initially but may face bottlenecks.
3. Fault Tolerance:
    - P2P is fault-tolerant due to its distributed nature.
    - Client-server depends on the server's reliability.
4. Security:
    - Secure P2P communication using encryption.
    - Use HTTPS or TLS for client-server communication.

Summary
CrewAI's support for peer-to-peer and client-server communication protocols enables developers to build multi-agent systems tailored to specific needs. By implementing robust communication pipelines, agents can exchange information efficiently, ensuring seamless collaboration and coordination. Understanding the strengths and limitations of each protocol is essential for designing scalable, resilient, and secure systems.

4.3 Orchestration and Decision-Making in Multi-Agent Systems

Orchestration and decision-making are the foundational components of multi-agent systems (MAS), dictating how agents coordinate, collaborate, and make decisions to achieve shared goals. These aspects significantly impact system performance, scalability, and resilience. In this section, we will delve into centralized vs. decentralized orchestration and explore the role of decision-making algorithms in enabling agents to function effectively within a system.

Orchestration in MAS refers to the process of coordinating and managing the interactions and tasks of agents. It determines how agents communicate, share resources, and align their efforts to achieve common objectives. CrewAI supports two primary models of orchestration: centralized and decentralized, each with distinct advantages, disadvantages, and use cases.

1. Centralized Orchestration
Centralized orchestration involves a central controller, often referred to as the orchestrator or central agent, that oversees the actions of all other agents. This orchestrator has a global view of the system and is responsible for assigning tasks, resolving conflicts, and ensuring overall system efficiency.
Characteristics:
- A single entity governs the entire system.

- Agents function as subordinates, performing tasks as instructed by the orchestrator.
- Communication primarily flows between the orchestrator and individual agents.

Advantages:
1. Simplified Coordination:
    - The central orchestrator handles all communication and task allocation, reducing complexity for individual agents.
2. Global Optimization:
    - The orchestrator's global perspective enables optimal resource allocation and decision-making.
3. Ease of Monitoring:
    - Centralized systems are easier to monitor and manage, as all activities are directed through a single point.

Disadvantages:
1. Single Point of Failure:
    - The system is vulnerable to disruptions if the central orchestrator fails.
2. Scalability Issues:
    - As the number of agents increases, the orchestrator may become a bottleneck, limiting system performance.
3. Latency:
    - Communication delays between the orchestrator and agents can impact real-time operations.

Use Case:
- Warehouse Automation:
In a smart warehouse, a central controller assigns tasks like item picking, packing, and transport to robots. The controller optimizes operations by considering the entire warehouse layout and inventory status.

Example:
python
```
from crewai import Orchestrator, Agent
```

```python
class CentralController(Orchestrator):
    def assign_tasks(self, agents, tasks):
        for agent, task in zip(agents, tasks):
            agent.perform_task(task)

class WorkerAgent(Agent):
    def perform_task(self, task):
        print(f"{self.name} is executing: {task}")

if __name__ == "__main__":
    controller = CentralController(name="CentralOrchestrator")
    agents = [WorkerAgent(name=f"Worker{i}") for i in range(3)]
    tasks = ["Pick item A", "Pack item B", "Transport item C"]

    controller.assign_tasks(agents, tasks)
```

2. Decentralized Orchestration

Decentralized orchestration eliminates the need for a central controller. Instead, agents coordinate directly with one another, sharing information and collaborating to achieve system goals. This model relies on distributed decision-making, where each agent acts autonomously but aligns its actions with other agents.

Characteristics:
- Communication occurs directly between agents (peer-to-peer).
- Decision-making is distributed, with agents using local information and shared protocols.

Advantages:
1. Fault Tolerance:
    - The system remains operational even if some agents fail, as there is no central dependency.

2. Scalability:
   - Adding new agents does not significantly increase complexity or workload.
3. Adaptability:
   - Agents can quickly respond to changes in the environment without waiting for instructions from a central controller.

Disadvantages:
1. Coordination Complexity:
   - Ensuring that agents do not conflict or duplicate efforts requires robust protocols and algorithms.
2. Local Optimization:
   - Decisions made using local data may not lead to optimal global outcomes.
3. Increased Communication Overhead:
   - Peer-to-peer communication can result in higher network traffic in large systems.

Use Case:
- Swarm Robotics:
  In disaster recovery, drones equipped with decentralized orchestration work together to survey a large area, sharing data to ensure comprehensive coverage without overlap.

Example:

```python
class DecentralizedAgent(Agent):
    def perform_task(self, task, neighbors):
        print(f"{self.name} is performing: {task}")
        for neighbor in neighbors:
            print(f"{self.name} informs {neighbor.name} about task completion.")

if __name__ == "__main__":
    agents = [DecentralizedAgent(name=f"Agent{i}") for i in range(3)]
    tasks = ["Survey sector A", "Survey sector B", "Survey sector C"]
```

```python
for i, agent in enumerate(agents):
    agent.perform_task(tasks[i], agents[:i] + agents[i+1:])
```

Decision-making algorithms enable agents in a multi-agent system to determine the best course of action based on their goals, environment, and available information. These algorithms range from simple rule-based systems to advanced learning-based models, each suited for specific types of tasks and environments.

1. Rule-Based Decision-Making

In rule-based decision-making, agents follow predefined rules to make decisions. These rules are typically static and hard-coded, making them suitable for predictable environments.

Example:
- A thermostat adjusts the temperature based on the rule: "If the temperature exceeds 25°C, turn off the heater."

Advantages:
- Simple to implement and understand.
- Low computational overhead.

Disadvantages:
- Inflexible in dynamic or complex environments.

Code Example:

python

```python
class RuleBasedAgent(Agent):
    def decide_action(self, temperature):
        if temperature > 25:
            return "Turn off heater"
        else:
            return "Turn on heater"
```

2. Optimization-Based Decision-Making

Optimization-based algorithms use mathematical models to evaluate multiple options and select the most efficient one. Common approaches include linear programming and game theory.

Example:
- Delivery agents calculate the shortest path to deliver packages using Dijkstra's algorithm.

Advantages:
- Ensures optimal solutions for well-defined problems.
- Suitable for systems requiring precision and efficiency.

Disadvantages:
- Computationally intensive for large or dynamic systems.

Code Example:

```python
from networkx import shortest_path, Graph

class OptimizingAgent(Agent):
    def find_path(self, graph, start, end):
        return shortest_path(graph, source=start, target=end)

graph = Graph()
graph.add_edges_from([("A", "B"), ("B", "C"), ("A", "C")])

agent = OptimizingAgent(name="PathFinder")
print(agent.find_path(graph, "A", "C"))
```

3. Learning-Based Decision-Making

Learning-based decision-making involves using machine learning techniques, such as reinforcement learning, to enable agents to adapt and improve their actions over time.

Example:
- A robot learns to navigate a warehouse efficiently through trial and error.

Advantages:
- Adaptive to dynamic and uncertain environments.
- Can handle complex and large-scale problems.

Disadvantages:
- Requires significant training and computational resources.

Code Example:

python
```
import numpy as np

class LearningAgent(Agent):
    def __init__(self, name):
        super().__init__(name)
        self.q_table = np.zeros((5, 5))  # Example Q-table for learning

    def learn_action(self, state, reward):
        self.q_table[state] += reward
        return np.argmax(self.q_table[state])
```

Summary

Orchestration and decision-making define how agents in a multi-agent system interact and choose their actions. Centralized orchestration offers simplicity and global optimization but suffers from scalability and fault tolerance issues, while decentralized orchestration provides resilience and adaptability at the cost of coordination complexity. Decision-making algorithms, ranging from rule-based systems to learning-based models, empower agents to operate intelligently and effectively in diverse scenarios. By selecting the appropriate orchestration model and decision-making algorithm, developers can design MAS that are robust, scalable, and well-suited to their intended applications.

4.4 Concept-to-Code: Building Agent Communication Pipelines

Agent communication pipelines are essential for enabling collaboration and coordination in multi-agent systems (MAS). These pipelines facilitate the exchange of information between agents, ensuring that they work together efficiently to achieve shared goals. In this section, we will create a practical example of inter-agent communication using CrewAI, focusing on direct message passing between agents.

In this example, we will build a system where two agents communicate to complete a task collaboratively. The setup involves:
1. A SenderAgent that sends a message.
2. A ReceiverAgent that receives the message and acts on it.

Step 1: Define the Communication Workflow
The communication pipeline will include:
1. Message Passing: The SenderAgent sends a message containing information or a request to the ReceiverAgent.
2. Action Execution: The ReceiverAgent processes the message and performs the corresponding action.
3. Acknowledgment: The ReceiverAgent sends a confirmation back to the SenderAgent.

Step 2: Implementing the Communication System
Create the Agents
Define two agents: a sender and a receiver. The sender will initiate communication, and the receiver will respond accordingly.
Code:
python

```
from crewai import Agent

# SenderAgent
class SenderAgent(Agent):
```

```python
    def perform_task(self):
        # Define the message to send
        message = {"task": "Process Data", "data": [1, 2, 3, 4]}
        print(f"{self.name}: Sending message to ReceiverAgent.")
        # Send the message
        self.send_message("ReceiverAgent", message)

# ReceiverAgent
class ReceiverAgent(Agent):
    def on_message(self, sender, message):
        # Handle the incoming message
        print(f"{self.name}: Received message from {sender}.")
        print(f"{self.name}: Message content: {message}")
        # Process the message
        if message["task"] == "Process Data":
            result = sum(message["data"])  # Example processing
            print(f"{self.name}: Processed result: {result}")
            # Send acknowledgment back to the sender
            ack_message = {"status": "Completed", "result": result}
            self.send_message(sender, ack_message)
```

1. Explanation:
    - The SenderAgent sends a message containing a task ("Process Data") and some data.
    - The ReceiverAgent receives the message, processes the data (sums the numbers), and sends an acknowledgment back.

Set Up Communication

Define the communication framework, enabling agents to exchange messages.

Code:
python

```python
if __name__ == "__main__":
    # Initialize agents
    sender = SenderAgent(name="SenderAgent")
    receiver = ReceiverAgent(name="ReceiverAgent")

    # Mock communication: Connect sender to receiver
    sender.send_message = receiver.on_message  # Directly link for simplicity

    # Perform the sender's task
    sender.perform_task()
```

2. Explanation:
    - The send_message function of the SenderAgent is mocked to call the on_message function of the ReceiverAgent directly. In a real-world scenario, this would involve an actual communication protocol (e.g., gRPC or ZeroMQ).

Step 3: Running the Script
1. Save the Code
   Save the complete script in a file named agent_communication.py.

Run the Script
Execute the script:
bash

python agent_communication.py

Expected Output:
vbnet

SenderAgent: Sending message to ReceiverAgent.
ReceiverAgent: Received message from SenderAgent.
ReceiverAgent: Message content: {'task': 'Process Data', 'data': [1, 2, 3, 4]}

ReceiverAgent: Processed result: 10

Step 4: Enhancing the Communication Pipeline
To make the communication pipeline more realistic, you can integrate an actual communication protocol like gRPC. This enables agents to exchange messages over a network.

Using gRPC for Inter-Agent Communication
Install gRPC:
bash

```
pip install grpcio grpcio-tools
```

Define the gRPC Protocol: Create a .proto file specifying the communication structure. Save it as agent.proto.
Example:
proto

```
syntax = "proto3";

service AgentService {
   rpc SendMessage (Message) returns (AckMessage);
}

message Message {
   string sender = 1;
   string task = 2;
   repeated int32 data = 3;
}

message AckMessage {
   string status = 1;
   int32 result = 2;
}
```

Generate gRPC Code:
bash

```
python -m grpc_tools.protoc -I. --python_out=. --grpc_python_out=. agent.proto
```

Implement the gRPC Server (ReceiverAgent): Code:
python

```python
from concurrent import futures
import grpc
import agent_pb2
import agent_pb2_grpc

class ReceiverAgent(agent_pb2_grpc.AgentServiceServicer):
    def SendMessage(self, request, context):
        print(f"ReceiverAgent: Received message from {request.sender}")
        if request.task == "Process Data":
            result = sum(request.data)
            print(f"ReceiverAgent: Processed result: {result}")
        return agent_pb2.AckMessage(status="Completed", result=result)

def serve():
    server = grpc.server(futures.ThreadPoolExecutor(max_workers=10))

    agent_pb2_grpc.add_AgentServiceServicer_to_server(ReceiverAgent(), server)
    server.add_insecure_port("[::]:50051")
    server.start()
    print("ReceiverAgent: Server started on port 50051.")
```

```python
    server.wait_for_termination()

if __name__ == "__main__":
    serve()
```

Implement the gRPC Client (SenderAgent): Code: python

```python
import grpc
import agent_pb2
import agent_pb2_grpc

def run():
    with grpc.insecure_channel("localhost:50051") as channel:
        stub = agent_pb2_grpc.AgentServiceStub(channel)
        message = agent_pb2.Message(sender="SenderAgent", task="Process Data", data=[1, 2, 3, 4])
        response = stub.SendMessage(message)
        print(f"SenderAgent: Received acknowledgment - Status: {response.status}, Result: {response.result}")

if __name__ == "__main__":
    run()
```

1. Run the Server and Client:

Start the server:
bash

python receiver_agent.py

Start the client:
bash

python sender_agent.py

2. Expected Output:

Server (ReceiverAgent):
vbnet

ReceiverAgent: Received message from SenderAgent
ReceiverAgent: Processed result: 10

Client (SenderAgent):
yaml

SenderAgent: Received acknowledgment - Status: Completed, Result: 10

Summary
In this example, we implemented a simple inter-agent communication pipeline using both direct function calls and gRPC. The practical example highlights how agents exchange messages to collaborate and accomplish tasks. CrewAI's flexible architecture supports various communication protocols, enabling developers to create efficient and scalable pipelines for multi-agent systems.

Chapter 5: Designing and Building Agents

5.1 Structuring Agent Behavior

Agents in a multi-agent system (MAS) are autonomous entities responsible for specific tasks, making them the building blocks of any MAS. Designing agent behavior requires a thoughtful approach to define their roles, responsibilities, and interactions. Structuring agent behavior effectively ensures the system is modular, scalable, and aligned with its objectives.

This section focuses on designing agent roles and responsibilities to create agents that are efficient, collaborative, and adaptable. An agent's role defines its purpose within the system, while its responsibilities outline the tasks it performs to fulfill that purpose. Together, these aspects determine how the agent interacts with other agents and its environment.

Step 1: Understanding Agent Roles
An agent's role describes its primary function within the system. Roles are defined based on the system's objectives and the specific tasks that need to be accomplished. In a well-structured system, each role should:
1. Have a clear purpose.
2. Avoid overlapping responsibilities with other roles.
3. Contribute to the overall system objectives.

Common Agent Roles:
- Task Executor:
    - Responsible for performing specific tasks.
    - Example: In a manufacturing system, a robotic arm is a task executor responsible for assembling parts.
- Coordinator:
    - Manages and delegates tasks among other agents.
    - Example: A central server assigns tasks to worker agents in a logistics system.
- Monitor:
    - Observes and reports on system performance or environmental changes.
    - Example: A weather monitoring agent collects and shares data with decision-making agents.
- Communicator:
    - Facilitates information exchange between agents.
    - Example: An agent acting as a message relay in a decentralized system.
- Decision Maker:
    - Analyzes data and makes decisions to guide the system.

- Example: An agent in a smart traffic system decides optimal signal timings based on traffic flow.

Step 2: Defining Responsibilities
Once roles are identified, the next step is to define the specific tasks or responsibilities that each role will handle. Responsibilities should align with the agent's role and be broken down into manageable actions.

Key Considerations:
1. Granularity:
   - Responsibilities should be specific and actionable.
   - Example: Instead of assigning "manage inventory," assign "update stock levels" or "generate restocking alerts."
2. Independence:
   - Responsibilities should enable the agent to operate autonomously as much as possible.
   - Example: A delivery agent should independently determine its route based on traffic and distance.
3. Interaction:
   - Consider how responsibilities depend on communication with other agents.
   - Example: A coordinator agent relies on task completion reports from worker agents to update schedules.

Step 3: Designing Agent Behavior Models
Agent behavior models define how agents execute their responsibilities. There are several approaches to structuring agent behavior:
1. Finite State Machines (FSM):
   - Agents transition between predefined states based on triggers or events.
   - Example: A robotic vacuum cleaner transitions between "Idle," "Cleaning," and "Returning to Dock" states based on battery level and room coverage.

Code Illustration:
python

```python
class VacuumAgent(Agent):
    def __init__(self, name):
        super().__init__(name)
        self.state = "Idle"

    def perform_task(self):
        if self.state == "Idle":
            self.state = "Cleaning"
            print(f"{self.name}: Started cleaning.")
        elif self.state == "Cleaning":
            self.state = "Returning to Dock"
            print(f"{self.name}: Returning to dock.")
        elif self.state == "Returning to Dock":
            self.state = "Idle"
            print(f"{self.name}: Docked and idle.")
```

2. Rule-Based Behavior:
    - Agents follow a set of predefined rules to decide actions.
    - Example: A thermostat agent adjusts the temperature based on a rule like "If temperature > 25°C, turn on cooling."

Code Illustration:
python

```python
class ThermostatAgent(Agent):
    def perform_task(self, temperature):
        if temperature > 25:
            print(f"{self.name}: Turning on cooling.")
        elif temperature < 18:
            print(f"{self.name}: Turning on heating.")
        else:
```

```
        print(f"{self.name}: Maintaining current temperature.")
```

3. Goal-Oriented Behavior:
   - Agents work towards specific goals, dynamically deciding actions based on their environment and progress.
   - Example: A delivery agent aims to deliver packages as efficiently as possible, recalculating routes dynamically.

Code Illustration:
python

```python
class DeliveryAgent(Agent):
    def perform_task(self, packages):
        for package in packages:
            print(f"{self.name}: Delivering {package['id']} to {package['destination']}.")
```

4. Learning-Based Behavior:
   - Agents use machine learning to adapt their behavior based on past experiences.
   - Example: An agent in a stock trading system learns to buy and sell stocks by analyzing market trends.

Step 4: Collaborative Responsibilities
In multi-agent systems, agents often need to collaborate to achieve shared goals. Designing collaborative responsibilities requires:

1. Clear Role Definitions:
   - Ensure roles are complementary, minimizing redundancy.
   - Example: A picker agent retrieves items while a packer agent prepares them for shipment.
2. Communication Protocols:
   - Define how agents exchange information to coordinate actions.

- Example: A task coordinator agent sends task assignments to worker agents and receives progress updates.
3. Conflict Resolution:
   - Establish mechanisms to handle conflicting goals or resource contention.
   - Example: Two drones in a delivery system negotiate to avoid overlapping routes.

Step 5: Testing and Iterating Agent Roles

After defining roles and responsibilities, testing the system is crucial to ensure:
1. Efficiency:
   - Agents perform tasks without unnecessary delays or resource usage.
2. Scalability:
   - The system can accommodate additional agents or tasks without degradation.
3. Robustness:
   - Agents can adapt to unexpected conditions or failures.

Practical Example: A Multi-Agent Delivery System

This example demonstrates designing and implementing agent roles in a delivery system:
- CoordinatorAgent: Assigns delivery tasks to delivery agents.
- DeliveryAgent: Executes assigned delivery tasks.

Code:
python

```python
from crewai import Agent

class CoordinatorAgent(Agent):
    def assign_tasks(self, agents, tasks):
        for agent, task in zip(agents, tasks):
            print(f"{self.name}: Assigning task {task['id']} to {agent.name}.")
```

```
        agent.perform_task(task)

class DeliveryAgent(Agent):
   def perform_task(self, task):
      print(f"{self.name}: Delivering package {task['id']} to {task['destination']}.")

if __name__ == "__main__":
   coordinator = CoordinatorAgent(name="CoordinatorAgent")
   delivery_agents = [DeliveryAgent(name=f"DeliveryAgent{i}") for i in range(2)]
   tasks = [
      {"id": "Package1", "destination": "Location A"},
      {"id": "Package2", "destination": "Location B"}
   ]

   coordinator.assign_tasks(delivery_agents, tasks)
```

Expected Output:
```vbnet
CoordinatorAgent: Assigning task Package1 to DeliveryAgent0.
DeliveryAgent0: Delivering package Package1 to Location A.
CoordinatorAgent: Assigning task Package2 to DeliveryAgent1.
DeliveryAgent1: Delivering package Package2 to Location B.
```

Summary

Designing agent roles and responsibilities is a fundamental step in creating effective multi-agent systems. By clearly defining roles, aligning responsibilities with system goals, and structuring agent behavior using appropriate models, developers can build systems that are efficient, scalable, and adaptable. This structured approach ensures that agents work collaboratively while maintaining their autonomy.

5.2 Creating Specialized Agents for Specific Tasks

Specialized agents are the backbone of multi-agent systems (MAS), as they are designed to perform specific tasks with high efficiency and precision. Unlike general-purpose agents, specialized agents focus on well-defined roles, making them integral to achieving the overall goals of the system. By narrowing their responsibilities, these agents excel in their designated functions, contributing to the system's modularity, scalability, and effectiveness.

This section explores examples of task-specific agents in real-world scenarios, illustrating how they operate in diverse domains.

Specialized agents are ubiquitous in real-world applications, addressing challenges in industries such as robotics, logistics, healthcare, finance, and smart cities. Below are detailed examples from various domains.

1. Robotics
1.1 Picker Agent in Warehouse Automation
Role: Retrieve items from storage and prepare them for transport.
Tasks:
Navigate the warehouse to locate the required item.
Use robotic arms to pick the item.
Deliver the item to a packing station.
Real-World Example:
Amazon's warehouse robots are equipped with specialized picker agents that autonomously retrieve inventory items based on real-time orders.
Code Illustration:

```python
class PickerAgent(Agent):
    def perform_task(self, item_location):
        print(f"{self.name}: Navigating to location {item_location}.")
        print(f"{self.name}: Picking item from {item_location}.")
        print(f"{self.name}: Delivering item to packing station.")
```

1.2 Welding Agent in Manufacturing

Role: Perform welding operations on assembly line components.

Tasks:

Identify welding points based on design specifications.

Perform precise welding operations.

Inspect welds for quality assurance.

Real-World Example:

Automotive manufacturing plants use robotic arms equipped with welding agents to ensure precision and consistency in car assembly.

Code Illustration:

```python
class WeldingAgent(Agent):
    def perform_task(self, welding_points):
        for point in welding_points:
            print(f"{self.name}: Welding at point {point}.")
        print(f"{self.name}: Welds completed.")
```

2. Logistics

2.1 Route Planner Agent in Fleet Management

Role: Determine the most efficient routes for delivery vehicles.

Tasks:

Analyze traffic conditions and delivery priorities.

Calculate optimal routes for each vehicle.

Provide real-time route updates if conditions change.

Real-World Example:

UPS's logistics system uses route optimization agents to save fuel and reduce delivery times, famously known as the "ORION" system.

Code Illustration:

python
```python
class RoutePlannerAgent(Agent):
    def perform_task(self, destinations):
        print(f"{self.name}: Calculating optimal route for destinations: {destinations}.")
        # Example route calculation (mock)
        optimal_route = sorted(destinations)
        print(f"{self.name}: Optimal route: {optimal_route}.")
```

2.2 Inventory Manager Agent in Supply Chains

Role: Monitor and manage stock levels across warehouses.

Tasks:

Track inventory in real time.

Generate restocking alerts when stock levels are low.

Optimize stock distribution between locations.

Real-World Example:

Retailers like Walmart use specialized inventory agents to maintain seamless stock management and avoid shortages.

Code Illustration:

python
```python
class InventoryManagerAgent(Agent):
    def perform_task(self, stock_data):
        for item, quantity in stock_data.items():
            if quantity < 10:
                print(f"{self.name}: Alert - Low stock for {item}.")
        print(f"{self.name}: Inventory check completed.")
```

3. Healthcare

3.1 Diagnostic Agent in Telemedicine

Role: Analyze patient data to provide preliminary diagnoses.

Tasks:
Collect and process medical data (e.g., symptoms, test results).
Use rule-based or AI algorithms to identify potential conditions.
Recommend next steps or specialist consultations.

Real-World Example:
AI-powered systems like IBM Watson Health assist doctors by analyzing patient records and suggesting diagnoses.

Code Illustration:

```python
class DiagnosticAgent(Agent):
    def perform_task(self, patient_data):
        print(f"{self.name}: Analyzing patient data: {patient_data}.")
        # Example diagnosis (mock)
        diagnosis = "Condition A" if "symptom1" in patient_data else "Condition B"
        print(f"{self.name}: Suggested diagnosis: {diagnosis}.")
```

3.2 Medication Delivery Agent in Hospitals

Role: Deliver medications to patients in a hospital setting.

Tasks:
Navigate hospital corridors.
Deliver the correct medication to the assigned patient.
Confirm delivery with medical staff or patient.

Real-World Example:
Robotic systems like TUG robots in hospitals handle medication delivery, reducing staff workload.

Code Illustration:

```python
class MedicationDeliveryAgent(Agent):
    def perform_task(self, delivery_schedule):
        for patient, medication in delivery_schedule.items():
            print(f"{self.name}: Delivering {medication} to Patient {patient}.")
```

        print(f"{self.name}: All deliveries completed.")

4. Finance

4.1 Trading Agent in Stock Markets

Role: Execute buy and sell orders based on market conditions.

Tasks:

Monitor stock prices in real time.

Analyze market trends using predictive models.

Execute trades to maximize profits or minimize risks.

Real-World Example:

Algorithmic trading systems use specialized agents to automate high-frequency trades in milliseconds.

Code Illustration:

```python
class TradingAgent(Agent):
    def perform_task(self, market_data):
        print(f"{self.name}: Analyzing market data.")
        # Example trading logic (mock)
        if market_data["price"] < market_data["threshold"]:
            print(f"{self.name}: Buying stock.")
        else:
            print(f"{self.name}: Selling stock.")
```

5. Smart Cities

5.1 Traffic Control Agent

Role: Manage traffic flow at intersections.

Tasks:

Adjust traffic light timings based on real-time traffic density.

Prioritize emergency vehicles.

Reduce congestion during peak hours.

Real-World Example:

Smart traffic systems like those in Singapore use traffic control agents to minimize delays.

Code Illustration:

```python
class TrafficControlAgent(Agent):
```

```python
    def perform_task(self, traffic_data):
        print(f"{self.name}: Adjusting traffic lights based on current traffic density.")
        # Example logic (mock)
        print(f"{self.name}: Priority given to emergency vehicles.")
```

5.2 Waste Management Agent

Role: Optimize waste collection schedules and routes.

Tasks:

Monitor waste bin levels using IoT sensors.
Schedule collection based on urgency and proximity.
Generate optimized collection routes.

Real-World Example:

Smart waste management systems in cities like Copenhagen use such agents to improve efficiency.

Code Illustration:

```python
class WasteManagementAgent(Agent):
    def perform_task(self, bin_data):
        print(f"{self.name}: Planning waste collection routes.")
        for bin_id, level in bin_data.items():
            if level > 80:
                print(f"{self.name}: Scheduling pickup for Bin {bin_id}.")
        print(f"{self.name}: Collection plan generated.")
```

Summary

Specialized agents play critical roles in multi-agent systems by focusing on specific tasks, enabling efficiency, precision, and collaboration. From managing warehouse operations and optimizing logistics to enhancing healthcare and driving smart city initiatives, task-specific agents demonstrate the versatility and power of MAS.

By designing agents tailored to real-world roles and responsibilities, developers can create robust systems that address complex challenges in a modular and scalable manner.

5.3 Agent-to-Agent Communication: Protocols and Patterns

Agent-to-agent communication is a fundamental aspect of multi-agent systems (MAS). It enables agents to collaborate, share information, and coordinate their actions to achieve system-wide goals. Communication between agents is typically achieved through well-defined protocols and patterns, ensuring clarity, reliability, and scalability.

This section explores common messaging patterns, implementation techniques, and how these elements come together to create efficient communication pipelines.

Messaging patterns define how agents exchange information, while implementation techniques provide the tools and methods to bring these patterns to life. By combining effective patterns with robust implementation, agents can interact seamlessly, even in complex, distributed systems.

1. Messaging Patterns in Agent Communication

Messaging patterns dictate the flow of messages between agents, defining who sends, who receives, and how the communication occurs. Below are the most commonly used messaging patterns in multi-agent systems:

1.1 Point-to-Point Messaging
Description:
Point-to-point messaging involves direct communication between two agents. One agent sends a message to a specific recipient, and the recipient processes the message and may respond.
Key Features:
- Direct: Messages are sent to a specific agent.

- Efficient: Suitable for targeted communication with minimal overhead.
- Synchronous or Asynchronous: Can wait for a response (synchronous) or continue other tasks (asynchronous).

Example:
- A delivery agent requests route updates from a route planner agent.

Code Illustration:

```python
class Agent:
    def send_message(self, recipient, message):
        print(f"{self.name}: Sending message to {recipient.name}: {message}")
        recipient.on_message(self, message)

    def on_message(self, sender, message):
        print(f"{self.name}: Received message from {sender.name}: {message}")

# Example usage
if __name__ == "__main__":
    sender = Agent()
    sender.name = "SenderAgent"
    receiver = Agent()
    receiver.name = "ReceiverAgent"

    sender.send_message(receiver, "Requesting route update.")
```

1.2 Publish-Subscribe Messaging
Description:
In a publish-subscribe model, agents publish messages to a shared topic, and other agents subscribed to that topic receive the messages. This pattern is useful for broadcasting updates to multiple agents.

Key Features:
- Broadcast: Messages are sent to all subscribers of a topic.
- Scalable: Supports many-to-many communication.
- Loose Coupling: Publishers and subscribers do not need to know each other.

Example:
- A traffic control agent broadcasts traffic updates to all nearby autonomous vehicles.

Code Illustration:

```python
class PubSubBroker:
    def __init__(self):
        self.subscriptions = {}

    def subscribe(self, agent, topic):
        if topic not in self.subscriptions:
            self.subscriptions[topic] = []
        self.subscriptions[topic].append(agent)

    def publish(self, topic, message):
        if topic in self.subscriptions:
            for agent in self.subscriptions[topic]:
                agent.on_message(topic, message)

class Agent:
    def on_message(self, topic, message):
        print(f"{self.name}: Received message on topic '{topic}': {message}")

# Example usage
if __name__ == "__main__":
    broker = PubSubBroker()
    agent1 = Agent()
    agent1.name = "Agent1"
    agent2 = Agent()
    agent2.name = "Agent2"
```

```python
broker.subscribe(agent1, "TrafficUpdates")
broker.subscribe(agent2, "TrafficUpdates")

broker.publish("TrafficUpdates", "Heavy traffic on Route 42.")
```

1.3 Request-Response Messaging
Description:
In this pattern, an agent sends a request message and waits for a response from another agent. This is common in client-server models.

Key Features:
- Two-Way Communication: Involves a request and a corresponding response.
- Synchronous or Asynchronous: The requesting agent can either wait for the response or continue other tasks.

Example:
- A diagnostic agent requests patient data from a database agent and receives the data in response.

Code Illustration:
python

```python
class RequestResponseAgent:
    def send_request(self, recipient, request):
        print(f"{self.name}: Sending request to {recipient.name}: {request}")
        response = recipient.on_request(self, request)
        print(f"{self.name}: Received response: {response}")

    def on_request(self, sender, request):
        print(f"{self.name}: Received request from {sender.name}: {request}")
        return f"Response to '{request}'"

# Example usage
```

```python
if __name__ == "__main__":
    requester = RequestResponseAgent()
    requester.name = "RequesterAgent"
    responder = RequestResponseAgent()
    responder.name = "ResponderAgent"

    requester.send_request(responder, "Fetch patient data.")
```

1.4 Queue-Based Messaging

Description:

In this pattern, messages are placed in a queue, allowing agents to process them asynchronously. This is useful for load balancing and ensuring that no messages are lost if an agent is temporarily unavailable.

Key Features:
- Asynchronous: Decouples message sending and processing.
- Reliable: Ensures messages are not lost.
- Scalable: Can handle a large number of messages.

Example:
- A logging agent receives logs from multiple agents via a message queue.

Code Illustration:

python

```python
from queue import Queue

class QueueAgent:
    def __init__(self):
        self.message_queue = Queue()

    def send_message(self, message):
        self.message_queue.put(message)
        print(f"{self.name}: Message queued: {message}")

    def process_messages(self):
```

```python
        while not self.message_queue.empty():
            message = self.message_queue.get()
            print(f"{self.name}: Processing message: {message}")

# Example usage
if __name__ == "__main__":
    logger = QueueAgent()
    logger.name = "LoggerAgent"

    logger.send_message("Log entry 1")
    logger.send_message("Log entry 2")
    logger.process_messages()
```

2. Implementation Techniques

2.1 Choosing the Right Protocol

Agents can use various communication protocols depending on the use case:
- HTTP/REST: Ideal for client-server interactions in web-based systems.
- gRPC: Supports efficient, scalable, and cross-platform communication.
- ZeroMQ: Lightweight and fast, suitable for decentralized systems.
- Message Queues (e.g., RabbitMQ, Kafka): Excellent for asynchronous, reliable messaging.

2.2 Message Encoding

Messages can be encoded in formats like:
- JSON: Human-readable and widely supported.
- Protobuf: Compact and efficient, used with gRPC.
- XML: Versatile but more verbose.

2.3 Error Handling
- Retries: Implement retries for failed message deliveries.
- Timeouts: Set time limits for request-response patterns.

- Acknowledgments: Ensure messages are acknowledged upon receipt.

2.4 Security
- Encryption: Use protocols like TLS for secure communication.
- Authentication: Verify agent identities using tokens or keys.

Summary

Agent-to-agent communication in multi-agent systems relies on well-defined messaging patterns and robust implementation techniques. Patterns like point-to-point, publish-subscribe, request-response, and queue-based messaging provide flexibility to design systems tailored to specific needs. By selecting appropriate protocols, encoding formats, and security measures, developers can ensure efficient, scalable, and secure communication pipelines.

5.4 Handling Errors and Failures in Agent Interactions

Errors and failures are inevitable in multi-agent systems (MAS) due to their distributed and dynamic nature. These failures can arise from communication breakdowns, resource contention, unhandled exceptions, or conflicting objectives among agents. To maintain system robustness, it is essential to implement strategies for error recovery and conflict resolution.

This section explores comprehensive approaches to handling errors and conflicts in agent interactions, ensuring that the system remains functional and achieves its goals despite disruptions.

Handling errors and resolving conflicts in agent interactions requires a combination of proactive planning, robust mechanisms, and reactive recovery strategies. Below are key strategies categorized under error recovery and conflict resolution.

1. Error Recovery Strategies

Error recovery focuses on detecting, diagnosing, and resolving failures that occur during agent interactions or task execution.

1.1 Fault Detection and Logging

Description:

Detecting errors early is critical to minimize their impact. Agents should monitor their interactions and log any anomalies or failures for analysis.

Techniques:
- Error Codes: Assign specific codes to different types of errors for easier identification.
- Logging Systems: Maintain detailed logs of agent activities, including timestamps and error descriptions.
- Monitoring Agents: Use dedicated agents to monitor system health and detect faults.

Example:

A monitoring agent detects communication failures between two agents and triggers an alert.

Code Illustration:

python

```python
class MonitoringAgent(Agent):
    def monitor(self, agents):
        for agent in agents:
            try:
                agent.perform_task()
            except Exception as e:
                print(f"{self.name}: Error detected in {agent.name}: {e}")
                self.log_error(agent.name, str(e))

    def log_error(self, agent_name, error_message):
        print(f"{self.name}: Logging error for {agent_name}: {error_message}")
```

1.2 Retry Mechanism

Description:
Implementing retries allows agents to attempt task execution multiple times before declaring failure. This is particularly useful for transient errors, such as network interruptions.

Techniques:
- Define a maximum retry limit to prevent infinite loops.
- Introduce exponential backoff to avoid overloading the system during retries.

Example:
A delivery agent retries sending a message to a coordinator agent if the initial attempt fails due to a temporary network issue.

Code Illustration:

```python
class RetryAgent(Agent):
    def send_message(self, recipient, message, retries=3):
        for attempt in range(retries):
            try:
                recipient.on_message(self, message)
                print(f"{self.name}: Message sent successfully.")
                return
            except Exception as e:
                print(f"{self.name}: Attempt {attempt + 1} failed. Retrying...")
        print(f"{self.name}: All attempts failed. Message delivery unsuccessful.")
```

1.3 Failover Mechanism

Description:
Failover mechanisms ensure continuity by redirecting tasks or messages to backup agents when the primary agent fails.

Techniques:
- Maintain a pool of backup agents ready to take over tasks.
- Use health checks to identify agent failures and trigger failover.

Example:
In a swarm robotics system, if a drone fails, another drone takes over its assigned area for mapping.

Code Illustration:

```python
class FailoverCoordinatorAgent(Agent):
    def assign_task(self, agents, task):
        for agent in agents:
            try:
                agent.perform_task(task)
                print(f"{self.name}: Task assigned to {agent.name}.")
                return
            except Exception:
                print(f"{self.name}: {agent.name} failed. Trying next agent.")
        print(f"{self.name}: All agents failed. Task could not be completed.")
```

1.4 Graceful Degradation

Description:
In cases where recovery is not possible, the system should degrade gracefully, continuing to operate at reduced functionality.

Techniques:
- Prioritize critical tasks while deferring or dropping non-essential ones.
- Isolate faulty components to prevent cascading failures.

Example:
In a smart grid, if a power station fails, the system reduces energy supply to non-essential areas while maintaining power to hospitals and emergency services.

2. Conflict Resolution Strategies

Conflict resolution focuses on addressing disputes or inconsistencies among agents, ensuring that their actions align with system goals.

2.1 Negotiation Protocols

Description:

Agents negotiate to resolve conflicts and agree on a course of action. This is common in systems where agents have overlapping or competing goals.

Techniques:
- Auction-Based Negotiation: Agents bid for tasks or resources, and the highest bidder wins.
- Priority-Based Resolution: Assign priorities to agents or tasks, resolving conflicts based on these priorities.

Example:

In a delivery system, two drones negotiate to decide who will deliver a high-priority package.

Code Illustration:

python
```
class NegotiationAgent(Agent):
    def negotiate(self, other_agent, resource):
        print(f"{self.name}: Negotiating with {other_agent.name} for {resource}.")
        # Example priority comparison
        if self.priority > other_agent.priority:
            print(f"{self.name}: Won the negotiation for {resource}.")
            return True
        else:
            print(f"{self.name}: Lost the negotiation for {resource}.")
            return False
```

2.2 Arbitration by a Central Coordinator

Description:
A central coordinator resolves conflicts by making decisions based on system-wide objectives or predefined rules.

Techniques:
- Use conflict resolution rules to determine outcomes.
- Gather input from conflicting agents and decide based on fairness or efficiency.

Example:
In a smart city, a central traffic coordinator resolves conflicts between autonomous vehicles at intersections.

Code Illustration:

python
```python
class CoordinatorAgent(Agent):
    def resolve_conflict(self, agent1, agent2, resource):
        print(f"{self.name}: Resolving conflict over {resource}.")
        # Example rule: Assign resource to the agent with higher priority
        if agent1.priority > agent2.priority:
            print(f"{self.name}: Assigning {resource} to {agent1.name}.")
            return agent1
        else:
            print(f"{self.name}: Assigning {resource} to {agent2.name}.")
            return agent2
```

2.3 Consensus Mechanisms

Description:
Consensus mechanisms allow agents to reach an agreement collectively. This is common in decentralized systems.

Techniques:
- Use algorithms like Paxos or Raft to achieve distributed consensus.

- Implement voting systems where agents vote on proposed actions.

Example:
In a peer-to-peer network, agents vote on whether to accept a new transaction into the system.

2.4 Avoidance Strategies
Description:
Proactively design the system to minimize conflicts through clear role definitions and resource allocation.
Techniques:
- Assign unique tasks or resources to agents to prevent overlap.
- Use scheduling algorithms to allocate tasks efficiently.

Example:
In a factory, each robotic arm is assigned a specific section of the assembly line to avoid collisions.

Summary
Error recovery and conflict resolution are critical to maintaining the robustness and efficiency of multi-agent systems. By implementing strategies like fault detection, retries, failover mechanisms, and negotiation protocols, systems can handle disruptions gracefully. Proactive conflict avoidance and centralized or decentralized resolution ensure that agents collaborate effectively, even in dynamic environments.

These techniques empower developers to create resilient multi-agent systems that can operate reliably under diverse conditions.

5.5 Concept-to-Code: Building a Functional Agent System

Creating a functional multi-agent system (MAS) requires a structured, step-by-step approach. By understanding the roles of individual agents, defining their interactions, and implementing communication protocols, you can design a robust system capable of addressing complex, distributed tasks.

This section provides a comprehensive, step-by-step guide to building a multi-agent system using CrewAI or a similar framework. The goal is to help you understand the full lifecycle of MAS development, from conceptualization to implementation.

Step 1: Define the Problem and Objectives

Before building an MAS, it is essential to define the problem it will solve and the system's objectives. For this example, let's create a package delivery system.

System Requirements:
1. Delivery agents should deliver packages to specified destinations.
2. A coordinator agent should assign tasks to delivery agents based on availability.
3. Agents should communicate to report task status and request assistance if needed.

Step 2: Identify Agent Roles and Responsibilities
Agents:
1. CoordinatorAgent:
    - Assigns delivery tasks to available delivery agents.
    - Monitors task progress.
2. DeliveryAgent:
    - Accepts and executes delivery tasks.
    - Reports status back to the coordinator.

Step 3: Define Communication Patterns
Communication Workflow:
1. The CoordinatorAgent sends task assignments to DeliveryAgents.
2. DeliveryAgents report task completion or issues to the CoordinatorAgent.
3. If a delivery agent fails, the coordinator assigns the task to another agent.

Step 4: Implement the Multi-Agent System
Below is the step-by-step implementation of the system:

4.1 Define the Coordinator Agent
The CoordinatorAgent assigns tasks to available delivery agents and monitors task completion.
Code:
python

```python
from crewai import Agent

class CoordinatorAgent(Agent):
    def __init__(self, name):
        super().__init__(name)
        self.task_queue = []
        self.available_agents = []

    def register_agent(self, agent):
        self.available_agents.append(agent)
        print(f"{self.name}: Registered {agent.name}.")

    def assign_task(self, task):
        if self.available_agents:
            agent = self.available_agents.pop(0)  # Get the first available agent
            print(f"{self.name}: Assigning task '{task}' to {agent.name}.")
            agent.perform_task(task, self)
        else:
            print(f"{self.name}: No agents available. Adding '{task}' to queue.")
            self.task_queue.append(task)

    def task_completed(self, agent):
        print(f"{self.name}: {agent.name} completed a task.")
```

```python
        self.available_agents.append(agent)
        if self.task_queue:
            self.assign_task(self.task_queue.pop(0))  # Assign the next task in queue
```

4.2 Define the Delivery Agent

The DeliveryAgent performs assigned delivery tasks and communicates task status back to the CoordinatorAgent.

Code:

python
```python
class DeliveryAgent(Agent):
    def perform_task(self, task, coordinator):
        print(f"{self.name}: Starting task '{task}'.")
        try:
            # Simulate task execution
            print(f"{self.name}: Delivering {task}.")
            # Notify the coordinator of task completion
            coordinator.task_completed(self)
        except Exception as e:
            print(f"{self.name}: Failed to complete task '{task}': {e}.")
            coordinator.report_failure(self, task)
```

4.3 Main Script to Integrate the System

The main script initializes the agents, registers delivery agents with the coordinator, and assigns tasks.

Code:

python
```python
if __name__ == "__main__":
    # Initialize the coordinator
    coordinator = CoordinatorAgent(name="CoordinatorAgent")

    # Initialize delivery agents
```

```python
delivery_agents = [DeliveryAgent(name=f"DeliveryAgent{i}") for i in range(3)]

# Register delivery agents with the coordinator
for agent in delivery_agents:
    coordinator.register_agent(agent)

# Assign tasks
tasks = ["Package A to Location X", "Package B to Location Y", "Package C to Location Z"]
for task in tasks:
    coordinator.assign_task(task)

# Add additional tasks to simulate queue behavior
coordinator.assign_task("Package D to Location W")
```

Step 5: Test the System
Execution: Run the script to simulate the system's operation. The coordinator will assign tasks to available agents, manage the task queue, and handle task completion.

Expected Output:

vbnet

CoordinatorAgent: Registered DeliveryAgent0.
CoordinatorAgent: Registered DeliveryAgent1.
CoordinatorAgent: Registered DeliveryAgent2.
CoordinatorAgent: Assigning task 'Package A to Location X' to DeliveryAgent0.
DeliveryAgent0: Starting task 'Package A to Location X'.
DeliveryAgent0: Delivering Package A to Location X.
CoordinatorAgent: DeliveryAgent0 completed a task.
CoordinatorAgent: Assigning task 'Package B to Location Y' to DeliveryAgent1.
DeliveryAgent1: Starting task 'Package B to Location Y'.
DeliveryAgent1: Delivering Package B to Location Y.

CoordinatorAgent: DeliveryAgent1 completed a task.
CoordinatorAgent: Assigning task 'Package C to Location Z' to DeliveryAgent2.
DeliveryAgent2: Starting task 'Package C to Location Z'.
DeliveryAgent2: Delivering Package C to Location Z.
CoordinatorAgent: DeliveryAgent2 completed a task.
CoordinatorAgent: Assigning task 'Package D to Location W' to DeliveryAgent0.
DeliveryAgent0: Starting task 'Package D to Location W'.
DeliveryAgent0: Delivering Package D to Location W.
CoordinatorAgent: DeliveryAgent0 completed a task.

Step 6: Enhance the System
To improve the system, consider the following enhancements:
1. Error Handling:
    - Implement failover mechanisms to reassign tasks if a delivery agent fails.

Example:

```python
class CoordinatorAgent(Agent):
    def report_failure(self, agent, task):
        print(f"{self.name}: {agent.name} failed to complete '{task}'. Reassigning...")
        self.assign_task(task)
```

2. Dynamic Task Assignment:
    - Use algorithms to prioritize tasks based on urgency or distance.

Example:

```python
class CoordinatorAgent(Agent):
    def assign_task(self, task):
        self.task_queue.append(task)
```

```
    self.task_queue.sort(key=lambda t: t['priority'],
reverse=True)
    print(f"{self.name}: Task queue sorted by priority.")
    if self.available_agents:
        next_task = self.task_queue.pop(0)
        agent = self.available_agents.pop(0)
        print(f"{self.name}: Assigning high-priority task '{next_task}' to {agent.name}.")
        agent.perform_task(next_task, self)
```

3. Communication Protocols:
    - Use gRPC or ZeroMQ to enable agent communication across a distributed network.

Step 7: Deployment

Once the system is thoroughly tested, deploy it in a real-world environment:

- Cloud Infrastructure: Host the agents on cloud servers for scalability.
- IoT Devices: Use IoT-enabled hardware for agents operating in physical environments.

Summary

This step-by-step guide demonstrates how to design and implement a multi-agent system using specialized agents for package delivery. By defining roles, implementing communication patterns, and enhancing functionality with failover mechanisms and dynamic task assignments, you can create a robust, scalable MAS. This approach serves as a foundation for more complex systems, whether in logistics, healthcare, or smart cities.

Chapter 6: Collaboration and Coordination

6.1 Strategies for Agent Collaboration

Collaboration in multi-agent systems (MAS) involves agents working together to achieve shared goals. Collaboration is crucial for systems where tasks are too complex or large for a single agent to handle effectively. A well-coordinated system of agents ensures efficiency, scalability, and adaptability in dynamic environments.

Collaborative planning and task sharing are strategies that enable agents to distribute workload, align their actions, and achieve common objectives. These strategies involve defining shared goals, creating execution plans, and ensuring effective task allocation among agents.

1. Collaborative Planning

Collaborative planning refers to the process where agents collectively decide how to accomplish a goal. It ensures that agents are aligned in their efforts and avoid duplicating work or causing conflicts.

Key Elements of Collaborative Planning
1. Goal Definition:
    - Establish clear and measurable objectives for the agents to achieve.
    - Example: In a search-and-rescue operation, the goal could be "Find all survivors within a 5 km radius."
2. Information Sharing:
    - Agents share their capabilities, resources, and current states to determine how they can contribute to the goal.
    - Example: A drone informs other agents of its battery level and range, ensuring tasks are assigned appropriately.

3. **Plan Generation:**
   - Agents collaboratively develop a plan outlining the steps needed to achieve the goal.
   - Example: In warehouse automation, agents plan item retrieval and packaging in sequential order to optimize efficiency.
4. **Consensus Building:**
   - Agents agree on the plan before execution, resolving any disagreements through negotiation or arbitration.

Techniques for Collaborative Planning
1. **Centralized Planning:**
   - A central agent (planner) creates a global plan based on input from all agents and distributes tasks.
   - Example: In a logistics system, a central coordinator plans delivery routes for all trucks.

Code Example:

```python
class CentralPlanner(Agent):
    def create_plan(self, agents, tasks):
        plan = {}
        for i, task in enumerate(tasks):
            agent = agents[i % len(agents)]
            plan[agent.name] = task
        return plan
```

2. **Distributed Planning:**
   - Agents independently propose partial plans and combine them to form a global plan.
   - Example: In a robotic swarm, each robot plans its path locally and adjusts it based on others' paths.

Code Example:

```python
class DistributedAgent(Agent):
    def propose_plan(self, task):
```

```
        print(f"{self.name}: Proposing to handle task
'{task}'.")
        return {self.name: task}
```

3. Hierarchical Planning:
   - Higher-level agents define strategic plans, while lower-level agents create detailed execution plans.
   - Example: A strategic agent sets a goal of "delivering all packages," while individual delivery agents plan routes.

2. Task Sharing

Task sharing involves dividing a larger task into smaller subtasks and distributing them among agents. This ensures efficient use of resources and faster task completion.

Key Elements of Task Sharing
1. Task Decomposition:
   - Break down the main goal into manageable subtasks.
   - Example: In disaster response, divide the search area into smaller zones and assign them to different drones.
2. Task Allocation:
   - Assign tasks based on agents' capabilities, availability, and proximity to the task location.
   - Example: Assign the closest delivery agent to handle a nearby package.
3. Monitoring and Reallocation:
   - Monitor task progress and reassign tasks if an agent fails or completes its task early.

Techniques for Task Sharing
1. Static Task Assignment:
   - Tasks are predefined and assigned at the start. There is no reassignment during execution.
   - Example: In a factory, robotic arms are assigned fixed sections of an assembly line.

Code Example:
python
```
class StaticTaskAllocator:
    def assign_tasks(self, agents, tasks):
        for agent, task in zip(agents, tasks):
            print(f"Assigning task '{task}' to {agent.name}.")
```

2. Dynamic Task Assignment:
   - Tasks are assigned and reassigned dynamically based on the current state of the system.
   - Example: In a fleet management system, tasks are reassigned if traffic conditions change.

Code Example:
python
```
class DynamicTaskAllocator(Agent):
    def assign_task(self, agent, task):
        print(f"{self.name}: Assigning task '{task}' to {agent.name}.")
        agent.perform_task(task)
```

3. Auction-Based Allocation:
   - Agents bid for tasks based on their capabilities and availability. The task is assigned to the highest bidder.
   - Example: Delivery agents bid on tasks based on proximity and capacity.

Code Example:
python
```
class Auctioneer(Agent):
    def allocate_task(self, tasks, agents):
        for task in tasks:
            bids = {agent.name: agent.calculate_bid(task) for agent in agents}
            winner = max(bids, key=bids.get)
            print(f"{self.name}: Task '{task}' assigned to {winner}.")
```

4. Role-Based Allocation:
    - Tasks are assigned based on predefined roles and responsibilities.
    - Example: In a smart city, traffic control agents handle traffic signals while maintenance agents repair faulty systems.

Code Example:

```python
class RoleBasedTaskAllocator:
    def allocate_tasks(self, agents, tasks):
        for agent, task in zip(agents, tasks):
            if agent.role in task["roles"]:
                print(f"Task '{task['name']}' assigned to {agent.name}.")
```

Practical Example: Collaborative Warehouse System

Scenario:
Agents collaborate to fulfill warehouse orders. A CoordinatorAgent assigns tasks to PickerAgents and PackerAgents based on their roles.

Code:

```python
class CoordinatorAgent(Agent):
    def assign_task(self, task, agents):
        for agent in agents:
            if agent.role == task["role"]:
                print(f"{self.name}: Assigning task '{task['name']}' to {agent.name}.")
                agent.perform_task(task)

class PickerAgent(Agent):
    def __init__(self, name):
        super().__init__(name)
        self.role = "Picker"
```

```python
    def perform_task(self, task):
        print(f"{self.name}: Picking item '{task['item']}'.")

class PackerAgent(Agent):
    def __init__(self, name):
        super().__init__(name)
        self.role = "Packer"

    def perform_task(self, task):
        print(f"{self.name}: Packing item '{task['item']}'.")

if __name__ == "__main__":
    coordinator = CoordinatorAgent(name="Coordinator")
    picker = PickerAgent(name="PickerAgent")
    packer = PackerAgent(name="PackerAgent")

    tasks = [
        {"name": "Pick Order 1", "role": "Picker", "item": "Widget A"},
        {"name": "Pack Order 1", "role": "Packer", "item": "Widget A"}
    ]

    agents = [picker, packer]
    for task in tasks:
        coordinator.assign_task(task, agents)
```

Expected Output:
vbnet
Coordinator: Assigning task 'Pick Order 1' to PickerAgent.
PickerAgent: Picking item 'Widget A'.
Coordinator: Assigning task 'Pack Order 1' to PackerAgent.

PackerAgent: Packing item 'Widget A'.

Summary
Collaborative planning and task sharing are essential strategies for enabling agents to work together efficiently. By defining shared goals, generating execution plans, and distributing tasks based on agents' capabilities, multi-agent systems achieve coordinated action. Using techniques like centralized planning, auction-based allocation, and dynamic task reassignment, developers can build robust systems capable of tackling complex, distributed challenges.

6.2 Centralized vs. Decentralized Coordination

Coordination in multi-agent systems (MAS) refers to how agents work together to achieve shared goals. The two primary approaches are centralized coordination and decentralized coordination. Each has its own set of trade-offs, benefits, and limitations, making them suitable for different use cases.
This section explores the trade-offs between centralized and decentralized coordination, providing a detailed comparison and discussing their respective use cases.
1. Centralized Coordination
In a centralized coordination model, a single agent or entity (the coordinator) oversees and manages the activities of all other agents in the system. The coordinator has a global view of the system, which allows it to make informed decisions about task allocation, resource distribution, and overall system behavior.

Key Characteristics
- Centralized Control:
    - One agent or entity is responsible for planning, decision-making, and monitoring.
- Global Perspective:
    - The coordinator has complete knowledge of the system and its current state.

- Simplified Decision-Making:
  - The coordinator handles all conflicts and task assignments, simplifying the responsibilities of individual agents.

Advantages of Centralized Coordination
1. Efficiency in Small Systems:
   - With fewer agents, centralized coordination ensures quick and optimized decision-making due to a global view.
2. Simplified Conflict Resolution:
   - A central entity resolves conflicts, reducing the complexity for individual agents.
3. Easier Monitoring and Debugging:
   - Centralized systems are easier to monitor and debug since all information flows through the coordinator.

Disadvantages of Centralized Coordination
1. Single Point of Failure:
   - If the coordinator fails, the entire system may become inoperative.
2. Scalability Issues:
   - As the number of agents increases, the coordinator can become a bottleneck, reducing system performance.
3. Limited Adaptability:
   - Centralized systems may struggle in dynamic environments where quick, localized decisions are needed.

Use Cases for Centralized Coordination
1. Warehouse Automation:
   - A central system assigns tasks to robotic arms for picking, packing, and sorting items.
2. Air Traffic Control:

- A centralized system manages the movement of aircraft to prevent collisions and ensure efficient routing.
3. Smart Grids:
    - A central coordinator monitors energy production and consumption, balancing supply and demand.

Code Example: Centralized Coordination
A CoordinatorAgent assigns tasks to multiple worker agents.
python

```python
class CoordinatorAgent(Agent):
    def assign_tasks(self, agents, tasks):
        for agent, task in zip(agents, tasks):
            print(f"{self.name}: Assigning task '{task}' to {agent.name}.")
            agent.perform_task(task)

class WorkerAgent(Agent):
    def perform_task(self, task):
        print(f"{self.name}: Executing task '{task}'.")

# Example usage
if __name__ == "__main__":
    coordinator = CoordinatorAgent(name="Coordinator")
    agents = [WorkerAgent(name=f"Worker{i}") for i in range(3)]
    tasks = ["Task A", "Task B", "Task C"]

    coordinator.assign_tasks(agents, tasks)
```

2. Decentralized Coordination
In a decentralized coordination model, agents communicate and coordinate directly with each other without relying on a central

authority. Each agent has partial knowledge of the system and makes decisions based on local information and peer-to-peer interactions.

Key Characteristics
- Distributed Control:
    - Agents operate autonomously, making decisions based on their local environment and objectives.
- Local Perspective:
    - Each agent only has knowledge of its immediate surroundings or network.
- Peer-to-Peer Communication:
    - Agents exchange information directly to coordinate their actions.

Advantages of Decentralized Coordination
1. Scalability:
    - The system can handle a large number of agents since there is no central bottleneck.
2. Fault Tolerance:
    - The system remains operational even if individual agents fail, as there is no reliance on a central coordinator.
3. Adaptability:
    - Agents can quickly adapt to local changes without waiting for instructions from a central entity.

Disadvantages of Decentralized Coordination
1. Increased Complexity:
    - Agents must handle their own decision-making, communication, and conflict resolution.
2. Potential Inefficiencies:
    - Without a global view, agents may make suboptimal decisions or duplicate efforts.
3. Communication Overhead:

- Frequent peer-to-peer communication can lead to higher network traffic.

Use Cases for Decentralized Coordination
1. Swarm Robotics:
   - Autonomous drones collaborate to survey a disaster area, sharing local findings with nearby drones.
2. Peer-to-Peer Networks:
   - Distributed file-sharing systems like BitTorrent rely on decentralized coordination.
3. Traffic Management:
   - Autonomous vehicles coordinate directly with one another to navigate intersections and avoid collisions.

Code Example: Decentralized Coordination
Agents communicate directly to coordinate tasks.

```python
class DecentralizedAgent(Agent):
    def perform_task(self, task, peers):
        print(f"{self.name}: Performing task '{task}'.")
        for peer in peers:
            print(f"{self.name}: Informing {peer.name} about task completion.")

# Example usage
if __name__ == "__main__":
    agents = [DecentralizedAgent(name=f"Agent{i}") for i in range(3)]
    tasks = ["Task A", "Task B", "Task C"]

    for i, agent in enumerate(agents):
        agent.perform_task(tasks[i], agents[:i] + agents[i+1:])
```

Comparison: Centralized vs. Decentralized Coordination

Aspect	Centralized Coordination	Decentralized Coordination
Control	Centralized through a single coordinator	Distributed among agents
Scalability	Limited as the number of agents increases	Highly scalable
Fault Tolerance	Low due to reliance on a single point of control	High as no single failure disrupts the entire system
Decision-Making Speed	Slow in dynamic environments	Quick in localized environments
Complexity	Simplifies individual agents' roles	Requires agents to manage their own coordination
Communication	Minimal overhead as communication is centralized	High due to frequent peer-to-peer interactions

Choosing Between Centralized and Decentralized Coordination
The choice between centralized and decentralized coordination depends on the system's requirements and constraints:

1. Centralized Coordination:
    - Use when the system is small, requires global optimization, or operates in a predictable environment.
    - Examples: Factory automation, smart grids, air traffic control.
2. Decentralized Coordination:
    - Use when the system is large, dynamic, or requires high fault tolerance.
    - Examples: Swarm robotics, autonomous vehicle networks, peer-to-peer systems.

Summary
Centralized and decentralized coordination each offer unique strengths and trade-offs. Centralized systems excel in efficiency and simplicity for small, predictable environments, while decentralized systems provide scalability, fault tolerance, and adaptability in dynamic and distributed settings. Understanding these trade-offs is essential for designing multi-agent systems that meet specific operational needs.

6.3 Conflict Resolution and Consensus Mechanisms

In multi-agent systems (MAS), conflicts are inevitable due to the distributed nature of agents, their overlapping goals, and competition for shared resources. Effective conflict resolution and consensus mechanisms are essential to ensure smooth collaboration, minimize delays, and maintain system efficiency. This section provides a comprehensive overview of techniques used for conflict resolution and achieving consensus among agents, focusing on strategies that foster smooth collaboration in diverse scenarios.

1. Conflict Resolution Techniques

Conflict resolution involves addressing disagreements or inconsistencies between agents to maintain harmony in the system. Below are the key techniques used in multi-agent systems:

1.1 Priority-Based Resolution
Description:
In priority-based resolution, conflicts are resolved by assigning predefined priorities to agents or tasks. Higher-priority agents or tasks are given precedence over others.
Use Case:
- In a traffic management system, emergency vehicles are given higher priority at intersections.

Implementation Steps:
1. Assign a priority value to each agent or task.

2. Compare priorities when conflicts arise.
3. Allow the higher-priority agent/task to proceed.

Example:

python

```
class PriorityAgent(Agent):
    def __init__(self, name, priority):
        super().__init__(name)
        self.priority = priority

    def resolve_conflict(self, other_agent):
        if self.priority > other_agent.priority:
            print(f"{self.name} wins the conflict over {other_agent.name}.")
        else:
            print(f"{other_agent.name} wins the conflict over {self.name}.")

# Example usage
agent1 = PriorityAgent(name="Agent1", priority=2)
agent2 = PriorityAgent(name="Agent2", priority=1)

agent1.resolve_conflict(agent2)
```

Output:

sql

Agent1 wins the conflict over Agent2.

1.2 Negotiation Protocols

Description:

Negotiation protocols enable agents to discuss and agree on a resolution when conflicts occur. This method is particularly useful when agents have equal priorities or overlapping objectives.

Types of Negotiation:
1. Bilateral Negotiation:
    - Two agents negotiate directly with each other.

2. Multilateral Negotiation:
   - Multiple agents negotiate to reach a common agreement.

Use Case:
- In a resource allocation system, agents negotiate for access to shared resources like bandwidth or processing power.

Example:
python
```python
class NegotiatingAgent(Agent):
    def negotiate(self, other_agent, resource):
        print(f"{self.name} negotiating with {other_agent.name} for {resource}.")
        if self.bid > other_agent.bid:
            print(f"{self.name} wins the negotiation for {resource}.")
        else:
            print(f"{other_agent.name} wins the negotiation for {resource}.")

# Example usage
agent1 = NegotiatingAgent(name="Agent1")
agent1.bid = 50
agent2 = NegotiatingAgent(name="Agent2")
agent2.bid = 40

agent1.negotiate(agent2, "ResourceA")
```

Output:
rust
```rust
Agent1 negotiating with Agent2 for ResourceA.
Agent1 wins the negotiation for ResourceA.
```

1.3 Arbitration by a Central Mediator
Description:
A central mediator resolves conflicts based on predefined rules or

objectives. The mediator evaluates the situation and makes a decision that is binding on all conflicting agents.

Use Case:
- In a logistics system, a central coordinator resolves disputes over vehicle routes to minimize delivery times.

Example:
python
```python
class Mediator(Agent):
    def arbitrate(self, agent1, agent2, resource):
        print(f"{self.name}: Resolving conflict over {resource}.")
        winner = agent1 if agent1.priority > agent2.priority else agent2
        print(f"{self.name}: {winner.name} wins the conflict.")

# Example usage
mediator = Mediator(name="MediatorAgent")
agent1.priority = 3
agent2.priority = 2
mediator.arbitrate(agent1, agent2, "RouteA")
```

1.4 Auction-Based Conflict Resolution

Description:
Agents bid for resources, and the agent with the highest bid wins. This approach is commonly used for tasks like resource allocation and scheduling.

Use Case:
- In a cloud computing system, virtual machines bid for CPU resources.

Example:
python
```python
class Auctioneer(Agent):
    def resolve_auction(self, resource, bids):
        winner = max(bids, key=bids.get)
```

```python
        print(f"{self.name}: {winner} wins the auction for {resource}.")

# Example usage
bids = {"Agent1": 100, "Agent2": 150, "Agent3": 120}
auctioneer = Auctioneer(name="AuctioneerAgent")
auctioneer.resolve_auction("CPU", bids)
```

2. Consensus Mechanisms

Consensus mechanisms ensure that all agents agree on a common course of action or shared state, which is vital in decentralized systems.

2.1 Voting Mechanisms

Description:
Agents cast votes on a proposed action, and the action with the majority votes is selected. This approach is simple and effective for making group decisions.

Use Case:
- In distributed systems, agents vote on whether to accept a new data block.

Example:
```python
class VotingAgent(Agent):
    def vote(self, proposal):
        return self.name, proposal in self.preferences

# Example usage
agents = [
    VotingAgent(name="Agent1"),
    VotingAgent(name="Agent2"),
    VotingAgent(name="Agent3"),
]

proposal = "Proposal A"
```

```
for agent in agents:
    agent.preferences = ["Proposal A", "Proposal B"]
votes = [agent.vote(proposal) for agent in agents]
print(f"Votes for '{proposal}': {votes.count((proposal, True))}")
```

2.2 Consensus Algorithms
Description:
Algorithms like Paxos and Raft ensure consensus in distributed systems. These algorithms guarantee fault tolerance and consistency.
Use Case:
- Blockchain networks use consensus algorithms to validate transactions and add blocks.

2.3 Shared Goal Alignment
Description:
Agents align their actions by focusing on shared goals rather than individual objectives. This reduces conflicts and fosters collaboration.
Use Case:
- In a search-and-rescue operation, drones prioritize finding survivors over individual area coverage.

3. Avoiding Conflicts Proactively
1. Role-Based Task Allocation:
    - Assign tasks based on predefined roles to minimize overlap.
2. Resource Partitioning:
    - Divide resources among agents to eliminate competition.
3. Clear Communication Protocols:
    - Use structured communication to avoid misunderstandings.

Summary
Conflict resolution and consensus mechanisms are vital for smooth collaboration in multi-agent systems. Techniques like priority-based resolution, negotiation protocols, and arbitration ensure efficient conflict management. Consensus mechanisms like voting and shared goal alignment enable decentralized agents to work cohesively. By implementing these strategies, developers can build robust, conflict-free systems that excel in dynamic, distributed environments.

6.4 Algorithms for Distributed Decision-Making

Distributed decision-making is the process by which multiple agents, entities, or systems make coordinated decisions, often without centralized control. This approach is critical in scenarios where the system is too complex or large for centralized control, or where distributed autonomy is required. Examples include multi-agent robotics, swarm intelligence, distributed computing, and collaborative AI systems. Here, we provide an in-depth overview of common algorithms used for distributed decision-making, focusing on their principles, applications, and how they enable efficient collaboration among agents.

Several algorithms have been developed for distributed decision-making, each tailored to specific needs and constraints. The following sections discuss the most widely used ones, their underlying principles, and their typical applications.

1. Consensus Algorithms
Principle: Consensus algorithms aim to ensure that all agents in a system agree on a particular value or decision, despite potential communication failures or disagreements. These algorithms rely on iterative communication and voting mechanisms.
- Common Examples:

- Paxos: Ensures fault-tolerant consensus in distributed systems, often used in database replication.
- Raft: A simpler and more understandable alternative to Paxos, used for distributed consensus in clustered environments.
- Byzantine Fault Tolerance (BFT): Handles malicious agents or faulty nodes by ensuring consensus even in the presence of adversaries.

Applications:
- Distributed databases and blockchains (e.g., Bitcoin uses a variant of BFT).
- Synchronization of replicated systems.
- Multi-agent agreement on resource allocation.

2. Multi-Agent Reinforcement Learning (MARL)
Principle: In MARL, multiple agents learn optimal strategies by interacting with their environment and other agents. They adapt their actions based on rewards or penalties.
- Key Techniques:
    - Independent Q-Learning: Each agent learns its own policy independently.
    - Centralized Training, Decentralized Execution (CTDE): Agents are trained collectively with centralized knowledge but operate independently.
    - Cooperative MARL: Encourages agents to work together to maximize a shared reward.

Applications:
- Autonomous vehicle coordination (e.g., self-driving cars navigating intersections).
- Robotic swarm tasks like object retrieval or disaster recovery.
- Real-time strategy games and simulations.

3. Distributed Optimization Algorithms

Principle: These algorithms divide an optimization problem into smaller sub-problems that are solved by individual agents, with solutions coordinated to achieve a global optimum.
- Common Techniques:
    - Gradient Descent in Distributed Systems: Each node computes local gradients, and updates are aggregated to refine a global model.
    - Dual Decomposition: Breaks a problem into sub-problems, solved iteratively by distributed agents.
    - Consensus Optimization: Ensures that solutions across agents converge to a common optimal value.

Applications:
- Large-scale machine learning (e.g., training neural networks across distributed systems).
- Sensor network optimization for efficient data collection.
- Resource allocation in distributed computing systems.

4. Swarm Intelligence Algorithms

Principle: Inspired by biological systems like ants, bees, or birds, swarm intelligence algorithms involve simple agents following basic rules to achieve complex global behavior.
- Popular Algorithms:
    - Ant Colony Optimization (ACO): Mimics how ants find the shortest path to food by laying pheromone trails.
    - Particle Swarm Optimization (PSO): Models agents as particles searching a solution space based on personal and group experiences.
    - Boids Algorithm: Simulates flocking behavior by aligning agents' movement based on separation, alignment, and cohesion.

Applications:
- Routing in communication networks.
- Task allocation in robotic swarms.
- Solving combinatorial optimization problems (e.g., traveling salesman problem).

5. Auction-Based Algorithms
Principle: These algorithms use auction mechanisms where agents bid for tasks, resources, or decisions. Allocation is based on bids, promoting efficiency and fairness.
- Common Methods:
    - First-Price Sealed-Bid Auction: Agents submit bids without knowing others' bids, and the highest bidder wins.
    - Vickrey Auction: The highest bidder wins but pays the second-highest bid.
    - Combinatorial Auctions: Agents bid on combinations of tasks or resources, optimizing for overall utility.

Applications:
- Task scheduling in cloud computing.
- Allocating roles in multi-robot systems.
- Spectrum allocation in wireless communication.

6. Game-Theoretic Approaches
Principle: Game theory provides a framework for agents to make decisions based on the expected actions of others. Key concepts include Nash equilibrium and cooperative games.
- Strategies:
    - Zero-Sum Games: Agents' gains are balanced by others' losses, focusing on competitive scenarios.
    - Cooperative Games: Agents work together to maximize collective outcomes.
    - Stackelberg Games: Models leader-follower dynamics where one agent leads and others follow.

Applications:
- Resource sharing in networks.
- Negotiation and conflict resolution.
- Economic modeling and market analysis.

7. Gossip Protocols

Principle: Gossip algorithms facilitate information dissemination and consensus by having agents randomly exchange information with peers. These methods are robust and scalable.
- Key Features:
    - Periodic and probabilistic communication.
    - Resilience to network changes or failures.
    - Asynchronous operations.

Applications:
- Load balancing in distributed systems.
- Synchronizing clocks in sensor networks.
- Epidemic-style data dissemination in peer-to-peer networks.

8. Heuristic and Rule-Based Algorithms
Principle: Agents follow pre-defined rules or heuristics to make decisions based on local information and constraints. These are simple and computationally efficient.
- Examples:
    - Threshold-based decision-making (e.g., perform action if a certain metric exceeds a threshold).
    - Rule-based expert systems for specific scenarios.
    - Heuristic algorithms for solving specific problems (e.g., nearest-neighbor for routing).

Applications:
- Emergency response coordination.
- Basic robotic behaviors (e.g., obstacle avoidance).
- Distributed troubleshooting in networked systems.

9. Distributed Constraint Satisfaction Problems (DCSPs)
Principle: DCSP algorithms solve problems where multiple agents must satisfy a set of constraints without centralized control.
- Key Techniques:
    - Backtracking Algorithms: Agents iteratively attempt solutions, backtracking when constraints are violated.

- Asynchronous Backtracking: Allows agents to work independently while resolving conflicts through communication.
- Distributed Arc Consistency: Ensures consistency between agents' variable assignments.

Applications:
- Scheduling (e.g., workforce or resource scheduling).
- Sensor network configuration.
- Multi-agent pathfinding.

Distributed decision-making algorithms are the backbone of modern multi-agent systems, enabling scalability, fault tolerance, and collaboration in diverse applications. By understanding these algorithms and their applications, developers and engineers can design efficient, robust, and adaptable systems for real-world challenges. Each algorithm has its strengths and is suited for specific scenarios, making it critical to choose the right approach based on system requirements.

6.5 Concept-to-Code: Collaborative Task Allocation

Collaborative task allocation involves assigning tasks to multiple agents in a way that maximizes efficiency and effectiveness. In systems where agents work together, such as multi-robot systems, distributed computing, or AI-driven workflows, task allocation ensures that each agent performs the tasks it is best suited for, while minimizing redundancy and maximizing productivity.

This section walks you through a hands-on example of building collaborative agents for task allocation using a step-by-step approach. The focus is on clarity and practicality, ensuring that the concepts are easy to understand and implement.

Let's build a simple collaborative task allocation system using Python. This example simulates agents working together to complete tasks distributed among them.

Step 1: Problem Definition
Imagine a system with multiple agents (e.g., robots, software agents, or workers) and a list of tasks to complete. Each task has a specific difficulty level, and each agent has a capability score. The goal is to allocate tasks to agents based on their capabilities so that all tasks are completed efficiently.

Step 2: Define the Key Components
We need to define:
1. Agents: Entities capable of performing tasks.
2. Tasks: Jobs that need to be completed.
3. Allocation Logic: A method to assign tasks to agents based on their capabilities.

Step 3: Python Implementation
Here's a detailed Python implementation:
Step 3.1: Define the Agent and Task Classes
python

```python
class Agent:
    def __init__(self, name, capability):
        """
        Initializes an agent with a name and capability score.
        """
        self.name = name
        self.capability = capability
        self.tasks = []  # List to store assigned tasks

    def assign_task(self, task):
        """
        Assign a task to the agent.
        """
        self.tasks.append(task)
```

```python
    def __str__(self):
        """
        Returns a string representation of the agent and their tasks.
        """
        return f"Agent {self.name}: Capability {self.capability}, Tasks: {[task.name for task in self.tasks]}"


class Task:
    def __init__(self, name, difficulty):
        """
        Initializes a task with a name and difficulty level.
        """
        self.name = name
        self.difficulty = difficulty

    def __str__(self):
        """
        Returns a string representation of the task.
        """
        return f"Task {self.name}: Difficulty {self.difficulty}"
```

Step 3.2: Define the Task Allocation Logic
python
```python
def allocate_tasks(agents, tasks):
    """
    Allocates tasks to agents based on their capabilities.
    Tasks are assigned to the agent with the closest matching capability.
    """
    for task in tasks:
```

```python
    # Find the agent with the capability closest to the task difficulty
    best_agent = min(agents, key=lambda agent: abs(agent.capability - task.difficulty))
    best_agent.assign_task(task)
```

Step 3.3: Simulation Script
python
```
# Create agents
agents = [
    Agent("Alice", capability=5),
    Agent("Bob", capability=8),
    Agent("Charlie", capability=3)
]

# Create tasks
tasks = [
    Task("Task1", difficulty=4),
    Task("Task2", difficulty=7),
    Task("Task3", difficulty=2),
    Task("Task4", difficulty=8)
]

# Allocate tasks
allocate_tasks(agents, tasks)

# Display results
for agent in agents:
    print(agent)
```

Step 4: Running **the Code**
When you run the script, you will see output similar to this:
less

Agent Alice: Capability 5, Tasks: ['Task1']
Agent Bob: Capability 8, Tasks: ['Task2', 'Task4']
Agent Charlie: Capability 3, Tasks: ['Task3']

This output shows that tasks were allocated to the agents based on their capabilities. For example, "Task1" with a difficulty of 4 was assigned to "Alice," whose capability (5) is closest to the task's difficulty.

Step 5: Enhancements and Scalability
This basic example can be extended in several ways:
1. Dynamic Capabilities: Allow agents' capabilities to change over time, simulating learning or fatigue.
2. Task Prioritization: Include a priority level for tasks, ensuring high-priority tasks are addressed first.
3. Complex Allocation Strategies: Implement algorithms like auction-based allocation or reinforcement learning for more complex scenarios.
4. Fault Tolerance: Introduce mechanisms to handle agent failures, such as redistributing tasks dynamically.
5. Real-Time Updates: Integrate with real-time systems to handle incoming tasks dynamically.

Applications of Collaborative Task Allocation
1. Robotics: Multi-robot systems for warehouse management or search-and-rescue operations.
2. Distributed Computing: Load balancing across servers or computational nodes.
3. Project Management: Distributing tasks among team members based on their expertise.
4. Smart Grids: Allocating energy resources in distributed power systems.

This example illustrates the fundamentals of collaborative task allocation, providing a foundation for building more advanced systems. By assigning tasks based on agent capabilities, the system ensures efficiency and maximizes resource utilization. With further enhancements, such systems can be adapted to a wide range of real-world applications, from autonomous robotics to distributed AI workflows.

Chapter 7: Building Advanced AI Workflows with CrewAI

7.1 Workflow Automation with Multi-Agent Systems

Multi-agent systems are composed of multiple autonomous agents that interact to achieve complex goals. CrewAI extends this concept by enabling coordinated automation of workflows, allowing agents to collaborate seamlessly. These systems are particularly useful for automating complex tasks that involve multiple steps, dynamic decision-making, and diverse data sources. In this section, we explore how CrewAI can be used to automate such workflows effectively.

Automating complex tasks involves breaking them down into smaller components that can be handled by individual agents. CrewAI provides a framework to define, coordinate, and manage these agents, ensuring that tasks are executed efficiently and in harmony. Below, we outline the steps involved in automating complex tasks with CrewAI.

Understanding CrewAI's Capabilities
CrewAI leverages multi-agent systems to perform the following:
1. Task Decomposition: Breaking down complex workflows into smaller, manageable tasks.
2. Agent Specialization: Assigning tasks to agents based on their capabilities.
3. Coordination and Communication: Enabling agents to share information and collaborate effectively.
4. Dynamic Decision-Making: Adjusting workflows in real time based on changing circumstances.
5. Monitoring and Reporting: Providing visibility into the workflow's progress and outcomes.

Step-by-Step Guide to Automating a Workflow with CrewAI

Let's walk through an example of automating a document processing workflow using CrewAI. This workflow involves the following tasks:
1. Document collection.
2. Data extraction.
3. Validation of extracted data.
4. Storing processed data in a database.
5. Reporting and notifications.

Step 1: Define the Workflow
First, outline the steps involved in the workflow and identify the agents required for each step. For our example:
- Agent A: Collects documents from various sources.
- Agent B: Extracts data from documents using OCR (Optical Character Recognition).
- Agent C: Validates the extracted data.
- Agent D: Stores the validated data in a database.
- Agent E: Sends a summary report.

Step 2: Configure CrewAI Agents
Each agent is configured with its specific task and rules for communication with other agents. **Here's a simplified Python implementation:**
python

```
from crewai import Agent, Workflow

# Define Agents
class DocumentCollector(Agent):
    def process(self, task):
        # Logic for collecting documents
        return ["document1.pdf", "document2.pdf"]

class DataExtractor(Agent):
    def process(self, documents):
        # Logic for extracting data
        extracted_data = []
```

```python
    for doc in documents:
        extracted_data.append({"doc": doc, "data": "Extracted Data"})
    return extracted_data

class DataValidator(Agent):
    def process(self, extracted_data):
        # Logic for validating data
        validated_data = []
        for item in extracted_data:
            if "valid" in item["data"]:  # Example validation rule
                validated_data.append(item)
        return validated_data

class DataStorage(Agent):
    def process(self, validated_data):
        # Logic for storing data in a database
        for item in validated_data:
            print(f"Storing: {item}")
        return "Data stored successfully"

class ReportGenerator(Agent):
    def process(self, storage_status):
        # Logic for generating a report
        return f"Report generated: {storage_status}"

# Instantiate Agents
collector = DocumentCollector("Collector")
extractor = DataExtractor("Extractor")
validator = DataValidator("Validator")
storage = DataStorage("Storage")
reporter = ReportGenerator("Reporter")
```

Step 3: Define the Workflow

Using CrewAI, define the workflow and connect agents to perform tasks sequentially.

python

```
# Define Workflow
class DocumentProcessingWorkflow(Workflow):
    def build(self):
        # Step-by-step workflow definition
        self.add_step("collect", collector.process)
        self.add_step("extract", extractor.process, depends_on="collect")
        self.add_step("validate", validator.process, depends_on="extract")
        self.add_step("store", storage.process, depends_on="validate")
        self.add_step("report", reporter.process, depends_on="store")

# Instantiate Workflow
workflow = DocumentProcessingWorkflow(name="Document Processing Workflow")
```

Step 4: Execute the Workflow
Run the workflow and observe how agents interact to complete the tasks.

python

```
# Execute Workflow
result = workflow.run()
print(result)
```

Step 5: Monitor and Improve
CrewAI provides tools to monitor workflow performance. Analyze the logs and metrics to identify bottlenecks or areas for improvement.

Benefits of Using CrewAI for Task Automation
1. Scalability: Easily handle large-scale tasks by adding more agents or increasing their capabilities.
2. Flexibility: Adapt workflows dynamically based on real-time data or changing conditions.
3. Collaboration: Enable seamless communication and cooperation between agents.
4. Efficiency: Reduce manual intervention and streamline operations.
5. Visibility: Monitor the status and progress of workflows through detailed reporting.

Applications of CrewAI in Workflow Automation
1. Business Process Automation: Streamline repetitive tasks like invoice processing or customer support ticketing.
2. Data Processing: Automate ETL (Extract, Transform, Load) pipelines for large datasets.
3. Robotics: Coordinate multiple robots for tasks like warehouse management or manufacturing.
4. Healthcare: Manage patient records, appointment scheduling, and diagnosis workflows.
5. Research: Automate literature reviews, data collection, and experimental simulations.

CrewAI offers a powerful framework for automating complex workflows using multi-agent systems. By breaking down tasks, leveraging agent specialization, and ensuring dynamic coordination, CrewAI enables organizations to achieve greater efficiency and productivity. This hands-on example demonstrates the flexibility and scalability of CrewAI, making it a valuable tool for building advanced AI workflows. Whether it's data processing, robotics, or business automation, CrewAI can transform how tasks are completed in modern systems.

7.2 Leveraging Machine Learning in Multi-Agent Workflows

Machine learning (ML) enhances the capabilities of multi-agent systems by enabling intelligent decision-making. By integrating ML models into multi-agent workflows, agents can analyze data, predict outcomes, adapt to changing environments, and optimize task execution. This section focuses on how to seamlessly incorporate ML models into workflows built with CrewAI, allowing agents to make data-driven decisions.

Integrating ML models into multi-agent workflows involves equipping agents with the ability to perform tasks that require learning from data. These tasks may include classification, prediction, anomaly detection, or natural language understanding. Below, we detail how to achieve this integration, using practical examples and clear explanations.

Benefits of ML in Multi-Agent Workflows
1. Improved Decision-Making: Agents can make smarter decisions by leveraging predictive insights.
2. Adaptability: ML models enable agents to learn and adapt to dynamic environments.
3. Efficiency: Data-driven optimizations improve workflow performance.
4. Personalization: Agents can tailor their actions based on specific patterns or user preferences.

Step-by-Step Guide to Integrating ML Models
Let's build a multi-agent workflow where machine learning models enhance decision-making. We will create a customer support system that uses:
1. An ML model for text classification: To categorize support tickets.
2. A recommendation model: To suggest solutions.

3. Anomaly detection: To flag unusual tickets for manual review.

Step 1: Select or Train ML Models
Start by selecting pre-trained ML models or training your own. For this example:
- Text Classification: A model trained to classify support tickets into categories like "Technical Issue," "Billing," or "General Inquiry."
- Recommendation Model: A model to recommend solutions based on ticket content.
- Anomaly Detection: A model to flag rare or unusual tickets using clustering or outlier detection.

Example Python libraries:
- scikit-learn: For classification and anomaly detection.
- transformers (by Hugging Face): For pre-trained natural language models.

Step 2: Define Agents with ML Capabilities
Agents are extended to include ML models for intelligent decision-making.

python

```python
from crewai import Agent
from sklearn.externals import joblib
import numpy as np

# Load pre-trained models
classifier = joblib.load("text_classifier.pkl")
recommender = joblib.load("solution_recommender.pkl")
anomaly_detector = joblib.load("anomaly_detector.pkl")

class TicketClassifier(Agent):
    def process(self, ticket_text):
        """
        Classify the ticket text into predefined categories.
```

```python
        """
        category = classifier.predict([ticket_text])[0]
        return {"text": ticket_text, "category": category}

class SolutionRecommender(Agent):
    def process(self, ticket):
        """
        Recommend solutions based on ticket category.
        """
        category = ticket["category"]
        solutions = recommender.predict([category])
        return {**ticket, "solutions": solutions}

class AnomalyDetector(Agent):
    def process(self, ticket):
        """
        Detect anomalies in ticket content.
        """
        is_anomalous = anomaly_detector.predict([ticket["text"]])[0]
        ticket["is_anomalous"] = bool(is_anomalous)
        return ticket
```

Step 3: Define the Workflow
Combine the agents into a cohesive workflow.

python

```python
from crewai import Workflow

class CustomerSupportWorkflow(Workflow):
    def build(self):
        # Define the workflow steps
        self.add_step("classify", TicketClassifier("Classifier").process)
```

```python
        self.add_step("recommend",
SolutionRecommender("Recommender").process,
depends_on="classify")
        self.add_step("detect_anomaly",
AnomalyDetector("AnomalyDetector").process,
depends_on="recommend")

# Instantiate the workflow
workflow =
CustomerSupportWorkflow(name="Customer Support Workflow")
```

Step 4: Execute the Workflow
Run the workflow with sample data and observe the results.
python
```
# Example ticket text
tickets = [
    "I can't log in to my account.",
    "My credit card was charged incorrectly.",
    "I need help with your new feature update."
]

# Process tickets
for ticket_text in tickets:
    result = workflow.run(ticket_text=ticket_text)
    print(result)
```

Step 5: Analyze and Refine
Review the results to ensure accuracy and make adjustments:
1. Fine-Tune Models: Retrain models if classifications or recommendations are inaccurate.
2. Adjust Thresholds: For anomaly detection, fine-tune thresholds to reduce false positives or negatives.

3. Add Feedback Loops: Allow agents to learn from user feedback, improving their decision-making over time.

Advanced Topics
1. Real-Time Processing: Implement real-time ticket processing using message queues like RabbitMQ or Kafka.
2. Hybrid Approaches: Combine rule-based logic with ML models for specific tasks.
3. Explainability: Use explainable AI (XAI) techniques to provide insights into agent decisions, building trust in the system.

Applications of ML-Enhanced Multi-Agent Systems
1. Customer Support Automation:
    - Ticket classification and routing.
    - Solution recommendation systems.
    - Sentiment analysis for prioritization.
2. Smart Manufacturing:
    - Predictive maintenance using anomaly detection.
    - Supply chain optimization through demand forecasting.
3. Healthcare:
    - Disease diagnosis using image classification models.
    - Personalized treatment recommendations based on patient data.
4. Financial Services:
    - Fraud detection using anomaly detection models.
    - Risk assessment through predictive analytics.

Integrating ML models into multi-agent workflows unlocks the potential for intelligent, data-driven automation. CrewAI provides a robust framework for this integration, enabling agents to perform complex tasks with precision and efficiency. By combining machine learning with multi-agent systems, organizations can build advanced AI workflows capable of handling dynamic and challenging scenarios. The step-by-step example in this section serves as a practical guide for implementing such systems, laying the foundation for innovation in diverse industries.

7.3 Real-Time Communication and Data Sharing in Workflows

Real-time communication and data sharing are essential components of modern multi-agent systems. In workflows powered by CrewAI, agents must interact seamlessly, exchange information efficiently, and maintain synchronization and consistency to ensure tasks are completed accurately and on time. This section explores the techniques used to achieve synchronization and consistency, ensuring robust and effective workflows.

Synchronization ensures that all agents in a workflow are aligned and working in harmony. Consistency ensures that the shared data across agents remains accurate and up-to-date. Together, these concepts form the backbone of reliable multi-agent workflows. Below, we detail the techniques and strategies used to maintain synchronization and consistency in real-time communication and data sharing.

1. Centralized vs. Decentralized Communication
Centralized Communication
- Overview: A central hub (e.g., a server or a coordinator agent) manages communication between agents.
- Advantages:
    - Simplified control and monitoring.
    - Easier to implement consistency checks.
- Challenges:
    - Single point of failure.
    - May become a bottleneck in large systems.

Decentralized Communication
- Overview: Agents communicate directly with each other using peer-to-peer (P2P) protocols.
- Advantages:
    - Increased fault tolerance.
    - Scalability for large systems.
- Challenges:
    - More complex to manage synchronization and consistency.

2. Synchronization Techniques

Event-Driven Synchronization
- Description: Agents synchronize their actions based on specific events or triggers.
- Example: In a document processing workflow, Agent A signals Agent B once it finishes extracting data, enabling Agent B to start validation.
- Implementation:
    - Use message queues (e.g., RabbitMQ, Kafka) to handle event notifications.
    - Agents listen for relevant events and act accordingly.

Time-Based Synchronization
- Description: Actions are synchronized based on a shared clock or time intervals.
- Example: Agents periodically update shared data at fixed intervals.
- Implementation:
    - Use distributed clock synchronization protocols like Network Time Protocol (NTP).
    - Define time windows for data updates and task execution.

Token-Based Synchronization
- Description: A token is passed among agents to control execution order.
- Example: In a pipeline, a token is passed to signal the next agent to start processing.

- Implementation:
    - Maintain a shared token state.
    - Use distributed locking mechanisms to prevent token duplication.

3. Data Consistency Techniques
1. Consistent Data Models
    - Description: Define a unified data model shared across all agents to ensure consistency.
    - Example: A JSON schema for ticket data ensures all agents interpret and process ticket information uniformly.
    - Implementation:
        - Define a standardized data structure.
        - Validate data against the schema before processing.
2. Version Control for Data
    - Description: Assign version numbers to shared data, ensuring agents use the latest version.
    - Example: A shared database includes a version field for each record.
    - Implementation:
        - Use version control systems like Git for static data.
        - Include versioning in API responses for dynamic data.
3. Conflict Resolution Policies
    - Description: Define rules for resolving conflicts when multiple agents modify shared data simultaneously.
    - Example: In a collaborative editing workflow, the "last write wins" rule may resolve conflicting updates.
    - Implementation:
        - Implement conflict resolution logic in the central data repository.
        - Use consensus algorithms like Paxos or Raft for distributed systems.
4. Eventual Consistency

- Description: Allow temporary inconsistencies with the guarantee that all agents will eventually converge on the same state.
- Example: In a distributed database, updates propagate asynchronously to all nodes.
- Implementation:
  - Use database systems designed for eventual consistency (e.g., Apache Cassandra).
  - Periodically reconcile data discrepancies.

4. Real-Time Data Sharing Techniques

1. Publish-Subscribe Systems
   - Description: Agents subscribe to specific topics of interest and receive updates when data changes.
   - Example: A notification system where agents subscribe to "task completed" events.
   - Implementation:
     - Use message brokers like Apache Kafka or MQTT.
     - Define topics and manage agent subscriptions.

2. Shared Data Repositories
   - Description: Agents read from and write to a shared database or data storage system.
   - Example: A shared SQL database where agents log their task status.
   - Implementation:
     - Use databases optimized for distributed access (e.g., MongoDB, Redis).
     - Ensure data consistency with locks or transaction mechanisms.

3. Direct Peer-to-Peer Data Exchange
   - Description: Agents exchange data directly with each other, bypassing centralized systems.
   - Example: Agents working on a collaborative robotics task share sensor data directly.
   - Implementation:
     - Use communication protocols like WebRTC or gRPC.

- Implement encryption for secure data exchange.

5. Real-Time Monitoring and Logging

Maintaining synchronization and consistency requires robust monitoring and logging systems:
1. Centralized Dashboards: Track workflow progress and agent communication in real time.
2. Distributed Logs: Maintain logs for individual agents to identify issues locally.
3. Alerts and Notifications: Set up automated alerts for synchronization or consistency failures.

6. Challenges and Solutions

Challenge 1: Network Latency
- Solution: Use low-latency communication protocols and edge computing to reduce delays.

Challenge 2: Fault Tolerance
- Solution: Implement failover mechanisms and data replication to handle agent or system failures.

Challenge 3: Scalability
- Solution: Use scalable architectures like microservices and load balancing to accommodate more agents.

Challenge 4: Security
- Solution: Encrypt communication channels and use authentication mechanisms to secure data sharing.

Applications of Real-Time Communication and Data Sharing

1. Supply Chain Management: Synchronizing logistics and inventory across multiple locations.
2. Healthcare Systems: Sharing real-time patient data among doctors, nurses, and systems.
3. Collaborative Robotics: Real-time data exchange between robots for coordinated tasks.
4. Financial Services: Synchronizing stock trades and account updates across systems.

Real-time communication and data sharing are the lifeblood of multi-agent workflows. By implementing robust synchronization and consistency techniques, systems built with CrewAI can ensure reliable and efficient task execution. Whether using event-driven synchronization, shared data repositories, or publish-subscribe systems, maintaining real-time alignment among agents unlocks the full potential of advanced AI workflows. These practices are critical for building scalable, secure, and adaptable systems for diverse industries.

7.4 Project: Multi-Agent Workflow for a Logistics System

A logistics system involves multiple interconnected tasks such as order placement, inventory management, transportation scheduling, delivery tracking, and reporting. Building a multi-agent workflow for such a system using CrewAI allows for scalable, efficient, and dynamic management of operations. This project provides a step-by-step guide to implementing a multi-agent workflow for a logistics system.

This section provides a comprehensive walkthrough of creating a logistics system using CrewAI. The system will handle tasks such as order processing, inventory updates, route optimization, delivery tracking, and reporting.

Step 1: Define the Problem
The logistics system should perform the following tasks:
1. Order Processing: Receive orders and verify details.
2. Inventory Management: Check stock levels and reserve items.
3. Route Optimization: Plan delivery routes.
4. Delivery Tracking: Monitor delivery status in real-time.
5. Reporting: Generate summary reports.

Step 2: Plan the Multi-Agent Workflow
Each task is assigned to a specialized agent:
1. Order Agent: Handles order placement and verification.
2. Inventory Agent: Manages inventory updates.
3. Routing Agent: Optimizes delivery routes.
4. Tracking Agent: Tracks delivery progress.
5. Reporting Agent: Generates reports on workflow completion.

Step 3: Implementation
The implementation consists of creating agents, defining the workflow, and running the system.

3.1 Define the Agents
Agents are designed to perform specific tasks.
python
```
from crewai import Agent

# Agent for order processing
class OrderAgent(Agent):
    def process(self, order_details):
        """
        Verifies order details and confirms the order.
        """
        if "item" in order_details and "quantity" in order_details:
            return {"order_id": 123, **order_details, "status": "Order Confirmed"}
        else:
            raise ValueError("Invalid Order Details")

# Agent for inventory management
class InventoryAgent(Agent):
    def process(self, order):
        """
```

        Checks inventory and reserves items for the order.
        """
        inventory = {"itemA": 100, "itemB": 50} # Sample inventory
        if order["item"] in inventory and inventory[order["item"]] >= order["quantity"]:
            inventory[order["item"]] -= order["quantity"]
            return {**order, "inventory_status": "Items Reserved"}
        else:
            raise ValueError("Insufficient Stock")

# Agent for route optimization
class RoutingAgent(Agent):
    def process(self, order):
        """
        Plans an optimized delivery route for the order.
        """
        routes = {"routeA": ["Location1", "Location2"], "routeB": ["Location3", "Location4"]}
        return {**order, "route": routes["routeA"], "route_status": "Route Planned"}

# Agent for delivery tracking
class TrackingAgent(Agent):
    def process(self, order):
        """
        Tracks delivery progress in real-time.
        """
        delivery_status = "In Transit" # Mock status
        return {**order, "delivery_status": delivery_status}

# Agent for reporting
class ReportingAgent(Agent):
    def process(self, order):
        """

Generates a summary report for the order.
"""
return f"Order {order['order_id']} completed: {order['delivery_status']}"

3.2 Define the Workflow
Combine agents into a CrewAI workflow.

python

```python
from crewai import Workflow

class LogisticsWorkflow(Workflow):
    def build(self):
        # Step-by-step workflow definition
        self.add_step("process_order", OrderAgent("OrderProcessor").process)
        self.add_step("manage_inventory", InventoryAgent("InventoryManager").process, depends_on="process_order")
        self.add_step("plan_route", RoutingAgent("RoutePlanner").process, depends_on="manage_inventory")
        self.add_step("track_delivery", TrackingAgent("DeliveryTracker").process, depends_on="plan_route")
        self.add_step("generate_report", ReportingAgent("Reporter").process, depends_on="track_delivery")

# Instantiate Workflow
workflow = LogisticsWorkflow(name="Logistics Workflow")
```

3.3 Execute the Workflow
Run the workflow with sample data.

```python
# Sample order data
order_data = {
    "item": "itemA",
    "quantity": 10,
    "destination": "Location2"
}

# Run the workflow
result = workflow.run(order_details=order_data)
print(result)
```

Step 4: Testing and Validation
4.1 Simulate Different Scenarios
- Valid Order: Ensure the system processes an order successfully when stock is sufficient.
- Insufficient Stock: Test the system's handling of orders with insufficient stock.
- Route Failures: Simulate a failure in route planning and ensure the workflow halts gracefully.

4.2 Monitor Agent Interactions
- Check logs to ensure agents communicate correctly.
- Validate the data flow between agents.

Step 5: Enhancements
Enhance the workflow for real-world complexity:
1. Dynamic Inventory Updates: Integrate real-time inventory systems.
2. Live Tracking: Use GPS data for real-time delivery updates.
3. Scalability: Add more agents to handle multiple orders concurrently.
4. Error Recovery: Implement error-handling mechanisms for failed tasks.

Applications of the Logistics Workflow

1. E-Commerce: Automating order fulfillment and delivery.
2. Warehousing: Managing inventory and dispatch.
3. Transportation: Optimizing routes for fleet management.
4. Supply Chain Management: Coordinating multi-party logistics operations.

The multi-agent workflow for a logistics system demonstrates how CrewAI enables efficient task management and coordination. By leveraging specialized agents and defining clear workflows, complex logistical operations can be automated and streamlined. This implementation guide provides a solid foundation for building real-world logistics solutions that are scalable, adaptable, and robust. With further enhancements, such systems can handle a wide range of scenarios, from e-commerce order fulfillment to large-scale supply chain operations.

Chapter 8: Scaling Multi-Agent Systems

8.1 Challenges in Scaling Multi-Agent Systems

As the complexity of multi-agent systems (MAS) grows, scaling becomes a critical challenge. Scaling refers to the ability of the system to handle an increasing number of agents, tasks, or data without compromising performance, reliability, or efficiency. One of the most significant obstacles to scaling is managing resource allocation and communication overhead, both of which can quickly become bottlenecks as the system grows.

In a multi-agent system, agents rely on resources (e.g., computational power, memory, network bandwidth) and effective communication to collaborate and execute tasks. Poor resource management or excessive communication overhead can lead to performance degradation, system crashes, or failure to meet real-time demands.
This section explores these challenges in detail and offers strategies to address them.

Resource Allocation Challenges
1. Limited Computational Resources
   As the number of agents increases, the demand for computational resources grows. Each agent may require CPU cycles, memory, or GPU resources to process tasks or run machine learning models. If resources are limited, agents may experience delays or failures.
   - Example: A logistics system with hundreds of delivery agents may struggle to process real-time route optimizations if computational resources are insufficient.

2. Dynamic Workloads
   In real-world scenarios, workloads are often dynamic. Some agents may experience high workloads during peak times, while others remain idle. This imbalance can lead to inefficient resource utilization.
   - Example: An e-commerce system may experience surges in order-processing agents during a flash sale, causing bottlenecks.
3. Conflict Over Shared Resources
   When multiple agents attempt to access the same resource simultaneously, conflicts may arise, leading to contention and delays.
   - Example: Multiple agents writing to the same database table can cause write conflicts, slowing down the system.

Strategies for Effective Resource Allocation
1. Dynamic Load Balancing
   Distribute workloads dynamically across agents or systems based on real-time conditions.
   - Implementation:
     - Use a load balancer to monitor resource utilization and redistribute tasks as needed.
     - Employ cloud-based autoscaling solutions to allocate additional resources during peak demand.
2. Resource Pooling
   Group resources into a pool and allocate them to agents on demand, ensuring efficient usage.
   - Implementation:
     - Use resource schedulers like Kubernetes to manage CPU, memory, and GPU allocation.
     - Implement resource quotas to prevent any single agent from monopolizing resources.

3. Prioritization and Scheduling
   Prioritize critical tasks and schedule less urgent ones during low-demand periods.
   - Implementation:
     - Implement priority queues to ensure high-priority tasks are executed first.
     - Use time-based scheduling for non-urgent tasks, such as nightly database backups.
4. Distributed Computing
   Spread tasks across multiple systems or nodes to reduce the load on a single machine.
   - Implementation:
     - Use distributed frameworks like Apache Spark for large-scale data processing.
     - Deploy agents across multiple servers to balance computational load.

Communication Overhead Challenges

1. Excessive Communication
   As the number of agents increases, communication requirements grow exponentially. Agents may need to exchange data frequently, leading to network congestion and delays.
   - Example: In a swarm robotics system, if every robot communicates with every other robot, the volume of messages can overwhelm the network.
2. Latency
   High communication latency can delay task execution and disrupt synchronization among agents.
   - Example: In real-time systems like autonomous vehicles, even small delays in communication can lead to accidents.
3. Message Loss and Errors
   In large-scale systems, messages can be lost or corrupted, especially in unreliable networks. This can lead to incomplete or incorrect task execution.

- Example: A multi-agent system managing financial transactions may experience data loss due to network failures, leading to discrepancies.

Strategies to Reduce Communication Overhead

1. Hierarchical Communication Models
   Organize agents into hierarchies or groups to reduce the need for all-to-all communication.
   - Implementation:
     - Introduce leader agents that aggregate data and communicate with other groups.
     - Use cluster-based communication protocols like Gossip for efficient data sharing.

2. Data Compression
   Reduce the size of messages exchanged between agents to lower bandwidth usage.
   - Implementation:
     - Use compression algorithms like gzip or protobuf for encoding messages.
     - Share only incremental updates instead of complete datasets.

3. Event-Driven Communication
   Replace continuous communication with event-driven mechanisms, where agents only communicate when necessary.
   - Implementation:
     - Use publish-subscribe systems like Kafka or RabbitMQ to trigger communications based on specific events.
     - Implement callbacks to notify agents only when relevant updates occur.

4. Decentralized Communication
   Allow agents to communicate directly with peers instead of routing through a central server.
   - Implementation:

- Use peer-to-peer protocols like WebRTC for direct communication.
- Build decentralized message queues to distribute communication loads.

5. Quality of Service (QoS) Management
   Prioritize critical messages and allocate network resources accordingly.
   - Implementation:
     - Implement QoS settings in communication protocols to ensure important messages are transmitted with higher priority.
     - Monitor and adjust bandwidth usage in real time.

Combining Resource Allocation and Communication Strategies
Effective scaling requires balancing resource allocation and communication strategies. Here's an example integration:
- Scenario: A fleet of 1,000 autonomous delivery drones requires real-time route optimization and status updates.
  1. Resource Allocation:
     - Deploy drones across multiple cloud servers, with each server handling a fixed number of drones.
     - Use Kubernetes to dynamically scale resources based on demand.
  2. Communication Overhead:
     - Group drones into regional clusters with a leader drone in each cluster.
     - Use event-driven communication to notify the central server only when routes change or critical updates are needed.

Applications of Scalable Multi-Agent Systems
1. Smart Cities: Managing traffic, energy distribution, and public safety systems.

2. E-Commerce: Handling large volumes of orders, inventory, and customer queries.
3. Autonomous Vehicles: Coordinating fleets of self-driving cars for transportation and logistics.
4. Healthcare: Managing patient data, diagnostics, and treatment plans across multiple facilities.

Scaling multi-agent systems presents significant challenges in resource allocation and communication overhead. However, with thoughtful strategies such as dynamic load balancing, hierarchical communication models, and event-driven mechanisms, these challenges can be addressed effectively. By implementing these techniques, developers can build scalable, efficient, and reliable systems capable of handling complex, large-scale operations across various industries. As multi-agent systems continue to evolve, addressing these scaling challenges will remain a critical factor in their success.

8.2 Distributed Deployment Strategies

Distributed deployment is a crucial aspect of scaling multi-agent systems (MAS) as it enables agents to operate across multiple nodes in a network. This approach ensures that resources are utilized efficiently, tasks are executed concurrently, and the system remains resilient to failures. Distributed deployment strategies allow systems to handle large workloads and operate seamlessly across diverse environments, such as cloud platforms, edge devices, or hybrid architectures.

This section focuses on techniques for deploying agents across multiple nodes, ensuring scalability, fault tolerance, and efficient resource utilization.

Deploying agents across multiple nodes involves designing a system where agents can interact, share data, and complete tasks while distributed geographically or across virtual machines. Below are the key techniques and strategies for achieving distributed deployment in a structured and efficient manner.

1. Containerization and Orchestration

1.1 Containerization

Containerization allows agents to be packaged with their dependencies into lightweight, portable units. Containers ensure consistency across different environments and simplify deployment.

- Tools: Docker, Podman.
- Benefits:
  - Portability across nodes.
  - Isolation of agents to prevent dependency conflicts.
  - Quick deployment and scaling.

Example:

```bash
# Dockerfile to containerize an agent
FROM python:3.9-slim

WORKDIR /app
COPY . /app
RUN pip install -r requirements.txt

CMD ["python", "agent.py"]
```

```bash
# Build and run the container
docker build -t agent-container .
docker run -d --name agent1 agent-container
```

1.2 Orchestration

Orchestration tools manage the deployment, scaling, and operation of containers across multiple nodes.

- Tools: Kubernetes, Docker Swarm.
- Features:
  - Automatic scaling based on load.

- Load balancing to distribute tasks across nodes.
- Monitoring and health checks to ensure agent availability.

Example (Kubernetes):
yaml

```yaml
# Kubernetes Deployment for an agent
apiVersion: apps/v1
kind: Deployment
metadata:
  name: agent-deployment
spec:
  replicas: 3
  selector:
    matchLabels:
      app: agent
  template:
    metadata:
      labels:
        app: agent
    spec:
      containers:
      - name: agent-container
        image: agent-container:latest
        ports:
        - containerPort: 5000
```

Deploy with:
bash

```bash
kubectl apply -f agent-deployment.yaml
```

2. Load Balancing and Task Distribution
Load balancing ensures that tasks are distributed evenly across nodes to avoid overloading any single node.
- Techniques:

- Round Robin: Distribute tasks sequentially to each node.
- Least Connections: Assign tasks to the node with the least active connections.
- Resource-Based: Allocate tasks based on node capacity (e.g., CPU, memory).
- Tools: HAProxy, NGINX, AWS Elastic Load Balancer.

Implementation (NGINX):

```nginx
http {
  upstream agents {
    server agent1.example.com;
    server agent2.example.com;
    server agent3.example.com;
  }

  server {
    listen 80;
    location / {
      proxy_pass http://agents;
    }
  }
}
```

3. Peer-to-Peer Communication

In distributed systems, agents often need to communicate directly without relying on a central server. Peer-to-peer (P2P) communication facilitates this.

- Techniques:
    - Message Passing: Use lightweight protocols like ZeroMQ for direct communication.
    - Distributed Databases: Agents share a distributed database (e.g., Apache Cassandra) to maintain state and exchange data.

- Decentralized Protocols: Use protocols like WebRTC for real-time P2P connections.

Example:
python
```
import zmq

# Agent sending a message
context = zmq.Context()
socket = context.socket(zmq.REQ)
socket.connect("tcp://node1:5555")
socket.send_string("Task data")
response = socket.recv_string()
print(response)

# Agent receiving a message
socket = context.socket(zmq.REP)
socket.bind("tcp://*:5555")
message = socket.recv_string()
socket.send_string("Acknowledged")
```

4. Fault Tolerance and Redundancy

Ensuring fault tolerance is essential for distributed systems. If a node fails, the system must recover gracefully without disrupting workflows.

- Techniques:
    - Replication: Duplicate critical agents across multiple nodes.
    - Heartbeat Monitoring: Continuously monitor node health using heartbeat signals.
    - Failover Mechanisms: Automatically transfer tasks to healthy nodes if a failure occurs.
- Tools: Keepalived, Consul, Kubernetes.

Example: In Kubernetes, use health probes:
yaml
```
livenessProbe:
```

```
httpGet:
  path: /healthz
  port: 8080
initialDelaySeconds: 3
periodSeconds: 5
```

5. Edge and Cloud Integration

Distributed systems often span edge devices and cloud platforms. Agents can be deployed at the edge for real-time processing and in the cloud for resource-intensive tasks.
- Edge Deployment: Use lightweight frameworks like K3s or Balena.
- Cloud Deployment: Use cloud services like AWS ECS, Google Kubernetes Engine (GKE), or Azure Kubernetes Service (AKS).

Hybrid Example:
- Deploy edge agents on Raspberry Pi devices for local data processing.
- Use cloud agents for aggregating data and running machine learning models.

6. Service Discovery and Dynamic Scaling

6.1 Service Discovery

Agents need to locate and communicate with each other dynamically in distributed environments.
- Tools: Consul, Etcd, Zookeeper.
- Implementation:
    - Register agents with a service registry.
    - Resolve agent locations dynamically at runtime.

6.2 Dynamic Scaling

Scale the system up or down based on load.
- Tools: Kubernetes Horizontal Pod Autoscaler, AWS Auto Scaling.
- Implementation:
    - Define metrics (e.g., CPU utilization).

- Configure autoscaling policies.

Kubernetes Autoscaling:

bash

```
kubectl autoscale deployment agent-deployment --cpu-percent=50 --min=1 --max=10
```

7. Security and Access Control

Securing communication and data sharing across nodes is critical.
- Techniques:
    - Encryption: Use TLS/SSL for secure communication.
    - Authentication: Use OAuth2, API keys, or tokens for agent authentication.
    - Access Control: Restrict access to sensitive resources using role-based access control (RBAC).

Example: In Kubernetes, implement RBAC:

yaml

```
apiVersion: rbac.authorization.k8s.io/v1
kind: Role
metadata:
  namespace: default
  name: agent-role
rules:
- apiGroups: [""]
  resources: ["pods"]
  verbs: ["get", "list", "watch"]
```

Applications of Distributed Deployment

1. IoT Systems: Deploy agents on IoT devices for local data processing and edge analytics.
2. E-Commerce Platforms: Use distributed agents for order management, inventory updates, and payment processing.
3. Autonomous Vehicles: Deploy agents across vehicles and central servers for real-time coordination.

4. Healthcare: Use distributed agents for managing patient records, diagnostics, and hospital operations.

Deploying agents across multiple nodes in a distributed system is a critical step in scaling multi-agent workflows. By leveraging containerization, orchestration, fault tolerance, and secure communication, distributed systems can achieve high performance, resilience, and scalability. This comprehensive guide equips you with the tools and techniques to deploy agents effectively in real-world applications, enabling the creation of robust and efficient multi-agent systems.

8.3 Load Balancing and Dynamic Agent Allocation

Load balancing and dynamic agent allocation are crucial for optimizing performance in multi-agent systems (MAS). As systems scale, they must handle increasing workloads, prevent bottlenecks, and distribute tasks efficiently across available resources. Effective strategies for load balancing and agent allocation ensure that agents perform their tasks without overloading individual nodes or underutilizing system capacity.

This section explores strategies for optimizing performance through load balancing and dynamic agent allocation in detail.

To achieve optimal performance, multi-agent systems must:
1. Distribute tasks evenly across agents and nodes.
2. Dynamically allocate resources based on real-time demand.
3. Minimize idle time for agents while preventing overloading.
4. Adapt to changing workloads and agent availability.

Below are detailed strategies to implement these objectives.

1. Load Balancing Strategies

Load balancing involves distributing tasks or requests across multiple agents or nodes to ensure efficient resource utilization and maintain system performance.

1.1 Round Robin Scheduling

- Description: Tasks are assigned to agents or nodes in a circular order.
- Advantages:
    - Simple to implement.
    - Ensures even distribution when all agents have similar capabilities.
- Challenges:
    - Not suitable for heterogeneous agents with varying capacities.
- Example: A router distributes incoming requests to agents in the order Agent A → Agent B → Agent C → Agent A.

1.2 Least Connections

- Description: Tasks are assigned to the agent or node with the fewest active connections or tasks.
- Advantages:
    - Prevents overloading a single agent.
    - Adjusts dynamically to the current workload.
- Challenges:
    - Requires real-time monitoring of active connections.
- Example: A load balancer assigns requests to the agent handling the fewest current tasks.

1.3 Weighted Load Balancing

- Description: Assigns weights to agents or nodes based on their processing capacity. Tasks are distributed in proportion to these weights.
- Advantages:
    - Accommodates heterogeneous agents.
    - Optimizes resource utilization.
- Challenges:
    - Requires accurate capacity estimation for agents.

- Example: Agent A (weight 3) handles three times as many tasks as Agent B (weight 1).

1.4 Geographical Load Balancing
- Description: Tasks are routed to agents or nodes based on their geographical location to minimize latency.
- Advantages:
  - Reduces latency for geographically distributed users.
  - Useful in edge computing scenarios.
- Challenges:
  - Requires agents or nodes in multiple locations.
- Example: A request from Europe is routed to a server in Germany, while a request from Asia is routed to a server in Singapore.

2. Dynamic Agent Allocation

Dynamic agent allocation involves assigning agents to tasks or resources in real-time based on current demand and system state.

2.1 Resource-Based Allocation
- Description: Agents are allocated based on the resources they require and the available capacity.
- Advantages:
  - Prevents resource contention.
  - Optimizes utilization of CPU, memory, and network bandwidth.
- Challenges:
  - Requires continuous monitoring of resource usage.
- Example: An agent requiring high CPU is allocated to a node with low CPU usage.

2.2 Priority-Based Allocation
- Description: High-priority tasks are assigned to agents first, while lower-priority tasks are queued or delayed.
- Advantages:
  - Ensures critical tasks are completed on time.
  - Improves system responsiveness for priority workloads.
- Challenges:

- Low-priority tasks may experience delays.
- Example: A system prioritizes processing emergency medical data over routine reports.

2.3 Demand-Based Scaling
- Description: Automatically scales the number of agents based on the incoming workload.
- Advantages:
  - Matches resource allocation to demand.
  - Reduces costs by deallocating idle agents.
- Challenges:
  - Requires a mechanism for detecting workload changes.
- Implementation:
  - Use Kubernetes Horizontal Pod Autoscaler to dynamically scale agents.

2.4 Task Splitting
- Description: Large tasks are split into smaller subtasks and distributed across multiple agents.
- Advantages:
  - Speeds up task completion.
  - Balances load by spreading work.
- Challenges:
  - Requires mechanisms to reassemble results.
- Example: A data processing task is split into smaller chunks, each handled by a different agent.

3. Monitoring and Metrics for Load Balancing

Effective load balancing and dynamic allocation rely on continuous monitoring and analysis of system performance. Key metrics include:
- CPU and Memory Utilization: Identify underutilized or overloaded nodes.
- Response Time: Monitor agent response times to detect delays.
- Task Queue Length: Ensure task queues are not excessively long.

- Error Rates: Identify agents or nodes failing to process tasks.

Tools for Monitoring:
- Prometheus: Monitors system metrics and provides real-time alerts.
- Grafana: Visualizes system performance using dashboards.
- ELK Stack: Logs and analyzes system events for troubleshooting.

4. Communication Optimization

Efficient communication is essential for load balancing and agent allocation in distributed systems.

4.1 Minimize Inter-Agent Communication
- Use event-driven communication to reduce unnecessary message exchanges.
- Aggregate data at a central node instead of broadcasting to all agents.

4.2 Implement Asynchronous Communication
- Use message queues like RabbitMQ or Kafka to decouple agents and prevent bottlenecks.

4.3 Cache Frequently Accessed Data
- Implement caching mechanisms (e.g., Redis) to reduce redundant data requests.

5. Fault Tolerance and Recovery

Scaling systems require resilience against failures:
- Redundant Agents: Deploy multiple instances of critical agents to prevent single points of failure.
- Failover Mechanisms: Automatically redirect tasks to healthy agents if one fails.
- Data Replication: Ensure data is replicated across nodes to avoid loss during failures.

Example: Load Balancing and Dynamic Allocation Workflow
Scenario: E-Commerce Order Processing

1. Task Types:
   - Order validation.
   - Inventory updates.
   - Payment processing.
   - Delivery scheduling.
2. Implementation:
   - Load Balancer:
     - Distributes incoming orders based on agent capacity.
   - Dynamic Scaling:
     - Adds agents during high traffic (e.g., holiday sales).
   - Priority Allocation:
     - Prioritizes payment processing tasks over delivery scheduling.
   - Fault Tolerance:
     - Redirects failed payment processing tasks to backup agents.

Applications of Load Balancing and Dynamic Allocation

1. Cloud Computing: Distributing tasks across virtual machines or containers.
2. IoT Systems: Balancing sensor data processing across edge devices.
3. Healthcare: Allocating computational resources for medical imaging or diagnostics.
4. Financial Services: Optimizing fraud detection and transaction processing workflows.

Load balancing and dynamic agent allocation are fundamental to optimizing performance in multi-agent systems. By employing strategies such as resource-based allocation, demand-based scaling, and priority scheduling, systems can achieve efficient resource utilization, minimize delays, and adapt to changing workloads. Monitoring metrics and implementing fault tolerance mechanisms further enhance the system's reliability and scalability. These strategies are essential for building robust and high-performing MAS across various industries.

8.4 Optimizing Performance and Resource Utilization

As multi-agent systems (MAS) scale, ensuring optimal performance and efficient use of resources becomes critical. Poorly optimized systems can lead to wasted computational resources, increased costs, and slower task execution. This section provides practical tips and strategies for improving the efficiency of MAS, focusing on real-world techniques to enhance performance while minimizing resource wastage.

The following practical tips are organized into key areas that impact performance and resource utilization in multi-agent systems.

1. Resource Management
Efficient resource management ensures that computational power, memory, and network bandwidth are used effectively.
1.1 Use Resource Quotas
- Description: Limit the resources allocated to each agent to prevent overuse.
- Implementation:

In Kubernetes, use resource quotas to allocate CPU and memory limits to containers running agents.
yaml

```yaml
resources:
  limits:
    cpu: "2"
    memory: "1Gi"
```

```
requests:
  cpu: "1"
  memory: "500Mi"
```

- Benefits: Prevents resource monopolization and ensures fair distribution.

1.2 Dynamic Scaling
- Description: Automatically scale the number of agents based on demand.
- Implementation:

Use tools like Kubernetes Horizontal Pod Autoscaler to add or remove agents dynamically.

bash

```
kubectl autoscale deployment my-agents --cpu-percent=50 --min=2 --max=10
```

- Benefits: Reduces costs during low demand and ensures availability during high demand.

1.3 Prioritize Resource Allocation
- Description: Allocate more resources to high-priority tasks or agents handling critical operations.
- Implementation:

Use priority classes in Kubernetes to prioritize workloads.

yaml

```
apiVersion: scheduling.k8s.io/v1
kind: PriorityClass
metadata:
  name: high-priority
value: 1000
```

- Benefits: Ensures critical tasks are completed without delays.

2. Task Scheduling

Efficient task scheduling optimizes agent workload and minimizes idle time.

2.1 Batch Processing
- Description: Group similar tasks into batches for agents to process together.
- Implementation:
    - Use tools like Apache Spark or custom scripts to handle batch processing.
- Benefits: Reduces communication overhead and improves throughput.

2.2 Use Task Queues
- Description: Maintain a queue of tasks to distribute among agents dynamically.
- Implementation:
    - Use message brokers like RabbitMQ, Kafka, or Celery for task management.
- Benefits: Ensures tasks are distributed evenly and reduces idle time.

2.3 Load Balancing
- Description: Distribute tasks evenly across agents or nodes.
- Implementation:
    - Use load balancers such as HAProxy or NGINX to distribute requests.
- Benefits: Prevents overloading of individual agents or nodes.

3. Communication Optimization

Reducing communication overhead improves system responsiveness and efficiency.

3.1 Use Asynchronous Communication
- Description: Decouple agents using message queues or asynchronous protocols.
- Implementation:
    - Use tools like ZeroMQ or RabbitMQ for asynchronous message passing.
- Benefits: Reduces blocking and improves scalability.

3.2 Minimize Data Transmission
- Description: Transmit only essential data between agents.
- Implementation:
    - Use data compression tools like gzip or protobuf for message payloads.
- Benefits: Reduces bandwidth usage and speeds up communication.

3.3 Optimize Data Sharing
- Description: Use shared memory or distributed data stores for frequently accessed data.
- Implementation:
    - Use caching tools like Redis or Memcached for shared data.
- Benefits: Reduces redundant requests and accelerates access.

4. Monitoring and Optimization

Continuous monitoring helps identify bottlenecks and inefficiencies.

4.1 Use Monitoring Tools
- Description: Monitor system metrics such as CPU, memory, and network usage.
- Implementation:
    - Use tools like Prometheus and Grafana for real-time monitoring and visualization.
- Benefits: Identifies performance issues and resource bottlenecks.

4.2 Implement Alerts
- Description: Set up alerts for resource usage thresholds or performance issues.
- Implementation:
    - Configure Prometheus Alertmanager to notify administrators of potential problems.
- Benefits: Allows proactive resolution of issues before they impact performance.

4.3 Analyze Logs

- Description: Use logs to debug and analyze system performance.
- Implementation:
    - Use the ELK Stack (Elasticsearch, Logstash, Kibana) for log management and analysis.
- Benefits: Provides insights into system behavior and helps optimize workflows.

5. Fault Tolerance and Redundancy

Ensuring fault tolerance minimizes downtime and resource wastage.

5.1 Replicate Critical Agents

- Description: Deploy multiple instances of critical agents for redundancy.
- Implementation:

Use Kubernetes ReplicaSets to maintain multiple agent instances.

yaml

```
kind: ReplicaSet
apiVersion: apps/v1
metadata:
  name: agent-replicaset
spec:
  replicas: 3
```

- Benefits: Ensures system availability even during failures.

5.2 Implement Checkpoints

- Description: Save agent states periodically to allow recovery after failures.
- Implementation:
    - Use checkpointing libraries like DMTCP (Distributed MultiThreaded CheckPointing).
- Benefits: Reduces resource wastage from failed tasks.

5.3 Use Distributed Databases

- Description: Store data in distributed databases for high availability and fault tolerance.

- Implementation:
    - Use systems like Cassandra or DynamoDB for resilient data storage.
- Benefits: Prevents data loss and ensures consistent performance.

6. Performance Tuning
Fine-tuning the system ensures agents perform tasks efficiently.

6.1 Optimize Code
- Description: Write efficient and lightweight agent code to reduce resource consumption.
- Implementation:
    - Profile code using tools like cProfile in Python to identify bottlenecks.
    - Optimize algorithms for computational efficiency.
- Benefits: Improves task execution speed and reduces resource usage.

6.2 Use Specialized Hardware
- Description: Leverage GPUs or TPUs for computationally intensive tasks.
- Implementation:
    - Deploy agents on GPU-enabled cloud instances for tasks like machine learning.
- Benefits: Accelerates processing and reduces execution time.

6.3 Implement Caching
- Description: Cache frequently accessed data or computation results.
- Implementation:
    - Use caching frameworks like Flask-Caching or Redis.
- Benefits: Speeds up repetitive tasks and reduces redundant computations.

7. Security and Access Control
Secure systems prevent unauthorized access and misuse of resources.

7.1 Use Encryption
- Description: Encrypt communication between agents to secure data.
- Implementation:
  - Use TLS/SSL for securing communication channels.
- Benefits: Prevents data breaches and unauthorized access.

7.2 Implement Role-Based Access Control (RBAC)
- Description: Limit resource access based on agent roles.
- Implementation:
  - Use Kubernetes RBAC to control access to resources.
- Benefits: Prevents misuse and ensures system integrity.

Applications of Resource Optimization
1. E-Commerce: Efficiently process high volumes of orders during peak sales.
2. IoT Systems: Optimize resource utilization for data collection and processing on edge devices.
3. Healthcare: Reduce response times for critical diagnostic tasks.
4. Finance: Improve throughput for real-time fraud detection and transaction processing.

Optimizing performance and resource utilization in multi-agent systems is essential for building scalable, cost-effective, and reliable systems. By implementing strategies like efficient resource management, task scheduling, communication optimization, and continuous monitoring, systems can handle complex workflows while minimizing overhead. Practical tips such as caching, dynamic scaling, and prioritizing critical tasks enable developers to maximize system efficiency, ensuring robust and adaptable performance across diverse applications.

8.5 Concept-to-Code: Scaling a Fleet of Agents

Scaling a fleet of agents in a multi-agent system involves designing and implementing a system that can handle an increasing number of agents, tasks, or users without compromising performance. This requires thoughtful strategies for task distribution, communication, resource allocation, and fault tolerance. In this section, we present a real-world implementation example of scaling a fleet of agents to solve a practical problem.

Scenario:
Imagine a logistics company managing a fleet of delivery drones. Each drone acts as an agent, responsible for tasks such as picking up packages, planning delivery routes, and tracking delivery status. The company wants to scale its operations to handle hundreds or thousands of drones operating across multiple regions, with the ability to dynamically allocate tasks, optimize performance, and ensure fault tolerance.
Below is a detailed, step-by-step implementation of this system.

Step 1: Define the Problem
The system must:
1. Manage tasks such as package pickup, delivery, and route optimization.
2. Handle scaling across multiple regions and drones.
3. Dynamically allocate tasks based on drone availability and location.
4. Optimize communication between drones and central servers.
5. Ensure fault tolerance in case of drone or server failures.

Step 2: Design the Architecture
The architecture is divided into the following components:
1. Task Management: A central task manager distributes tasks to drones.
2. Drone Agents: Each drone is an independent agent capable of executing tasks.
3. Communication Layer: Ensures real-time communication between drones and the task manager.

4. Monitoring and Scaling: Tracks system performance and scales resources dynamically.

Step 3: Implementation

3.1 Define the Drone Agent

Each drone agent performs specific tasks such as picking up packages and delivering them. It communicates with the central task manager to receive assignments.

python

```python
from crewai import Agent

class DroneAgent(Agent):
    def process(self, task):
        """
        Executes the assigned task and reports status back.
        """
        try:
            if task["type"] == "pickup":
                return f"Drone {self.name} picked up package {task['package_id']} from {task['location']}"
            elif task["type"] == "delivery":
                return f"Drone {self.name} delivered package {task['package_id']} to {task['destination']}"
            else:
                raise ValueError("Unknown task type")
        except Exception as e:
            return f"Error: {str(e)}"
```

3.2 Create the Task Manager

The task manager distributes tasks to available drones based on their location and availability.

python

```python
from queue import PriorityQueue

class TaskManager:
```

```python
    def __init__(self):
        self.task_queue = PriorityQueue()
        self.drones = {}

    def register_drone(self, drone):
        """
        Registers a drone agent with the task manager.
        """
        self.drones[drone.name] = drone

    def assign_task(self, task):
        """
        Assigns a task to the most suitable drone.
        """
        closest_drone = self.find_closest_drone(task["location"])
        if closest_drone:
            return closest_drone.process(task)
        else:
            return "No available drones to assign the task"

    def find_closest_drone(self, location):
        """
        Finds the closest available drone to the task location.
        """
        # Mock implementation: Select the first available drone
        for drone in self.drones.values():
            return drone
        return None
```

3.3 Define the Workflow
Combine the drones and task manager into a scalable workflow.
python
```python
from crewai import Workflow
```

```python
class DroneFleetWorkflow(Workflow):
    def build(self):
        # Define steps in the workflow
        self.add_step("assign_task", task_manager.assign_task)

# Instantiate the task manager and workflow
task_manager = TaskManager()
workflow = DroneFleetWorkflow(name="Drone Fleet Workflow")
```

3.4 Simulate the System

Register multiple drones and assign tasks.

python
```python
# Register drones
drones = [
    DroneAgent("Drone1"),
    DroneAgent("Drone2"),
    DroneAgent("Drone3"),
]

for drone in drones:
    task_manager.register_drone(drone)

# Simulate tasks
tasks = [
    {"type": "pickup", "package_id": "PKG1", "location": "Warehouse1"},
    {"type": "delivery", "package_id": "PKG1", "destination": "Customer1"},
]

# Assign tasks
for task in tasks:
```

```
result = task_manager.assign_task(task)
print(result)
```

Step 4: Scaling the System

4.1 Use Containerization for Drones
- Package each drone agent in a Docker container.
- Deploy containers on a Kubernetes cluster for scalability.

Example Dockerfile:
Dockerfile

```
FROM python:3.9-slim
WORKDIR /app
COPY . /app
RUN pip install crewai
CMD ["python", "drone_agent.py"]
```

4.2 Dynamic Task Allocation
- Use a priority queue to handle task urgency.
- Monitor drone availability in real-time and dynamically allocate tasks.

4.3 Communication Optimization
- Use MQTT or WebSocket for real-time communication between drones and the task manager.
- Compress messages to reduce bandwidth usage.

Step 5: Monitoring and Fault Tolerance

5.1 Monitor System Performance
- Use Prometheus and Grafana to track drone activity, task completion times, and resource utilization.

5.2 Implement Fault Tolerance
- Deploy redundant task managers to ensure continuity in case of failures.
- Replicate task data across multiple nodes using a distributed database (e.g., Cassandra).

Applications of the Scaled Fleet
1. Logistics: Automating package delivery across large geographical areas.
2. Disaster Relief: Coordinating drones for delivering supplies in emergencies.
3. Agriculture: Deploying drones for crop monitoring and pesticide spraying.
4. Surveillance: Managing a fleet of drones for security or wildlife monitoring.

Scaling a fleet of agents requires careful planning, robust task management, and real-time communication. By combining efficient agent design, dynamic task allocation, containerized deployment, and fault-tolerant architectures, multi-agent systems can handle complex and large-scale operations. The example provided demonstrates how to implement and scale a logistics system, showcasing the power of CrewAI in building efficient, reliable, and scalable solutions. With these strategies, organizations can deploy multi-agent systems across industries, unlocking new possibilities for automation and innovation.

Chapter 9: Debugging and Monitoring Multi-Agent Systems

9.1 Tools and Techniques for Debugging CrewAI Applications

Debugging multi-agent systems (MAS) is a critical step in ensuring that agents, workflows, and communication channels operate correctly. MAS like those built with CrewAI involve complex interactions among agents, dynamic workflows, and real-time data exchange, making debugging a potentially challenging task. This section explores tools and techniques for debugging agents, workflows, and inter-agent communication to identify and resolve issues effectively.

Debugging CrewAI applications requires a systematic approach, as issues can arise at various levels:
1. Agent-Level Debugging: Debugging the logic and behavior of individual agents.
2. Workflow Debugging: Ensuring workflows are correctly defined and executed.
3. Communication Debugging: Troubleshooting issues in the exchange of data between agents.

1. Debugging Agents
Agents are the core building blocks of any CrewAI system. Debugging them involves verifying their logic, data processing, and error-handling capabilities.
1.1 Logging
- Description: Logging is a primary method for understanding agent behavior during runtime. By adding log statements, you can trace the flow of data and identify where issues occur.

Implementation:
python

```python
import logging

class MyAgent(Agent):
    def process(self, data):
        logging.info(f"Processing data: {data}")
        try:
            # Agent logic
            result = data["key"] * 2
            logging.info(f"Result: {result}")
            return result
        except Exception as e:
            logging.error(f"Error in processing: {str(e)}")
```

```
            raise
```

- Benefits:
    - Helps trace execution flow.
    - Captures errors and warnings for analysis.

1.2 Unit Testing
- Description: Write unit tests to validate agent functionality in isolation.

Implementation:
python

```python
import unittest

class TestMyAgent(unittest.TestCase):
    def test_process(self):
        agent = MyAgent("TestAgent")
        result = agent.process({"key": 5})
        self.assertEqual(result, 10)
```

- Benefits:
    - Ensures agents behave as expected.
    - Allows quick detection of issues during development.

1.3 Debugging Tools
- Description: Use interactive debugging tools to step through agent code.
- Tools:

Python Debugger (pdb): Insert breakpoints and examine variable states.
python

```python
import pdb; pdb.set_trace()
```

- IDE Debuggers: Debug directly within IDEs like PyCharm or VSCode.

2. Debugging Workflows

Workflows define how agents interact and execute tasks. Debugging workflows ensures the system behaves as intended and tasks flow correctly.

2.1 Workflow Validation
- Description: Validate the workflow structure before execution to catch configuration errors.

Implementation:
python

```python
workflow.validate()
```

2.2 Step-by-Step Execution
- Description: Execute workflows step-by-step to isolate issues in specific steps.

Implementation:
python

```python
result = workflow.execute_step("step_name", input_data)
print(result)
```

2.3 Workflow Logs
- Description: Enable detailed logging for workflows to capture execution flow and errors.

Implementation:
python

```python
workflow.enable_logging(level=logging.DEBUG)
```

2.4 Workflow Visualization
- Description: Use visualization tools to analyze the workflow structure and execution.
- Implementation:
    - Generate a visual representation of the workflow using libraries like Graphviz.

Example:
python

```
from graphviz import Digraph

dot = Digraph()
dot.node("Step1", "Collect Data")
dot.node("Step2", "Process Data")
dot.edge("Step1", "Step2")
dot.render("workflow", format="png")
```

3. Debugging Communication

Inter-agent communication is critical for collaboration in multi-agent systems. Debugging communication involves verifying that data is transmitted and received correctly.

3.1 Message Logging
- Description: Log all messages sent and received by agents to trace communication.

Implementation:
python

```
class CommunicatingAgent(Agent):
    def send_message(self, recipient, message):
        logging.info(f"Sending message to {recipient}: {message}")
        super().send_message(recipient, message)

    def receive_message(self, message):
        logging.info(f"Received message: {message}")
        return super().receive_message(message)
```

3.2 Message Validation
- Description: Validate message formats and contents to prevent errors.

Implementation:
python

```python
def validate_message(message):
    if "type" not in message or "data" not in message:
        raise ValueError("Invalid message format")
```

3.3 Network Monitoring
- Description: Monitor network traffic to analyze message exchange patterns.
- Tools:
    - Wireshark: Analyze packet-level communication.
    - Netstat: Monitor active network connections.

3.4 Simulated Communication Testing
- Description: Simulate communication scenarios to identify potential issues.

Implementation:
python

```python
def test_communication():
    agent1 = CommunicatingAgent("Agent1")
    agent2 = CommunicatingAgent("Agent2")
    agent1.send_message("Agent2", {"type": "greet", "data": "Hello"})
    assert agent2.receive_message() == {"type": "greet", "data": "Hello"}
```

4. Common Issues and Solutions

Issue 1: Agent Crashes
- Cause: Unhandled exceptions or invalid input data.
- Solution: Add robust error handling and validate inputs.

Issue 2: Workflow Deadlocks
- Cause: Circular dependencies between workflow steps.
- Solution: Analyze the workflow graph and break dependency cycles.

Issue 3: Communication Failures
- Cause: Network issues or message format mismatches.
- Solution: Use retry mechanisms and validate message formats.

5. Debugging Tools

CrewAI integrates with several tools to simplify debugging:
1. Integrated Logs: Centralized logging for agents and workflows.
2. Metrics Dashboards: Tools like Prometheus and Grafana to monitor system performance.
3. Distributed Tracing: Use tools like OpenTelemetry to trace inter-agent communication.

6. Debugging in a Distributed Environment

In distributed systems, debugging becomes more complex due to multiple nodes and asynchronous communication.

6.1 Centralized Logging
- Use centralized logging systems like ELK Stack (Elasticsearch, Logstash, Kibana) to aggregate logs from all agents.

6.2 Distributed Debugging
- Use tools like Jaeger or Zipkin to trace distributed workflows and communication paths.

6.3 Test Environments
- Set up a test environment that mimics the production environment for debugging.

Debugging multi-agent systems like those built with CrewAI requires a structured approach that addresses issues at the agent, workflow, and communication levels. By leveraging tools like logging, unit testing, workflow visualization, and distributed tracing, developers can identify and resolve issues effectively. A combination of best practices, robust error handling, and advanced debugging tools ensures that multi-agent systems perform reliably, even as they scale.

9.2 Setting Up Real-Time Monitoring and Logging

Real-time monitoring and logging are essential for maintaining the stability, reliability, and performance of multi-agent systems (MAS). These tools enable developers and system administrators to track agent behavior, measure performance metrics, and detect issues in real-time. By implementing effective monitoring and logging practices, MAS can operate efficiently while quickly identifying and resolving potential problems.
This section provides an in-depth guide to tools and techniques for setting up real-time monitoring and logging, specifically focusing on tracking agent behavior and performance.

Real-time tracking of agent behavior and system performance involves collecting, analyzing, and visualizing key metrics. The following sections detail the most effective tools and strategies.

1. Logging: The Foundation of Real-Time Monitoring
Logging is a critical component of tracking agent behavior. Logs capture detailed records of events, agent activities, and errors.
1.1 Local Logging with Python
- Description: Use Python's built-in logging module to capture and store logs for agents.

Implementation:
python

```
import logging

# Configure logging
logging.basicConfig(
    filename="agent.log",
```

```python
    level=logging.INFO,
    format="%(asctime)s - %(name)s - %(levelname)s - %(message)s"
)

class Agent:
    def perform_task(self, task):
        logging.info(f"Starting task: {task}")
        try:
            result = task["value"] * 2
            logging.info(f"Task completed successfully: {result}")
            return result
        except Exception as e:
            logging.error(f"Task failed: {e}")
            raise
```

1.2 Centralized Logging
- Description: Aggregate logs from multiple agents to a centralized location for easy analysis.
- Tools:
    - ELK Stack (Elasticsearch, Logstash, Kibana):
        - Elasticsearch: Stores and indexes logs.
        - Logstash: Processes and forwards logs.
        - Kibana: Visualizes logs in dashboards.
    - Fluentd: An open-source tool for collecting and forwarding logs.

1.3 Structured Logging
- Description: Use structured log formats like JSON to simplify searching and filtering.

Implementation:
python

```python
import json
logging.info(json.dumps({"agent": "Agent1", "event": "task_started", "task_id": 123}))
```

Benefits:
- Simplifies debugging.
- Improves searchability and analysis of logs.

2. Metrics Monitoring: Real-Time Agent Performance Tracking
Metrics provide quantitative data on system performance, helping identify bottlenecks and inefficiencies.

2.1 Prometheus
- Description: A powerful open-source tool for real-time metrics collection and alerting.
- Features:
    - Customizable metrics collection using exporters.
    - Query language (PromQL) for data analysis.
    - Integration with Grafana for visualization.

Implementation:
python

```python
from prometheus_client import Counter, start_http_server

# Define a counter metric
task_counter = Counter("tasks_completed", "Number of tasks completed by the agent")

def perform_task(task):
    task_counter.inc()  # Increment the counter
    return task["value"] * 2

if __name__ == "__main__":
    start_http_server(8000)  # Start metrics server
    perform_task({"value": 5})
```

2.2 Grafana

- Description: A visualization tool that integrates with Prometheus and other data sources to create real-time dashboards.
- Features:
  - Customizable dashboards for metrics visualization.
  - Alerts for abnormal metric values.
- Example: Display metrics like CPU usage, memory utilization, and task completion rates in a real-time dashboard.

2.3 Resource Monitoring Tools
- Tools:
  - cAdvisor: Tracks container-level resource usage (CPU, memory, network).
  - Node Exporter: Provides system-level metrics for Prometheus.

3. Workflow Monitoring: Tracking Task Execution

Workflow monitoring ensures that tasks are executed correctly and efficiently across agents.

3.1 Execution Logs
- Description: Log the execution details of each workflow step.

Implementation:
python

```
workflow.log_step("Task1", status="completed", execution_time=5.2)
```

3.2 Workflow Visualization
- Description: Visualize workflows to track dependencies, task progress, and potential bottlenecks.
- Tools:

Graphviz:
python

```
from graphviz import Digraph
```

```python
dot = Digraph()
dot.node("Start", "Step 1: Collect Data")
dot.node("End", "Step 2: Process Data")
dot.edge("Start", "End")
dot.render("workflow", format="png")
```

4. Communication Monitoring

Efficient communication is critical for MAS. Monitoring communication helps detect latency, errors, and message loss.

4.1 Message Logs
- Description: Log all incoming and outgoing messages for troubleshooting.

Implementation:
python

```python
class CommunicatingAgent:
    def send_message(self, recipient, message):
        logging.info(f"Sending message to {recipient}: {message}")

    def receive_message(self, message):
        logging.info(f"Received message: {message}")
```

4.2 Distributed Tracing
- Description: Trace communication paths across agents to identify bottlenecks or failures.
- Tools:
    - Jaeger: Provides end-to-end tracing for distributed systems.
    - Zipkin: Tracks message flows and identifies latency issues.

4.3 Network Monitoring
- Tools:
    - Wireshark: Analyzes packet-level communication.

- Netstat: Monitors active connections.

5. Alerts and Notifications

Set up alerts to notify administrators of critical issues.

5.1 Prometheus Alertmanager
- Description: Configures alerts for metrics exceeding predefined thresholds.

Example:
yaml

```yaml
groups:
- name: alert_rules
  rules:
  - alert: HighTaskLatency
    expr: task_latency_seconds > 2
    for: 1m
    labels:
      severity: critical
    annotations:
      summary: "Task latency exceeded 2 seconds"
```

5.2 Slack and Email Notifications
- Integrate alerts with Slack, PagerDuty, or email for real-time notifications.

6. Best Practices for Monitoring and Logging
   1. Log Retention Policies:
      - Retain logs for a reasonable period based on compliance and storage costs.
   2. Use Log Levels:
      - Apply appropriate log levels (DEBUG, INFO, WARNING, ERROR) to reduce noise.
   3. Real-Time Dashboards:
      - Regularly update dashboards to reflect the latest system state.
   4. Proactive Alerts:

- Configure alerts for potential issues like high CPU usage or task failures.
5. Continuous Monitoring:
    - Regularly audit monitoring tools and configurations for accuracy.

Applications of Monitoring and Logging
1. E-Commerce: Monitor order processing workflows and server performance.
2. Healthcare: Track diagnostic workflows and ensure system uptime.
3. IoT Systems: Monitor device performance and data collection efficiency.
4. Finance: Detect anomalies in transaction processing and fraud detection.

Real-time monitoring and logging are indispensable for managing multi-agent systems. Tools like Prometheus, Grafana, ELK Stack, and Jaeger provide comprehensive solutions for tracking agent behavior and system performance. By implementing these tools effectively, developers can ensure robust operations, promptly detect and resolve issues, and optimize performance. These practices are foundational for building scalable, reliable, and efficient MAS that meet real-world demands.

9.3 Ensuring System Stability and Reliability

System stability and reliability are critical in multi-agent systems (MAS), where complex interactions between agents, workflows, and communication channels can introduce potential bottlenecks and failure points. Identifying and mitigating these bottlenecks ensures smooth operation, scalability, and robustness. This section focuses on strategies for identifying system bottlenecks and implementing effective solutions to maintain stability and reliability.

A bottleneck is a point in the system where the flow of tasks, data, or communication is restricted, causing delays and reducing overall performance. Bottlenecks can occur at various levels, including resource allocation, workflow execution, agent communication, or system design.

1. Identifying System Bottlenecks
The first step in ensuring system stability is detecting and analyzing bottlenecks. The following techniques can be used:
1.1 Monitoring System Metrics
- Description: Track key metrics to identify areas of high resource consumption or performance degradation.
- Metrics to Monitor:
    - CPU and Memory Utilization: High usage can indicate resource contention.
    - Task Latency: Increased task execution times signal workflow delays.
    - Network Bandwidth Usage: Overloaded communication channels can cause delays.
    - Error Rates: Frequent errors may point to systemic issues.

Tools:
- Prometheus: Monitor system metrics in real-time.
- Grafana: Visualize trends and detect anomalies.
- cAdvisor: Monitor container resource usage.

Example:

yaml

```yaml
- alert: HighCPUUsage
  expr: process_cpu_seconds_total > 100
  for: 5m
  labels:
    severity: critical
  annotations:
    summary: "High CPU usage detected"
```

1.2 Workflow Analysis
- Description: Analyze workflows to identify steps with excessive delays or high failure rates.
- Techniques:
  - Step Timing: Log the execution time of each step in a workflow.
  - Dependency Graphs: Use tools like Graphviz to visualize workflow dependencies and locate bottlenecks.

Example:
python
```
import time

def workflow_step(task):
    start_time = time.time()
    result = process_task(task)
    execution_time = time.time() - start_time
    logging.info(f"Step executed in {execution_time} seconds")
    return result
```

1.3 Communication Trace Analysis
- Description: Trace message paths to identify latency or dropped messages.
- Tools:
  - Jaeger: Provides distributed tracing for identifying slow communication paths.
  - Wireshark: Captures and analyzes network traffic to detect bottlenecks.

Example: Trace communication between agents:
python
```
class Agent:
    def send_message(self, recipient, message):
        start_time = time.time()
```

```
    response = super().send_message(recipient, message)
    latency = time.time() - start_time
    logging.info(f"Message latency: {latency} seconds")
    return response
```

2. Mitigating System Bottlenecks

Once bottlenecks are identified, the next step is implementing solutions to address them.

2.1 Resource Optimization

- Description: Ensure adequate resources are allocated to tasks and agents.
- Techniques:

Dynamic Scaling: Use tools like Kubernetes to scale agents based on demand.

bash

```bash
kubectl autoscale deployment agent-deployment --cpu-percent=50 --min=1 --max=10
```

Resource Quotas: Limit resource usage per agent to prevent overconsumption.

yaml

```yaml
resources:
  limits:
    cpu: "2"
    memory: "2Gi"
```

  - Priority Allocation: Assign higher priority to critical tasks.

2.2 Workflow Optimization

- Description: Improve workflow design to reduce delays and inefficiencies.
- Techniques:

Parallel Execution: Execute independent steps in parallel to save time.

python

```
from concurrent.futures import ThreadPoolExecutor

def parallel_execution(tasks):
    with ThreadPoolExecutor() as executor:
        results = executor.map(process_task, tasks)
    return results
```

- Task Batching: Group similar tasks for processing to reduce overhead.

2.3 Communication Optimization
- Description: Enhance the efficiency of inter-agent communication.
- Techniques:

Message Compression: Compress large messages to reduce bandwidth usage.

python

```
import gzip

def compress_message(message):
    return gzip.compress(message.encode())

def decompress_message(compressed_message):
    return gzip.decompress(compressed_message).decode()
```

- Event-Driven Communication: Use event-based systems to minimize unnecessary messages.
- Caching: Cache frequently requested data to reduce repeated transmissions.

2.4 Fault Tolerance and Recovery
- Description: Ensure the system can handle failures without significant impact.
- Techniques:
    - Redundancy: Deploy multiple instances of critical agents to prevent downtime.
    - Checkpointing: Save the state of workflows periodically to allow recovery after failures.

Retry Mechanisms: Implement automatic retries for failed tasks or messages.

python

```python
def retry_task(task, retries=3):
    for attempt in range(retries):
        try:
            return process_task(task)
        except Exception as e:
            logging.warning(f"Attempt {attempt+1} failed: {e}")
    raise Exception("Task failed after retries")
```

2.5 Load Balancing
- Description: Distribute tasks evenly across agents or nodes to prevent overloading.
- Techniques:
    - Round Robin: Assign tasks in a circular order.
    - Weighted Load Balancing: Allocate tasks based on agent capacity.
    - Geographical Load Balancing: Route tasks to the nearest agent for lower latency.

Tools:
NGINX: Configures load balancing for task distribution.
nginx

```nginx
upstream agents {
```

```
    server agent1.example.com;
    server agent2.example.com;
}

server {
  listen 80;
  location / {
    proxy_pass http://agents;
  }
}
```

2.6 Monitoring and Alerts
- Description: Continuously monitor the system and set up alerts for potential bottlenecks.
- Techniques:
    - Dashboards: Use Grafana to visualize real-time metrics and trends.
    - Alert Rules: Configure alerts for abnormal conditions (e.g., high latency, error spikes).

3. Best Practices for Ensuring Stability
   1. Regular Testing: Perform load testing and stress testing to ensure the system can handle peak loads.
      - Tools: Apache JMeter, Locust.
   2. Proactive Scaling: Anticipate workload spikes and scale resources in advance.
   3. Documentation: Maintain detailed documentation of workflows, agent roles, and communication protocols to simplify debugging and optimization.

Applications of Bottleneck Mitigation
   1. E-Commerce: Ensure fast order processing during high-traffic events like sales.
   2. IoT Systems: Handle data streams from thousands of devices efficiently.

3. Healthcare: Maintain system responsiveness for critical patient diagnostics.
4. Autonomous Vehicles: Prevent communication delays between vehicles and control systems.

Identifying and mitigating bottlenecks is essential for ensuring the stability and reliability of multi-agent systems. By monitoring system metrics, optimizing workflows, improving communication, and implementing fault tolerance mechanisms, MAS can achieve high performance and resilience. Proactive measures such as dynamic scaling, load balancing, and efficient resource management further enhance system reliability, enabling seamless operation even under demanding conditions.

9.4 Example: Debugging a Faulty Agent Interaction

Debugging faulty interactions in a multi-agent system (MAS) can be challenging due to the distributed nature of the system and the interdependencies between agents. Identifying and resolving issues requires a systematic approach to troubleshooting, focusing on communication protocols, task execution, and error handling mechanisms.

This section provides a practical troubleshooting walkthrough for debugging a faulty interaction between agents in a simulated environment.

Scenario: Faulty Agent Interaction
System Description:

A CoordinatorAgent assigns tasks to multiple WorkerAgents. Each WorkerAgent reports task completion back to the CoordinatorAgent.

The system logs all task statuses for monitoring.
Fault:
One of the WorkerAgents fails to report task completion, causing the CoordinatorAgent to incorrectly assume the task is incomplete.

Step-by-Step Troubleshooting Walkthrough
Step 1: Understand the Problem
Symptoms:

Tasks are assigned but not marked as complete.
The CoordinatorAgent keeps the task in its queue, leading to duplication or delays.
Hypothesis: The issue may stem from:

A failure in the WorkerAgent's task execution.
A breakdown in the communication between the WorkerAgent and the CoordinatorAgent.
Incorrect error handling in the CoordinatorAgent.
Step 2: Set Up Debugging Tools
Logging:

Add detailed logs to both the CoordinatorAgent and WorkerAgent to track their interactions.
Message Inspection:

Capture and inspect messages exchanged between agents to verify communication integrity.
Task State Validation:

Track the state of each task to ensure proper transitions (e.g., from "Assigned" to "In Progress" to "Completed").
Step 3: Simulate the System
Code Implementation:

python
```
class CoordinatorAgent(Agent):
```

```python
    def __init__(self, name):
        super().__init__(name)
        self.tasks = {}
        self.available_agents = []

    def register_agent(self, agent):
        self.available_agents.append(agent)
        print(f"{self.name}: Registered {agent.name}.")

    def assign_task(self, task):
        if self.available_agents:
            agent = self.available_agents.pop(0)
            print(f"{self.name}: Assigning task '{task}' to {agent.name}.")
            self.tasks[task] = "Assigned"
            agent.perform_task(task, self)
        else:
            print(f"{self.name}: No available agents for task '{task}'.")

    def task_completed(self, task, agent):
        print(f"{self.name}: Task '{task}' completed by {agent.name}.")
        self.tasks[task] = "Completed"
        self.available_agents.append(agent)

class WorkerAgent(Agent):
    def perform_task(self, task, coordinator):
        print(f"{self.name}: Starting task '{task}'.")
        try:
            # Simulate task execution
            if task == "FaultyTask":
                raise Exception("Simulated failure")
            print(f"{self.name}: Completed task '{task}'.")
            coordinator.task_completed(task, self)
        except Exception as e:
```

```
        print(f"{self.name}: Failed to complete task '{task}': {e}")
        # Report failure to coordinator
        coordinator.report_failure(task, self)
```

Step 4: Run the Simulation Script:

```python
if __name__ == "__main__":
    coordinator = CoordinatorAgent(name="Coordinator")
    agents = [WorkerAgent(name=f"Worker{i}") for i in range(2)]

    # Register agents
    for agent in agents:
        coordinator.register_agent(agent)

    # Assign tasks
    tasks = ["Task1", "FaultyTask", "Task3"]
    for task in tasks:
        coordinator.assign_task(task)
```

Expected Output:

```vbnet
Coordinator: Registered Worker0.
Coordinator: Registered Worker1.
Coordinator: Assigning task 'Task1' to Worker0.
Worker0: Starting task 'Task1'.
Worker0: Completed task 'Task1'.
Coordinator: Task 'Task1' completed by Worker0.
Coordinator: Assigning task 'FaultyTask' to Worker1.
Worker1: Starting task 'FaultyTask'.
Worker1: Failed to complete task 'FaultyTask': Simulated failure
```

Coordinator: Assigning task 'Task3' to Worker0.
Worker0: Starting task 'Task3'.
Worker0: Completed task 'Task3'.
Coordinator: Task 'Task3' completed by Worker0.

Step 5: Identify the Fault
Observations:

Worker1 encounters a failure during "FaultyTask". CoordinatorAgent does not handle the failure appropriately; the task remains incomplete.

Step 6: Debug the Issue
Inspect Logs:

Review logs to identify where the failure occurs and how it propagates.

Verify Communication:

Check if the WorkerAgent sends a failure message to the CoordinatorAgent.
Ensure the CoordinatorAgent logs and processes the failure correctly.

Validate State Transitions:

Ensure tasks transition properly from "Assigned" to "In Progress" to "Completed" or "Failed".

Step 7: Fix the Issue
Improvement in Code:

Add a report_failure method in the CoordinatorAgent:

```python
def report_failure(self, task, agent):
    print(f"{self.name}: Task '{task}' failed by {agent.name}. Reassigning...")
    self.tasks[task] = "Failed"
    self.assign_task(task)
```

Modify the WorkerAgent to handle task failure more gracefully:

python

```python
def perform_task(self, task, coordinator):
    print(f"{self.name}: Starting task '{task}'.")
    try:
        # Simulate task execution
        if task == "FaultyTask":
            raise Exception("Simulated failure")
        print(f"{self.name}: Completed task '{task}'.")
        coordinator.task_completed(task, self)
    except Exception as e:
        print(f"{self.name}: Failed to complete task '{task}': {e}")
        coordinator.report_failure(task, self)
```

Step 8: Re-Test the System
Expected Output After Fix:

vbnet

```
Coordinator: Registered Worker0.
Coordinator: Registered Worker1.
Coordinator: Assigning task 'Task1' to Worker0.
Worker0: Starting task 'Task1'.
Worker0: Completed task 'Task1'.
Coordinator: Task 'Task1' completed by Worker0.
Coordinator: Assigning task 'FaultyTask' to Worker1.
Worker1: Starting task 'FaultyTask'.
Worker1: Failed to complete task 'FaultyTask': Simulated failure
Coordinator: Task 'FaultyTask' failed by Worker1. Reassigning...
Coordinator: Assigning task 'FaultyTask' to Worker0.
Worker0: Starting task 'FaultyTask'.
Worker0: Completed task 'FaultyTask'.
Coordinator: Task 'FaultyTask' completed by Worker0.
```

Coordinator: Assigning task 'Task3' to Worker1.
Worker1: Starting task 'Task3'.
Worker1: Completed task 'Task3'.
Coordinator: Task 'Task3' completed by Worker1.

Step 9: Finalize and Document

Document Changes:

Record updates to the CoordinatorAgent and WorkerAgent code. Include failure scenarios and how they are handled.

Monitor in Production:

Add additional logs and monitoring to detect similar issues in real-world deployments.

Summary

Debugging faulty agent interactions involves systematically identifying issues, analyzing logs, and testing fixes. In this walkthrough:

A faulty WorkerAgent interaction was identified and resolved by adding error reporting and re-assignment mechanisms in the CoordinatorAgent.

Techniques like logging, message inspection, and state validation played a crucial role in pinpointing the issue.

This structured approach ensures robust and fault-tolerant multi-agent systems.

Chapter 10: Security and Ethical Considerations

10.1 Security Challenges in Multi-Agent Systems

Multi-agent systems (MAS) are increasingly used in critical applications, including healthcare, autonomous vehicles, and smart cities. However, their distributed nature, autonomous decision-making, and reliance on communication channels make them vulnerable to various security threats. Ensuring the security of MAS is crucial to prevent malicious attacks, data breaches, and system failures.

Understanding potential vulnerabilities in MAS and implementing effective mitigation strategies are essential to safeguard these systems. Below are detailed discussions on key vulnerabilities and how to address them.

1. Potential Vulnerabilities in Multi-Agent Systems
MAS are exposed to several security risks due to their reliance on communication, autonomy, and inter-agent interactions.

1.1 Communication Vulnerabilities
   1. Eavesdropping:
       - Unauthorized agents or attackers intercept messages between agents to gain access to sensitive information.
       - Example: In a logistics system, an attacker intercepts delivery instructions to learn shipment routes.
   2. Man-in-the-Middle (MITM) Attacks:
       - An attacker secretly relays or alters communications between agents.
       - Example: In a swarm of drones, an attacker manipulates navigation commands to cause collisions.

3. Message Tampering:
    - Messages are modified during transmission, leading to incorrect task execution.
    - Example: A malicious agent alters resource allocation messages in a smart grid.

Mitigation Strategies:
- Encryption:
    - Use end-to-end encryption (e.g., TLS) to protect messages during transmission.
    - Example: Encrypt all inter-agent messages using AES or RSA algorithms.
- Authentication:
    - Verify the identity of agents before communication.
    - Example: Use digital signatures or certificates to authenticate agents.
- Message Integrity Checks:
    - Use cryptographic hashes (e.g., SHA-256) to ensure messages are not tampered with.

1.2 Autonomy Vulnerabilities
1. Compromised Agents:
    - Malicious actors can take control of an agent, using it to disrupt the system.
    - Example: A hacked drone in a surveillance system misreports data, misleading other agents.
2. Unauthorized Decision-Making:
    - An attacker manipulates an agent's decision-making algorithm.
    - Example: In a financial MAS, a malicious agent triggers unauthorized transactions.

Mitigation Strategies:
- Behavior Monitoring:
    - Continuously monitor agents' actions for anomalies.
    - Example: Detect unusual task assignments or excessive resource usage.
- Sandboxing:

- Run agents in isolated environments to limit the impact of compromised behavior.
- Example: Use virtualized containers like Docker to isolate agents.
- Periodic Validation:
    - Periodically verify that agents are executing authorized tasks only.
    - Example: Use predefined rules or policies to check task legitimacy.

1.3 Resource Vulnerabilities

1. Denial-of-Service (DoS) Attacks:
    - Attackers overwhelm the system by flooding it with tasks or communication requests.
    - Example: In a smart traffic system, a malicious agent sends excessive data to jam the network.
2. Resource Contention:
    - Multiple agents compete for limited resources, causing delays or failures.
    - Example: In a cloud computing MAS, agents overload a server by requesting excessive CPU power.

Mitigation Strategies:
- Rate Limiting:
    - Limit the number of requests an agent can make in a given time.
    - Example: Allow each agent to send only 10 requests per minute.
- Load Balancing:
    - Distribute resource requests across multiple servers or agents.
    - Example: Use load balancers to ensure fair distribution of computational tasks.
- Access Control:
    - Restrict resource access based on agent roles and permissions.

- Example: Only authorized agents can access critical resources.

1.4 Inter-Agent Collaboration Vulnerabilities
1. Spoofing:
   - A malicious agent impersonates another agent to gain unauthorized access.
   - Example: An attacker spoofs the identity of a coordinator agent to issue fake commands.
2. Conflict Exploitation:
   - Malicious agents exploit conflicts between agents to disrupt coordination.
   - Example: In a robotic swarm, an attacker triggers conflicting navigation commands.

Mitigation Strategies:
- Identity Verification:
  - Use secure tokens or certificates to validate agent identities.
  - Example: Implement OAuth2 for authentication and authorization.
- Consensus Mechanisms:
  - Require agents to reach consensus before executing critical actions.
  - Example: Use distributed algorithms like Paxos or Raft.

1.5 Data Vulnerabilities
1. Data Breaches:
   - Unauthorized access to sensitive data shared between agents.
   - Example: In a healthcare MAS, patient records are accessed by an attacker.
2. Data Poisoning:
   - An attacker feeds malicious or incorrect data to agents, causing erroneous decisions.

- Example: In a machine learning MAS, an attacker injects biased training data.

Mitigation Strategies:
- Data Encryption:
  - Encrypt sensitive data at rest and in transit.
  - Example: Use database encryption for stored information and SSL for transmitted data.
- Data Validation:
  - Validate data before use to ensure its accuracy and integrity.
  - Example: Implement checks to detect anomalous input data.
- Access Control:
  - Restrict access to sensitive data based on agent roles.
  - Example: Use role-based access control (RBAC) to limit data access.

2. Threat Mitigation Framework

To comprehensively address security challenges, adopt the following framework:

1. Risk Assessment:
   - Identify and prioritize potential risks in the MAS.
   - Example: Use threat modeling techniques like STRIDE to evaluate vulnerabilities.
2. Secure Design Principles:
   - Incorporate security measures during the design phase.
   - Example: Use the principle of least privilege to minimize access rights for agents.
3. Continuous Monitoring:
   - Monitor agent activities and communication for anomalies.
   - Example: Use intrusion detection systems (IDS) to detect suspicious behavior.
4. Incident Response:

- Develop a response plan to mitigate the impact of security incidents.
- Example: Define procedures for isolating compromised agents and restoring system functionality.
5. Periodic Updates:
    - Regularly update agents and system components to patch vulnerabilities.
    - Example: Deploy updates to address newly discovered security flaws.

Case Study: Securing a Multi-Agent Logistics System
Scenario:
A logistics MAS consists of delivery drones and a central coordinator. The system faces potential threats, including message tampering, compromised drones, and resource contention.

Implementation:
1. Encryption:
    - Encrypt all communications between drones and the coordinator using TLS.
2. Authentication:
    - Use digital certificates to authenticate drones before assigning tasks.
3. Behavior Monitoring:
    - Monitor drone activities for anomalies, such as unauthorized routes or excessive task failures.
4. Access Control:
    - Restrict access to delivery schedules and sensitive customer data.

Outcome: The system becomes more resilient to security threats, ensuring reliable and secure delivery operations.

Summary

Multi-agent systems face diverse security challenges, ranging from communication vulnerabilities to resource contention and data breaches. Mitigation strategies such as encryption, authentication, access control, and behavior monitoring are essential to protect MAS from malicious attacks and ensure system integrity. By adopting a secure-by-design approach and implementing a robust threat mitigation framework, developers can build resilient and trustworthy multi-agent systems.

10.2 Securing Communication Between Agents

In multi-agent systems (MAS), agents communicate extensively to share information, coordinate tasks, and achieve common goals. The security of this communication is critical, as vulnerabilities can lead to data breaches, unauthorized access, or malicious attacks that disrupt system operations. Encryption and secure communication protocols are fundamental tools for protecting inter-agent communication.

Encryption and secure protocols ensure the confidentiality, integrity, and authenticity of messages exchanged between agents. This section explores these concepts in detail and provides practical implementation techniques for securing agent communication.

1. Encryption in Multi-Agent Systems
Encryption is the process of converting plaintext messages into unreadable ciphertext, ensuring that only authorized recipients can decipher and access the information. Encryption plays a crucial role in securing agent communication by protecting data from eavesdropping and tampering.

1.1 Types of Encryption
   1. Symmetric Encryption:
      - A single key is used for both encryption and decryption.
      - Example Algorithms: AES (Advanced Encryption Standard), DES (Data Encryption Standard).

- Advantages:
    - Faster than asymmetric encryption.
- Disadvantages:
    - Requires secure key distribution.

Code Example:

```python
from cryptography.fernet import Fernet

# Generate a symmetric key
key = Fernet.generate_key()
cipher = Fernet(key)

# Encrypt a message
message = "Task: Deliver Package A"
encrypted_message = cipher.encrypt(message.encode())
print(f"Encrypted: {encrypted_message}")

# Decrypt the message
decrypted_message = cipher.decrypt(encrypted_message).decode()
print(f"Decrypted: {decrypted_message}")
```

Output:
```vbnet
Encrypted: b'gAAAAABl...'
Decrypted: Task: Deliver Package A
```

2. Asymmetric Encryption:
    - Uses a pair of keys: a public key for encryption and a private key for decryption.
    - Example Algorithms: RSA (Rivest–Shamir–Adleman), ECC (Elliptic Curve Cryptography).
    - Advantages:
        - No need to share private keys.

- Disadvantages:
  - Slower than symmetric encryption.

Code Example:

```python
from cryptography.hazmat.primitives.asymmetric import rsa
from cryptography.hazmat.primitives.asymmetric import padding
from cryptography.hazmat.primitives import hashes

# Generate RSA key pair
private_key = rsa.generate_private_key(
    public_exponent=65537,
    key_size=2048,
)
public_key = private_key.public_key()

# Encrypt a message
message = b"Task: Collect Sensor Data"
ciphertext = public_key.encrypt(
    message,
    padding.OAEP(
        mgf=padding.MGF1(algorithm=hashes.SHA256()),
        algorithm=hashes.SHA256(),
        label=None,
    ),
)
print(f"Encrypted: {ciphertext}")

# Decrypt the message
plaintext = private_key.decrypt(
    ciphertext,
    padding.OAEP(
        mgf=padding.MGF1(algorithm=hashes.SHA256()),
        algorithm=hashes.SHA256(),
        label=None,
```

```python
    ),
)
print(f"Decrypted: {plaintext.decode()}")
```

Output:
vbnet
```
Encrypted: b'\x91\xe6...\xb7'
Decrypted: Task: Collect Sensor Data
```

1.2 Best Practices for Using Encryption
1. Use strong encryption algorithms (e.g., AES-256, RSA-2048).
2. Regularly update and rotate encryption keys.
3. Securely store and transmit encryption keys using key management systems (e.g., AWS KMS, HashiCorp Vault).
4. Implement forward secrecy to protect past communications even if keys are compromised.

2. Secure Communication Protocols

Secure protocols provide a framework for encrypted and authenticated communication between agents. These protocols combine encryption with other security measures to ensure data protection.

2.1 Common Secure Protocols
1. Transport Layer Security (TLS):
    - Provides encryption, authentication, and integrity for communication over networks.
    - Widely used in web-based systems and agent communication frameworks.

Implementation Example:
python
```python
import ssl
import socket
```

```python
# Create a secure socket using TLS
context = ssl.create_default_context(ssl.Purpose.CLIENT_AUTH)
server_socket = socket.socket(socket.AF_INET, socket.SOCK_STREAM)
secure_socket = context.wrap_socket(server_socket, server_side=True)

secure_socket.bind(('localhost', 8443))
secure_socket.listen(5)
print("Secure server running on port 8443.")
```

2. Message Queue Telemetry Transport (MQTT) with TLS:
    - A lightweight messaging protocol suitable for IoT and MAS.
    - Supports secure communication using TLS.

Implementation Example:
python
```python
import paho.mqtt.client as mqtt

def on_connect(client, userdata, flags, rc):
    print("Connected with result code " + str(rc))

# Create MQTT client and configure TLS
client = mqtt.Client()
client.tls_set(ca_certs="ca.crt", certfile="client.crt", keyfile="client.key")

client.on_connect = on_connect
client.connect("mqtt.example.com", 8883, 60)
client.loop_start()
```

3. gRPC with TLS:

- A high-performance, open-source RPC framework that supports secure communication.
- Useful for agent interactions in distributed systems.

Implementation Example:

```python
import grpc
from concurrent import futures
import time
import agent_pb2
import agent_pb2_grpc

class SecureAgent(agent_pb2_grpc.AgentServiceServicer):
    def SendMessage(self, request, context):
        print(f"Received message: {request.message}")
        return agent_pb2.ResponseMessage(message="Acknowledged")

# Create a secure gRPC server
server = grpc.server(futures.ThreadPoolExecutor(max_workers=10))
agent_pb2_grpc.add_AgentServiceServicer_to_server(SecureAgent(), server)

# Load server certificate and key
with open("server.crt", "rb") as f:
    cert = f.read()
with open("server.key", "rb") as f:
    key = f.read()

server_credentials = grpc.ssl_server_credentials(((key, cert),))
server.add_secure_port("[::]:50051", server_credentials)
```

```
server.start()
print("Secure gRPC server running on port 50051.")
```

2.2 Best Practices for Secure Protocols
1. Use the latest protocol versions (e.g., TLS 1.3).
2. Validate certificates to prevent man-in-the-middle attacks.
3. Enable mutual authentication for two-way verification between agents.

3. Integrating Encryption and Secure Protocols in MAS
   1. Message Encryption:
      - Encrypt all inter-agent messages before sending them.
      - Decrypt messages upon receipt and validate their integrity.
   2. Protocol Selection:
      - Use gRPC or MQTT for secure communication in distributed systems.
      - Choose HTTPS for web-based interactions.
   3. Authentication:
      - Implement token-based authentication (e.g., JWT) for agent verification.
      - Use OAuth2 or similar frameworks for secure access control.
   4. Auditing and Monitoring:
      - Log all communication events and monitor for anomalies.
      - Use intrusion detection systems (IDS) to identify potential breaches.

Summary
Securing communication between agents is vital for protecting data integrity, confidentiality, and authenticity in multi-agent systems. Encryption methods, such as AES and RSA, safeguard messages, while secure protocols like TLS, MQTT, and gRPC

ensure robust communication channels. By adopting encryption, secure protocols, and best practices, developers can create resilient systems capable of withstanding malicious attacks and unauthorized access.

10.3 Designing Resilient Systems to Handle Attacks

Building resilient systems capable of withstanding attacks is a critical requirement in multi-agent systems (MAS). Resilience refers to the ability of a system to continue functioning correctly and efficiently in the presence of malicious attacks, system faults, or failures. To achieve this, developers must employ a combination of design principles, defensive techniques, and recovery mechanisms.

The following techniques provide a comprehensive framework for designing resilient multi-agent systems:

1. Proactive Design for Security and Resilience
Proactive design involves embedding security and resilience measures into the system architecture from the outset.
1.1 Defense-in-Depth
- Description: Implement multiple layers of security to protect against a wide range of attacks.
- Key Components:
    1. Network Security: Use firewalls, VPNs, and secure protocols to protect communication.
    2. Agent Security: Authenticate agents using robust identity verification mechanisms.
    3. Data Security: Encrypt sensitive data at rest and in transit.

Example: In a warehouse MAS, communication between the coordinator and worker agents is secured with TLS encryption, while agent identities are verified using digital certificates.

1.2 Principle of Least Privilege
- Description: Agents are granted only the permissions necessary to perform their tasks, minimizing the impact of compromised agents.
- Implementation:
    - Restrict resource access based on agent roles.
    - Use role-based access control (RBAC) or attribute-based access control (ABAC).

Example: A delivery agent can access route information but is restricted from modifying warehouse inventory data.

1.3 Secure Software Development Lifecycle (SDLC)
- Description: Integrate security practices into all phases of the software development lifecycle.
- Key Practices:
    - Conduct threat modeling during the design phase.
    - Perform static and dynamic code analysis for vulnerabilities.
    - Use automated tools to scan dependencies for known security issues.

2. Real-Time Threat Detection and Mitigation

Monitoring and responding to attacks in real-time are essential for maintaining system integrity.

2.1 Intrusion Detection Systems (IDS)
- Description: Deploy IDS to monitor agent activity and detect suspicious behavior.
- Types:
    1. Signature-Based IDS: Detect known attack patterns.
    2. Anomaly-Based IDS: Identify deviations from normal behavior.

Example: An IDS detects excessive communication requests from a single agent, flagging it as a potential denial-of-service (DoS) attack.

2.2 Behavioral Analysis
- Description: Continuously analyze agent behavior to identify anomalies, such as unauthorized actions or unexpected communication patterns.
- Implementation:
  - Define baseline behavior for each agent.
  - Trigger alerts for deviations.

Example: A robotic arm in a manufacturing MAS suddenly begins moving outside its assigned area, triggering an alert for further investigation.

2.3 Honeypots for Attack Detection
- Description: Deploy decoy agents or systems to attract and monitor attackers, gaining insights into their methods.
- Implementation:
  - Use low-priority resources as honeypots.
  - Log all interactions for analysis.

Example: A decoy agent in a smart grid system simulates a control panel, capturing data about attempted breaches.

3. Fault Tolerance and Recovery Mechanisms
Building fault tolerance ensures the system can recover quickly and continue operating after an attack or failure.

3.1 Redundancy
- Description: Duplicate critical components to ensure availability even if one component fails.
- Types:
  1. Agent Redundancy: Deploy backup agents to take over tasks if a primary agent fails.
  2. Communication Redundancy: Use multiple communication channels for resilience.

Example: In a drone swarm, if one drone fails to complete its mapping task, another drone automatically takes over.

3.2 Failover Mechanisms

- Description: Implement automatic switching to backup components during failures.
- Implementation:
    - Use health checks to detect agent failures.
    - Redirect tasks to functioning agents.

Example: In a package delivery MAS, if a delivery agent is unreachable, its tasks are reassigned to an available agent.

3.3 Checkpointing and State Recovery
- Description: Periodically save the system state to enable recovery after failures or attacks.
- Implementation:
    - Store agent states in a distributed database.
    - Implement recovery protocols to reload states after a crash.

Example: A financial MAS saves transaction states every minute, ensuring no data is lost in case of a system restart.

4. Resilient Communication Mechanisms
Securing agent communication is vital for preventing attacks such as eavesdropping, tampering, and spoofing.

4.1 Encrypted Communication
- Use strong encryption protocols (e.g., TLS, AES) to secure messages.
- Rotate encryption keys periodically to enhance security.

4.2 Authentication and Authorization
- Authenticate agents using certificates, tokens, or biometrics.
- Implement fine-grained access control to prevent unauthorized actions.

4.3 Distributed Consensus Algorithms
- Description: Use consensus algorithms to ensure agents agree on critical decisions, even in the presence of malicious agents.
- Examples:

- Paxos and Raft for distributed decision-making.
- Byzantine Fault Tolerance (BFT) for systems with potential malicious agents.

Example: In a blockchain MAS, BFT ensures that the system remains operational even if some nodes act maliciously.

5. System Testing and Continuous Improvement

5.1 Penetration Testing
- Simulate attacks on the system to identify vulnerabilities.
- Example: Test for SQL injection, cross-site scripting, or man-in-the-middle attacks.

5.2 Chaos Engineering
- Introduce faults into the system intentionally to test its resilience.
- Example: Simulate agent failures or network partitions in a controlled environment.

5.3 Continuous Monitoring and Updates
- Monitor the system for emerging threats and apply patches regularly.
- Example: Deploy a centralized logging system to aggregate and analyze agent activities.

6. Case Study: Designing a Resilient Smart Grid MAS

Scenario:
A smart grid MAS manages energy distribution among multiple regions. The system is vulnerable to DoS attacks, compromised agents, and data tampering.

Resilience Measures:
1. Encryption and Authentication:
   - Encrypt all communications using TLS.
   - Authenticate agents using digital certificates.
2. Redundancy:
   - Deploy backup agents to monitor energy usage.
   - Use redundant communication channels.
3. Intrusion Detection:
   - Implement IDS to detect abnormal energy requests.

4. Consensus Mechanisms:
    - Use Paxos to ensure agreement on energy distribution decisions.
5. State Recovery:
    - Store the state of energy transactions in a distributed database for recovery.

Outcome:
The smart grid remains operational despite malicious attacks, ensuring uninterrupted energy supply.

Summary
Designing resilient systems involves proactive security measures, real-time threat detection, fault tolerance, and robust communication mechanisms. By implementing techniques like defense-in-depth, redundancy, and consensus algorithms, developers can build multi-agent systems capable of handling attacks and ensuring continuous operation. Regular testing and monitoring further enhance the system's ability to adapt to evolving threats.

10.4 Ethical Design of Agent Behaviors

Ethical considerations play a crucial role in the design of multi-agent systems (MAS), particularly as these systems are increasingly deployed in sensitive areas such as healthcare, finance, autonomous vehicles, and law enforcement. Ethical design ensures that agent behaviors align with societal values, respect user rights, and promote accountability and transparency in their decision-making processes.
This section explores the principles of ethical design for agent behaviors, with a focus on transparency and accountability, two pillars of trustworthiness in MAS.

Transparency and accountability are essential for ensuring that MAS operate ethically and can be trusted by users. Below is an in-depth look at how these principles can be embedded in agent behaviors.

1. Transparency in Agent Behaviors
Transparency refers to the ability of agents to clearly communicate their actions, decisions, and underlying reasoning to stakeholders. Transparent systems make it easier for users to understand why agents act in a particular way, fostering trust and reducing the risk of misuse.

1.1 Principles of Transparency
1. Explainable Decision-Making:
    - Agents should provide clear and understandable explanations for their decisions.
    - Example: A financial advisor agent explains why it recommends a particular investment portfolio.
2. Access to System Logic:
    - Users should have access to high-level details of the algorithms governing agent behaviors.
    - Example: An autonomous vehicle agent discloses how it prioritizes safety over speed during navigation.
3. Visibility of Goals and Objectives:
    - Agents should clearly state their goals and objectives to avoid misinterpretation.
    - Example: A medical diagnostic agent explicitly states that its goal is to assist doctors, not replace them.

1.2 Techniques to Achieve Transparency
1. Implementing Explainable AI (XAI):
    - Use techniques like decision trees, rule-based systems, or visualizations to explain agent decisions.
    - Example: An AI assistant uses a flowchart to show how it arrived at a suggested action.

Code Example:
python

```python
class TransparentAgent(Agent):
    def explain_decision(self, input_data, decision):
        explanation = f"Based on input {input_data}, the agent chose '{decision}' because it optimizes for cost and efficiency."
        return explanation

# Example usage
agent = TransparentAgent(name="AdvisorAgent")
print(agent.explain_decision(input_data="Stock Market Data", decision="Buy Stock A"))
```

Output:
vbnet
Based on input Stock Market Data, the agent chose 'Buy Stock A' because it optimizes for cost and efficiency.

2. Audit Logs:
    - Maintain detailed logs of agent actions and decisions for review by users or auditors.
    - Example: A security system logs every access decision made by an agent.

Implementation:
python
```python
class AuditAgent(Agent):
    def log_action(self, action, reason):
        with open("audit_log.txt", "a") as log_file:
            log_file.write(f"Action: {action}, Reason: {reason}\n")

agent = AuditAgent(name="SecurityAgent")
agent.log_action("Denied Access", "Invalid credentials")
```

3. User-Friendly Interfaces:

- Provide interfaces that display agent decisions and their justifications in a comprehensible format.
- Example: A dashboard shows the recommendations of a smart energy management agent.

1.3 Challenges in Transparency
1. Complexity of Algorithms:
   - Advanced models like deep learning can be difficult to interpret.
   - Solution: Use interpretable models or surrogate models to approximate explanations.
2. Balancing Transparency and Security:
   - Revealing too much information can expose the system to attacks.
   - Solution: Share sufficient details for user understanding without compromising security.

2. Accountability in Agent Behaviors

Accountability ensures that agents and their developers can be held responsible for the system's actions. This is critical in building systems that operate ethically and lawfully.

2.1 Principles of Accountability
1. Traceability:
   - Actions and decisions of agents should be traceable to specific inputs and algorithms.
   - Example: A loan approval agent records the data and rules used to make its decision.
2. Responsibility Assignment:
   - Define who is accountable for the actions of agents (e.g., developers, operators, or the organization).
   - Example: In a healthcare system, the hospital is accountable for the decisions of its diagnostic agents.
3. Error Reporting and Correction:
   - Agents should identify errors in their actions and provide mechanisms for correction.

- Example: A chatbot acknowledges when it misunderstands a query and allows the user to rephrase it.

2.2 Techniques to Ensure Accountability
1. Accountability Frameworks:
    - Define policies and procedures for monitoring and evaluating agent actions.
    - Example: Develop an accountability policy that specifies how agents handle user data and decisions.
2. Ethical Guidelines:
    - Incorporate ethical guidelines into system design, such as fairness, non-discrimination, and respect for privacy.
    - Example: A hiring agent is programmed to avoid bias by anonymizing applicant data before evaluation.

Code Example:

```python
class EthicalAgent(Agent):
    def evaluate_candidate(self, candidate_data):
        # Remove personal identifiers to ensure fairness
        anonymized_data = {key: value for key, value in candidate_data.items() if key != "name"}
        return self.decision_logic(anonymized_data)

    def decision_logic(self, data):
        # Example decision logic
        return "Hired" if data["score"] > 80 else "Rejected"
```

3. External Audits:
    - Allow third parties to review agent behaviors and ensure compliance with ethical standards.
    - Example: A financial MAS undergoes annual audits to ensure it follows regulations.
4. Feedback Mechanisms:

- Provide users with the ability to report issues or provide feedback on agent actions.
- Example: A recommendation agent includes a button for users to flag incorrect or inappropriate suggestions.

2.3 Challenges in Accountability
1. Shared Responsibility:
   - In complex systems, it can be difficult to assign accountability to a single entity.
   - Solution: Clearly define roles and responsibilities for all stakeholders.
2. Evolving Legal and Ethical Standards:
   - Rapid technological advancements often outpace existing regulations.
   - Solution: Stay updated with new legal frameworks and industry best practices.

3. Real-World Applications of Ethical Design
1. Healthcare:
   - A diagnostic agent provides a detailed explanation of its diagnosis and allows doctors to override its suggestions.
2. Autonomous Vehicles:
   - A navigation agent logs all decisions, including why it chose a specific route, for post-incident analysis.
3. Finance:
   - A trading agent ensures accountability by recording the data and algorithms used for each trade.

Summary

Ethical design of agent behaviors is essential for building trustworthy and user-centric multi-agent systems. Transparency enables users to understand and trust agent decisions, while accountability ensures that agents operate responsibly and ethically. By implementing explainable AI, audit mechanisms, and ethical guidelines, developers can design systems that align with societal values and legal standards.

10.5 Mitigating Risks of Unintended Outcomes

Unintended outcomes in multi-agent systems (MAS) can result from errors in decision-making, agent miscommunication, or unforeseen interactions between agents. These outcomes can undermine system performance, user trust, and safety. To mitigate such risks, it is essential to adopt a systematic approach that addresses potential errors at every stage of system design, implementation, and operation.

This section explores strategies for minimizing errors in agent decision-making and actions, ensuring that MAS operate reliably and predictably.

1. Sources of Errors in Multi-Agent Systems
Understanding the root causes of errors is the first step in mitigating their risks. Common sources of errors include:

1.1 Flawed Decision-Making Logic
- Description: Errors in algorithms or rules used by agents for decision-making.
- Example: A warehouse robot chooses an inefficient path due to incorrect prioritization logic.
- Impact: Suboptimal performance or system inefficiency.

1.2 Incomplete or Inaccurate Data
- Description: Agents make decisions based on incomplete or incorrect information.
- Example: A diagnostic agent misdiagnoses a condition due to missing patient data.
- Impact: Incorrect decisions with potentially severe consequences.

1.3 Poor Communication Between Agents
- Description: Miscommunication or lack of coordination between agents.
- Example: Two drones in a swarm collide due to conflicting navigation instructions.
- Impact: Task failures, system downtime, or physical damage.

1.4 Environmental Changes
- Description: Dynamic or unpredictable changes in the environment that agents fail to account for.
- Example: An autonomous car fails to detect a newly installed traffic sign.
- Impact: Errors in action or decision-making.

1.5 Emergent Behaviors
- Description: Unintended behaviors arising from the interaction of multiple agents.
- Example: In a pricing system, competing agents create a price war, reducing profitability.
- Impact: Loss of control over system outcomes.

2. Techniques to Avoid Errors in Decision-Making and Actions
To avoid errors, MAS should be designed with robust error-prevention and handling mechanisms.

2.1 Building Robust Decision-Making Logic
2.1.1 Implementing Fail-Safe Mechanisms
- Description: Design agents to revert to safe states when an error is detected.
- Example: A delivery drone lands safely in a pre-designated area if it encounters a navigation error.

Implementation:
python
```
class Agent:
```

```python
def perform_task(self):
    try:
        # Task logic
        print("Task performed successfully.")
    except Exception as e:
        self.fail_safe(e)

def fail_safe(self, error):
    print(f"Error detected: {error}. Reverting to safe state.")
```

2.1.2 Decision Validation
- Description: Validate agent decisions against predefined rules or criteria before execution.
- Example: A trading agent verifies that a transaction aligns with risk limits before proceeding.

Implementation:
python
```
class ValidatorAgent:
    def validate_decision(self, decision):
        if decision["risk"] > 5:
            raise ValueError("Decision exceeds risk limits.")
        return True
```

2.2 Ensuring Data Quality

2.2.1 Data Validation and Preprocessing
- Description: Validate and preprocess input data to ensure accuracy and consistency.
- Example: A medical agent validates patient records to ensure all required fields are populated.

Implementation:
python
```
def validate_data(data):
    required_fields = ["name", "age", "symptoms"]
```

```python
for field in required_fields:
    if field not in data:
        raise ValueError(f"Missing field: {field}")
return True
```

2.2.2 Redundancy in Data Sources
- Description: Use multiple data sources to ensure accuracy and mitigate errors.
- Example: A weather forecasting agent uses data from satellites, ground stations, and radar.

2.3 Improving Agent Communication
2.3.1 Standardized Communication Protocols
- Description: Use standardized protocols to reduce miscommunication.
- Example: Agents in a swarm use a common messaging format for navigation commands.

Implementation:

```python
class Message:
    def __init__(self, sender, receiver, content):
        self.sender = sender
        self.receiver = receiver
        self.content = content
```

2.3.2 Conflict Resolution Mechanisms
- Description: Implement mechanisms to resolve conflicts between agents.
- Example: In a robotic warehouse, a coordinator agent resolves conflicts over the use of shared pathways.

2.4 Adapting to Environmental Changes
2.4.1 Real-Time Sensing and Monitoring

- Description: Use sensors to monitor the environment and update agent actions dynamically.
- Example: An autonomous car uses LiDAR to detect obstacles in real-time.

2.4.2 Dynamic Replanning
- Description: Allow agents to replan tasks in response to environmental changes.
- Example: A delivery agent reroutes when encountering traffic congestion.

Implementation:
python
```python
class DynamicAgent:
    def replan(self, current_plan, new_data):
        print(f"Updating plan based on {new_data}.")
        # Logic for replanning
```

2.5 Managing Emergent Behaviors

2.5.1 Agent Behavior Constraints
- Description: Impose constraints on agent actions to prevent harmful emergent behaviors.
- Example: A pricing agent is restricted from setting prices below a minimum threshold.

2.5.2 Simulations and Testing
- Description: Simulate agent interactions extensively to identify and mitigate emergent behaviors.
- Example: Test swarm behavior in simulated environments before deployment.

3. Monitoring and Continuous Improvement

3.1 Real-Time Monitoring
- Use monitoring tools to track agent actions and system performance in real-time.

- Example: A dashboard shows the status of all agents and alerts operators to anomalies.

3.2 Feedback Loops
- Implement feedback mechanisms to refine agent behaviors based on past outcomes.
- Example: A delivery agent learns from past errors to improve route planning.

3.3 Regular Updates and Patches
- Update agents regularly to fix bugs and improve performance.
- Example: Deploy patches to address vulnerabilities identified during testing.

Case Study: Avoiding Errors in an Autonomous Warehouse
Scenario:
An autonomous warehouse uses MAS to manage inventory, picking, and packing. Unintended outcomes include:
1. Misplaced inventory due to faulty data.
2. Robot collisions from poor communication.

Solutions:
1. Data Validation: Validate inventory data before processing.
2. Conflict Resolution: Use a coordinator agent to assign tasks and resolve conflicts.
3. Redundancy: Employ backup robots to handle failed tasks.
4. Simulation: Test robot interactions in simulated environments before deployment.

Outcome:
Errors are minimized, and the warehouse operates efficiently.

Summary
Mitigating risks of unintended outcomes in MAS involves addressing errors in decision-making, ensuring data quality, improving communication, and adapting to environmental changes. By implementing robust validation mechanisms,

standardized communication protocols, and real-time monitoring, developers can build reliable systems that minimize errors and foster trust.

Chapter 11: Integrating Machine Learning with CrewAI

11.1 Using Machine Learning for Agent Optimization

Machine learning (ML) can significantly enhance the capabilities of agents in multi-agent systems (MAS) like CrewAI. By leveraging ML techniques, agents can learn from past interactions, adapt to dynamic environments, and improve their decision-making and performance over time.

This section explores how machine learning can be applied to optimize agent behaviors, with a focus on training agents to improve performance.

Training agents involves applying machine learning algorithms to enable them to make better decisions, execute tasks efficiently, and adapt to changing conditions. Below is a detailed breakdown of how this process works and the key considerations involved.

1. Why Train Agents with Machine Learning?

Traditional rule-based agents operate on predefined logic, which limits their ability to adapt to new scenarios or improve over time. Machine learning addresses these limitations by enabling agents to:

1. Learn from Experience:
    - Agents analyze historical data to identify patterns and improve future actions.
    - Example: A delivery agent learns the most efficient routes based on traffic patterns.
2. Adapt to Dynamic Environments:
    - ML enables agents to adjust to new conditions without requiring manual reprogramming.

- Example: A warehouse robot dynamically adjusts its path based on real-time obstacles.
3. Enhance Decision-Making:
    - Agents use predictive models to anticipate outcomes and make informed decisions.
    - Example: A trading agent predicts stock price trends to optimize investments.
4. Improve Efficiency:
    - Training helps agents minimize resource consumption while maximizing output.
    - Example: An energy management agent reduces power consumption during peak hours.

2. Machine Learning Approaches for Training Agents

There are several machine learning techniques that can be applied to train agents. These include:

2.1 Supervised Learning

Description:
Agents are trained on labeled datasets containing input-output pairs. The goal is to learn a mapping between inputs and the desired outputs.

Use Case:

- Training a diagnostic agent to classify medical conditions based on patient data.

Example:

python

```python
from sklearn.ensemble import RandomForestClassifier
from sklearn.model_selection import train_test_split
from sklearn.metrics import accuracy_score

# Dataset: Features and labels
X = [[1, 0, 1], [0, 1, 1], [1, 1, 0], [0, 0, 0]]
y = [1, 0, 1, 0]  # Labels

# Train-test split
X_train, X_test, y_train, y_test = train_test_split(X, y, test_size=0.25, random_state=42)

# Train a supervised learning model
model = RandomForestClassifier()
model.fit(X_train, y_train)

# Make predictions
y_pred = model.predict(X_test)
print(f"Accuracy: {accuracy_score(y_test, y_pred)}")
```

2.2 Reinforcement Learning (RL)

Description:
Agents learn by interacting with their environment and receiving feedback in the form of rewards or penalties. The goal is to maximize cumulative rewards.

Use Case:

- Training a delivery agent to optimize routes by rewarding shorter delivery times.

Key Components:

1. State: The agent's current situation.
2. Action: The decisions the agent can make.
3. Reward: Feedback based on the agent's actions.

Example:

python

```python
import gym
import numpy as np
from stable_baselines3 import PPO

# Environment: CartPole (for demonstration)
env = gym.make("CartPole-v1")

# Train the agent using PPO (Proximal Policy Optimization)
model = PPO("MlpPolicy", env, verbose=1)
```

```python
model.learn(total_timesteps=10000)

# Test the trained agent
obs = env.reset()
for _ in range(1000):
    action, _states = model.predict(obs, deterministic=True)
    obs, reward, done, info = env.step(action)
    env.render()
    if done:
        obs = env.reset()
env.close()
```

2.3 Unsupervised Learning

Description:
Agents identify patterns in data without labeled outputs, enabling them to group or cluster similar observations.

Use Case:

- Training a surveillance agent to detect unusual activity by clustering normal behavior patterns.

Example:

python

```python
from sklearn.cluster import KMeans

# Data: Features
X = [[1, 2], [1, 4], [1, 0], [10, 2], [10, 4], [10, 0]]

# Train an unsupervised learning model
kmeans = KMeans(n_clusters=2, random_state=42)
kmeans.fit(X)

# Predict cluster for a new data point
print(f"Cluster assignment: {kmeans.predict([[0, 0]])}")
```

3. Steps to Train Agents

To successfully train agents, follow these steps:

3.1 Define the Objective

- Clearly specify what the agent is expected to achieve.
- Example: Maximize task completion efficiency in a warehouse setting.

3.2 Prepare the Dataset

- Collect and preprocess relevant data.
- Example: For a traffic management agent, gather data on traffic flow, accident reports, and weather conditions.

3.3 Select the Appropriate ML Technique

- Choose supervised, unsupervised, or reinforcement learning based on the problem.
- Example: Use reinforcement learning for adaptive decision-making in dynamic environments.

3.4 Train the Model

- Train the agent using the selected algorithm and dataset.
- Monitor training performance and adjust hyperparameters as needed.

3.5 Test and Evaluate

- Validate the agent's performance on unseen data or in simulated environments.
- Example: Test a delivery agent's routing decisions in a virtual city.

3.6 Deploy and Monitor

- Deploy the trained agent in a real-world environment.
- Continuously monitor its performance and retrain as needed.

4. Challenges and Considerations

Training agents with ML involves several challenges:

1. Data Quality:
   - Inaccurate or biased data can lead to poor model performance.
   - Mitigation: Use data preprocessing and validation techniques.
2. Computational Requirements:
   - Training ML models, especially deep learning, requires significant computational resources.

- Mitigation: Use cloud-based platforms like AWS, Google Cloud, or Azure.
3. Dynamic Environments:
    - Agents may struggle to adapt to rapidly changing conditions.
    - Mitigation: Use online learning or continuous training techniques.
4. Ethical Concerns:
    - Ensure that trained agents do not exhibit biased or harmful behaviors.
    - Mitigation: Audit training datasets and algorithms for fairness and inclusivity.

5. Practical Applications

1. Healthcare:
    - Train agents to predict patient outcomes or recommend treatments.
2. Logistics:
    - Optimize delivery routes and warehouse operations.
3. Finance:
    - Predict stock prices or detect fraudulent transactions.
4. Autonomous Vehicles:
    - Improve navigation and collision avoidance.

Case Study: Training a Warehouse Robot

Scenario:
A warehouse robot learns to navigate efficiently and avoid obstacles while picking items.

Steps:

1. Data Collection:
    - Gather data on warehouse layouts, item locations, and robot movements.

2. Reinforcement Learning:
   - Use RL to reward shorter paths and penalize collisions.
3. Testing:
   - Simulate the robot's movements in a virtual warehouse.
4. Deployment:
   - Deploy the trained model in a real-world warehouse.

Outcome:

The robot reduces task completion time by 30% and avoids collisions.

Summary

Training agents with machine learning empowers them to adapt, improve, and optimize their performance. Techniques like supervised learning, reinforcement learning, and unsupervised learning provide powerful tools for training agents to achieve specific objectives. By following structured steps and addressing challenges proactively, developers can integrate ML into MAS to unlock their full potential.

11.2 Reinforcement Learning in Multi-Agent Systems

Reinforcement Learning (RL) is a branch of machine learning that enables agents to learn optimal behaviors through trial and error. In multi-agent systems (MAS), RL is particularly powerful because it allows agents to adapt dynamically, interact with their environment, and improve their decision-making processes collaboratively or competitively.

This section explains how reinforcement learning is used in MAS to teach agents to adapt through trial and error, providing practical insights, real-world applications, and challenges.

Reinforcement Learning operates on the principle of learning from feedback. Agents perform actions in an environment, receive feedback in the form of rewards or penalties, and update their strategies to maximize cumulative rewards over time.

1. Core Components of Reinforcement Learning

   1. Agent:
      - The decision-making entity that interacts with the environment.
      - Example: A delivery drone learning the fastest route to a destination.
   2. Environment:
      - The external system with which the agent interacts.
      - Example: A simulated city for testing drone navigation.
   3. State (S):
      - The current situation or context of the agent in the environment.
      - Example: A drone's position and battery level.
   4. Action (A):
      - A set of possible decisions or moves the agent can make.
      - Example: Turn left, turn right, or move forward.
   5. Reward (R):
      - Feedback from the environment based on the agent's action.
      - Example: +10 for delivering a package on time, -10 for exceeding the battery limit.
   6. Policy (π):
      - A strategy that defines how the agent selects actions based on its current state.
      - Example: "If the drone is low on battery, prioritize recharging."
   7. Value Function (V):

- A measure of the long-term reward an agent can expect from a given state.
- Example: The drone estimates the benefit of moving closer to a delivery destination.

2. Types of Reinforcement Learning in MAS

1. Single-Agent RL:
   - Focuses on training one agent in a static environment.
   - Example: A robotic arm learning to assemble parts.
2. Multi-Agent RL (MARL):
   - Involves multiple agents interacting with each other and the environment.
   - Example: A fleet of autonomous cars coordinating to avoid traffic congestion.

MARL Approaches:

1. Cooperative Learning:
   - Agents collaborate to maximize a shared reward.
   - Example: Robots in a warehouse optimizing item retrieval together.
2. Competitive Learning:
   - Agents compete against each other to maximize individual rewards.
   - Example: Trading bots competing in a financial market.
3. Mixed Learning:
   - A combination of cooperative and competitive strategies.
   - Example: Traffic management where vehicles cooperate to avoid collisions but compete for faster routes.

3. Teaching Agents Through Trial and Error

The trial-and-error approach in RL involves the following steps:

3.1 Initialization

- Define the environment, agent, states, actions, and reward function.
- Example: A drone in a city simulation with actions like "move forward" or "turn left."

3.2 Exploration vs. Exploitation

- Exploration: The agent tries new actions to discover better strategies.
- Exploitation: The agent uses its learned strategy to maximize rewards.
- Example: A delivery agent explores alternative routes initially but later sticks to the fastest route.

3.3 Feedback Loop

- The agent performs an action, observes the outcome, and receives feedback.
- Example: A drone receives a penalty for crashing into an obstacle and updates its strategy to avoid such paths.

3.4 Policy Optimization

- The agent refines its policy to maximize cumulative rewards.
- Algorithms: Q-Learning, Deep Q-Networks (DQN), Proximal Policy Optimization (PPO).

Code Example: Q-Learning for a Gridworld Environment:

python

```python
import numpy as np

# Define environment
states = 5
actions = 2  # 0: Left, 1: Right
q_table = np.zeros((states, actions))
alpha = 0.1  # Learning rate
gamma = 0.9  # Discount factor
epsilon = 0.2  # Exploration rate

# Define rewards
rewards = [-1, -1, -1, -1, 10]

# Q-Learning process
for episode in range(100):
    state = 0  # Start state
    while state != 4:  # Goal state
        if np.random.rand() < epsilon:  # Explore
            action = np.random.choice(actions)
        else:  # Exploit
```

```
        action = np.argmax(q_table[state])

    # Transition to next state
    next_state = state + 1 if action == 1 else max(0, state - 1)
    reward = rewards[next_state]

    # Update Q-value
    q_table[state, action] = q_table[state, action] + alpha * (
        reward + gamma * np.max(q_table[next_state]) - q_table[state, action]
    )

    state = next_state  # Move to next state

print("Trained Q-Table:")
print(q_table)
```

4. Applications of RL in Multi-Agent Systems

1. Traffic Management:
   - Agents (cars) learn to optimize their routes while avoiding congestion.

2. Warehouse Automation:
   - Robots collaborate to pick and pack items efficiently.
3. Energy Management:
   - Smart grid agents balance energy supply and demand dynamically.
4. Game AI:
   - Agents learn to cooperate or compete in games like chess or StarCraft.

5. Challenges and Considerations

1. Scalability:
   - Training multiple agents simultaneously increases computational complexity.
   - Solution: Use distributed training frameworks like Ray RLlib.
2. Non-Stationary Environments:
   - Dynamic environments can make learned strategies obsolete.
   - Solution: Implement online learning or transfer learning.
3. Credit Assignment Problem:
   - Determining which actions led to a reward in multi-agent settings is challenging.
   - Solution: Use techniques like Shapley values for fair credit assignment.
4. Ethical Concerns:
   - RL agents might exploit loopholes in the reward function.
   - Solution: Design reward functions carefully to align with desired outcomes.

6. Case Study: Reinforcement Learning in Drone Swarms

Scenario:

A drone swarm is tasked with mapping a disaster area while avoiding obstacles and covering maximum ground.

Solution:

1. Environment Setup:
   - A simulated gridworld where drones can move in four directions.
2. Reward Function:
   - +10 for mapping a new area, -5 for collisions, +5 for avoiding obstacles.
3. Algorithm:
   - Train drones using Proximal Policy Optimization (PPO).

Outcome:

- The drones learn to collaborate, avoid redundant mapping, and complete the task efficiently.

Summary

Reinforcement learning provides a powerful framework for teaching agents to adapt through trial and error. By interacting with their environment and refining their policies, agents can improve their performance over time. In multi-agent systems, RL enables both cooperation and competition, unlocking advanced capabilities in fields like traffic management, logistics, and robotics. While challenges such as scalability and credit assignment exist, careful design and robust algorithms ensure successful applications.

11.3 Combining CrewAI with Pretrained Models

Integrating CrewAI with pretrained machine learning models can significantly enhance the functionality of multi-agent systems

(MAS). Pretrained models provide specialized capabilities like natural language processing (NLP), computer vision, and decision-making, enabling agents to perform complex tasks without requiring extensive training from scratch. By leveraging these models, CrewAI agents can quickly gain advanced skills and adapt to diverse applications such as autonomous systems, smart assistants, and real-time analytics.

Integrating pretrained models into CrewAI involves connecting agents with state-of-the-art machine learning frameworks, APIs, or libraries that deliver specific capabilities. Below is a detailed exploration of how pretrained models are integrated, their applications, and practical implementation techniques.

1. Why Use Pretrained Models with CrewAI?

Pretrained models provide several benefits that make them ideal for integration with CrewAI:

1. Time Efficiency:
    - Reduce the time required to train models from scratch.
    - Example: Use a pretrained NLP model for text classification instead of developing a model from the ground up.
2. Cost Savings:
    - Save computational resources by reusing models trained on large datasets.
    - Example: Leverage a vision model like ResNet for object detection without needing massive GPU resources.
3. High Accuracy:
    - Benefit from the expertise and resources of top research teams who created these models.

- Example: Utilize OpenAI's GPT for text generation tasks.
4. Domain-Specific Expertise:
   - Pretrained models are often specialized for tasks like sentiment analysis, image recognition, or audio processing.
   - Example: Use BERT for sentiment analysis in customer service chatbots.

2. Types of Pretrained Models Commonly Integrated

1. Natural Language Processing (NLP) Models:
   - Examples: GPT, BERT, T5, RoBERTa.
   - Applications:
     - Language translation, text summarization, sentiment analysis, and question answering.
   - Integration Use Case:
     - A customer service agent uses GPT to generate human-like responses to user queries.
2. Computer Vision Models:
   - Examples: ResNet, YOLO, MobileNet, EfficientNet.
   - Applications:
     - Object detection, image classification, facial recognition, and scene segmentation.
   - Integration Use Case:
     - A delivery robot uses YOLO to detect and avoid obstacles in real time.
3. Audio Processing Models:
   - Examples: DeepSpeech, Wav2Vec, Whisper.
   - Applications:
     - Speech-to-text, voice recognition, and sound classification.
   - Integration Use Case:

- A voice assistant uses DeepSpeech for real-time transcription of spoken commands.
4. Reinforcement Learning (RL) Models:
   - Examples: AlphaZero, DQN, PPO.
   - Applications:
     - Decision-making in games, autonomous vehicles, and robotics.
   - Integration Use Case:
     - An autonomous car uses a pretrained RL policy for lane navigation.

3. How to Integrate Pretrained Models with CrewAI

Integrating pretrained models with CrewAI involves designing agents that can communicate with or embed these models to perform specific tasks. Below is a detailed step-by-step guide.

Step 1: Define the Agent's Role

- Identify the agent's primary function and the capabilities it needs from the pretrained model.
- Example: A warehouse robot requires object detection for identifying and picking items.

Step 2: Select the Pretrained Model

- Choose a model suited to the agent's task.
- Example: Use YOLO for real-time object detection or GPT for text generation.

Step 3: Integrate the Model into the Agent

1. **API Integration:**
   - Use APIs provided by platforms like OpenAI, Hugging Face, or Google Cloud to access pretrained models.
   - Example: Call GPT's API for generating responses in a chatbot agent.

Code Example: Integrating GPT with CrewAI:

python

```python
import openai

class ChatAgent:
    def __init__(self, name):
        self.name = name

    def generate_response(self, user_input):
        openai.api_key = "your_api_key"
        response = openai.Completion.create(
            engine="text-davinci-003",
            prompt=user_input,
            max_tokens=100
        )
        return response.choices[0].text.strip()
```

```python
# Example usage
agent = ChatAgent(name="CustomerServiceAgent")
print(agent.generate_response("What is the status of my order?"))
```

2. Direct Integration:
    - Import pretrained models from machine learning libraries like TensorFlow, PyTorch, or Hugging Face.
    - Example: Use a pretrained YOLO model for object detection.

Code Example: Integrating YOLO for Object Detection:

python

```python
import cv2
import torch

# Load YOLO model
model = torch.hub.load('ultralytics/yolov5', 'yolov5s')

class VisionAgent:
    def detect_objects(self, image_path):
        results = model(image_path)
        results.show()  # Display detected objects
        return results.pandas().xyxy
```

```python
# Example usage
agent = VisionAgent()
results = agent.detect_objects("warehouse_image.jpg")
print(results)
```

3. Hybrid Approaches:
    - Combine pretrained models with CrewAI-specific logic.
    - Example: Use an NLP model for intent detection and CrewAI logic for task execution.

Step 4: Test and Evaluate

- Validate the model's performance in the agent's environment.
- Example: Test a vision agent's object detection accuracy in different lighting conditions.

Step 5: Deploy and Monitor

- Deploy the integrated agent and continuously monitor its performance for improvements.
- Example: Monitor a customer service agent's response accuracy using user feedback.

4. Applications of CrewAI with Pretrained Models

1. **Customer Service Automation:**
   - Use GPT for natural language understanding and response generation.
2. **Autonomous Navigation:**
   - Integrate computer vision models like YOLO for real-time obstacle detection.
3. **Healthcare Diagnostics:**
   - Combine computer vision (for imaging) with NLP (for patient notes) to assist in diagnostics.
4. **Retail:**
   - Use vision models for inventory tracking and NLP models for personalized customer recommendations.
5. **Security Systems:**
   - Deploy vision models for anomaly detection and NLP models for automated reporting.

5. Challenges and Considerations

1. **Model Compatibility:**
   - Pretrained models may require additional adaptation to fit into CrewAI's architecture.
2. **Resource Constraints:**
   - Large models like GPT-4 require significant computational resources.
   - Solution: Use optimized versions or cloud-based APIs.
3. **Data Privacy:**
   - Ensure that data shared with APIs or models complies with privacy regulations.
   - Solution: Use on-premise models or encrypted communication.
4. **Model Updates:**
   - Pretrained models evolve, requiring periodic updates in the integration pipeline.

5. Performance Trade-offs:
   - Balancing accuracy with latency is critical, especially for real-time applications.

6. Case Study: Integrating CrewAI with Computer Vision

Scenario:
A warehouse robot uses a pretrained YOLO model for object detection to identify items and navigate efficiently.

Steps:

1. Load the YOLO model using PyTorch.
2. Design the robot's logic to process YOLO's outputs and execute navigation.
3. Test the system in simulated and real-world environments.

Outcome:
The robot reduces item retrieval time by 40% and avoids collisions with obstacles.

Summary

Integrating CrewAI with pretrained models like GPT, YOLO, and BERT enhances the capabilities of multi-agent systems, enabling them to tackle complex tasks in NLP, computer vision, and more. By leveraging APIs, libraries, and hybrid approaches, developers can rapidly deploy agents with advanced functionalities. While challenges like compatibility and resource constraints exist, careful planning and optimization ensure seamless integration and improved system performance.

11.4 Project: Reinforcement Learning in Multi-Agent Environments

This project demonstrates an end-to-end implementation of Reinforcement Learning (RL) in a multi-agent environment. By combining the principles of reinforcement learning and multi-agent systems (MAS), you will learn to train multiple agents to collaborate or compete within a simulated environment. This practical guide provides step-by-step instructions to design, implement, and evaluate a multi-agent RL system.

Overview of the Project

Goal:

Train multiple agents to perform tasks collaboratively in a gridworld environment. Agents must learn to optimize their actions to achieve a common objective while avoiding collisions or resource conflicts.

Scenario:

A gridworld is represented as a 2D grid where agents move to collect resources. Each agent receives rewards for collecting resources and penalties for collisions or stepping into forbidden areas.

Key Components:

1. Environment: A gridworld with multiple agents, resources, and obstacles.
2. Agents: Autonomous entities that interact with the environment.
3. Reward Function: Defines the feedback agents receive for their actions.

4. Policy: The strategy agents use to decide their actions.

Step 1: Setting Up the Environment

1. Install Required Libraries:
   - Use Python along with libraries like Gym (for RL environments) and Stable-Baselines3 (for RL algorithms).

bash

```
pip install gym stable-baselines3 numpy matplotlib
```

2. Design the Gridworld Environment:
   - Define a grid of size $N \times N$ with cells representing empty spaces, obstacles, resources, or agents.
   - Create a custom Gym environment for the simulation.

Code Example: Custom Gridworld Environment:
python

```python
import gym
from gym import spaces
import numpy as np

class GridworldEnv(gym.Env):
    def __init__(self, grid_size=5, n_agents=2):
        super().__init__()
```

```python
        self.grid_size = grid_size
        self.n_agents = n_agents
        self.state = None
        self.action_space = spaces.Discrete(4)  # 0: Up, 1: Down, 2: Left, 3: Right
        self.observation_space = spaces.Box(
            low=0, high=1, shape=(grid_size, grid_size, n_agents), dtype=np.float32
        )
        self.reset()

    def reset(self):
        self.state = np.zeros((self.grid_size, self.grid_size, self.n_agents))
        # Place agents randomly
        for agent in range(self.n_agents):
            x, y = np.random.randint(0, self.grid_size, size=2)
            self.state[x, y, agent] = 1
        return self.state

    def step(self, actions):
        rewards = []
```

```python
        for agent, action in enumerate(actions):
            x, y = np.where(self.state[:, :, agent] == 1)
            x, y = x[0], y[0]
            self.state[x, y, agent] = 0
            if action == 0: x = max(x - 1, 0)  # Up
            if action == 1: x = min(x + 1, self.grid_size - 1)  # Down
            if action == 2: y = max(y - 1, 0)  # Left
            if action == 3: y = min(y + 1, self.grid_size - 1)  # Right
            self.state[x, y, agent] = 1
            rewards.append(1 if np.random.random() > 0.9 else -1)  # Example reward logic
        return self.state, rewards, False, {}


env = GridworldEnv()
print(env.reset())
```

Step 2: Defining the Multi-Agent System

Agents will operate within the environment and learn using reinforcement learning. Each agent's goal is to maximize its cumulative reward by collecting resources and avoiding penalties.

1. Action Space:

- Define the possible actions (e.g., move up, down, left, right).
2. Observation Space:
   - Represent the environment from each agent's perspective, including the positions of resources and other agents.
3. Rewards:
   - Reward agents for achieving goals (e.g., collecting resources) and penalize them for collisions.

Step 3: Choosing an RL Algorithm

- Proximal Policy Optimization (PPO) is a commonly used algorithm for multi-agent RL due to its stability and scalability.

Install Stable-Baselines3 and train agents with PPO:

bash

```bash
pip install stable-baselines3[extra]
```

Code Example: PPO Training:

python

```python
from stable_baselines3 import PPO
from stable_baselines3.common.env_util import make_vec_env


# Create a vectorized environment
env = make_vec_env(lambda: GridworldEnv(grid_size=5, n_agents=2), n_envs=1)
```

```python
# Define the PPO model
model = PPO("MlpPolicy", env, verbose=1)

# Train the model
model.learn(total_timesteps=10000)

# Save the model
model.save("multi_agent_ppo")
```

Step 4: Simulating Multi-Agent Behavior

Load the Trained Model:
python

```python
model = PPO.load("multi_agent_ppo")
```

1. Run Simulations:
   - Visualize agents interacting in the environment.

Code Example: Simulation:

python

```python
state = env.reset()

done = False
```

```python
while not done:
    actions, _ = model.predict(state)
    state, rewards, done, _ = env.step(actions)
    print("Rewards:", rewards)
```

Step 5: Visualizing Results

Use matplotlib to create a visualization of the agents' movements and interactions within the gridworld.

Code Example: Visualization:

python

```python
import matplotlib.pyplot as plt

def render_grid(state):
    grid = np.sum(state, axis=2)
    plt.imshow(grid, cmap='cool', interpolation='nearest')
    plt.show()

# Render the environment after training
state = env.reset()
for _ in range(10):
    actions, _ = model.predict(state)
```

```
state, _, _, _ = env.step(actions)

render_grid(state)
```

Step 6: Evaluating Performance

1. Metrics:
    - Cumulative rewards: Measure the total rewards collected by agents.
    - Task completion rate: Evaluate how often agents complete their objectives.
    - Collision rate: Track the number of collisions between agents.
2. Analysis:
    - Compare performance across different training durations and algorithms.
    - Test the system under varying environmental conditions (e.g., increasing obstacles or agents).

Step 7: Enhancing the System

1. Advanced Reward Functions:
    - Design rewards to encourage collaboration (e.g., shared rewards for group success).
2. Communication Between Agents:
    - Allow agents to share information to improve coordination.
3. Dynamic Environments:
    - Introduce real-time changes to the environment, such as moving obstacles.

Applications

1. Logistics:
    - Optimize warehouse robots for item retrieval and delivery.
2. Traffic Management:
    - Coordinate autonomous vehicles to reduce congestion.
3. Disaster Response:
    - Train drones to collaborate in search-and-rescue missions.

Summary

This end-to-end project illustrates how reinforcement learning can be applied to train agents in multi-agent environments. By following the steps outlined above—defining the environment, training with PPO, simulating behavior, and evaluating performance—you can create a robust multi-agent system capable of solving complex tasks collaboratively or competitively. With further enhancements, these systems can be deployed in real-world scenarios like logistics, traffic management, and robotics.

Chapter 12: Real-World Applications and Case Studies

12.1 Automation and Robotics

Automation and robotics are some of the most prominent domains where multi-agent systems like CrewAI are transforming workflows and operations. By enabling autonomous agents to collaborate, communicate, and make decisions, CrewAI enhances the efficiency, adaptability, and intelligence of both industrial and household robotic systems.

This section provides an in-depth exploration of real-world applications of CrewAI in automation and robotics, detailing its role in industrial and household settings.

1. Industrial Robotics

Industrial environments demand high efficiency, precision, and scalability, making them ideal for CrewAI-powered robotic systems. These systems excel in managing complex tasks that require multiple agents working together.

1.1 Collaborative Robots (Cobots) in Manufacturing

Application:
Cobots, or collaborative robots, work alongside human operators to perform tasks such as assembly, quality inspection, and packaging.

Role of CrewAI:

- Enables cobots to coordinate with each other and with humans.
- Ensures efficient task allocation based on real-time data.

Example:

1. In an automotive assembly line:
    - One cobot handles welding, while another performs part inspection.
    - CrewAI ensures seamless task handovers and adjusts schedules dynamically based on production rates.

Benefits:

- Reduces human workload and errors.
- Increases production speed and precision.

1.2 Warehouse Automation

Application:
CrewAI manages fleets of robots in warehouses to optimize inventory management, picking, and packing.

Role of CrewAI:

- Coordinates robotic agents for efficient item retrieval and delivery.
- Prevents collisions and resource conflicts through intelligent navigation and communication.

Example:

1. In an e-commerce warehouse:
    - Robots equipped with CrewAI retrieve items from shelves and deliver them to packing stations.
    - CrewAI dynamically reroutes robots to avoid congestion and prioritizes high-demand orders.

Benefits:

- Improves order fulfillment speed.

- Reduces operational costs by minimizing human intervention.

1.3 Material Handling in Construction

Application:
Autonomous robots transport heavy materials across construction sites.

Role of CrewAI:

- Assigns routes and tasks to each robot based on load capacity and site layout.
- Coordinates actions to avoid delays and ensure worker safety.

Example:

1. In a building construction project:
    - Robots move concrete blocks to specific areas.
    - CrewAI optimizes robot schedules and monitors real-time progress.

Benefits:

- Enhances construction efficiency.
- Reduces accidents by minimizing human involvement in hazardous tasks.

2. Household Robotics

Household robotics represents a growing field where CrewAI-powered agents improve convenience and automation for everyday users. These systems focus on simplifying tasks, enhancing safety, and providing personalized services.

2.1 Smart Cleaning Robots

Application:
Autonomous vacuum cleaners and mops collaborate to clean households efficiently.

Role of CrewAI:

- Coordinates multiple cleaning agents to divide and conquer cleaning tasks.
- Monitors progress and adjusts operations based on room layouts and dirt levels.

Example:

1. In a large household:
   - One robot cleans the living room while another handles the kitchen.
   - CrewAI ensures they do not overlap and communicates cleaning status to the homeowner via a smartphone app.

Benefits:

- Saves time and energy for users.
- Provides more thorough cleaning coverage.

2.2 Home Security Systems

Application:
Robots equipped with cameras and sensors patrol homes to enhance security.

Role of CrewAI:

- Manages communication between security robots and other smart devices like cameras and alarms.
- Analyzes data to detect unusual activities and respond appropriately.

Example:

1. In a residential property:
   - One robot monitors the front yard, while another checks the backyard.
   - CrewAI raises an alert if a suspicious movement is detected and directs robots to focus on that area.

Benefits:

- Increases safety through constant monitoring.
- Reduces the need for manual security checks.

2.3 Personal Assistant Robots

Application:
Robots provide assistance in daily activities, such as carrying items, setting reminders, or entertaining users.

Role of CrewAI:

- Integrates with smart home ecosystems to deliver personalized services.
- Enables robots to share tasks and prioritize user requests effectively.

Example:

1. In a smart home:
   - One robot assists a user by fetching groceries from the fridge.

- Another robot sets up a video call based on the user's schedule.
- CrewAI ensures both robots operate without interfering with each other.

Benefits:

- Enhances user experience with seamless automation.
- Provides companionship and support for elderly or disabled individuals.

3. Advanced Applications of CrewAI in Robotics

  1. Search and Rescue Operations:
     - Drones equipped with CrewAI coordinate to locate survivors in disaster-struck areas.
     - Example: In earthquake zones, drones map affected regions and relay real-time data to rescue teams.
  2. Healthcare Robots:
     - Robots assist in delivering medicines and monitoring patient health in hospitals.
     - Example: CrewAI ensures robots prioritize critical patients during emergencies.
  3. Agricultural Robots:
     - Autonomous machines plant, irrigate, and harvest crops.
     - Example: CrewAI optimizes resource usage by coordinating irrigation schedules among robotic tractors.
  4. Retail Automation:
     - Robots provide personalized shopping assistance and manage inventory in stores.
     - Example: CrewAI helps multiple robots navigate crowded aisles while maintaining inventory records.

4. Benefits of CrewAI in Robotics

    1. Efficiency:
        o Optimizes resource utilization and task allocation.
    2. Scalability:
        o Easily scales to manage large fleets of robots in diverse environments.
    3. Adaptability:
        o Responds dynamically to changing conditions, such as traffic in warehouses or obstacles in homes.
    4. Cost Savings:
        o Reduces operational costs by minimizing downtime and manual intervention.
    5. Safety:
        o Mitigates risks by automating hazardous tasks and enhancing human-robot collaboration.

5. Challenges and Solutions

    1. Challenge: Integration with Legacy Systems.
        o Solution: Develop modular architectures to integrate CrewAI seamlessly with existing infrastructures.
    2. Challenge: Real-Time Decision-Making.
        o Solution: Use high-performance computing and edge AI for faster processing.
    3. Challenge: Ethical and Privacy Concerns.
        o Solution: Implement robust encryption and access controls to protect user data.
    4. Challenge: Hardware Limitations.
        o Solution: Optimize algorithms to operate efficiently on resource-constrained devices.

Summary

CrewAI is revolutionizing both industrial and household robotics by enabling intelligent, autonomous, and collaborative behaviors. From improving manufacturing efficiency with cobots to enhancing daily life with smart assistants, the integration of CrewAI with robotics is unlocking unprecedented possibilities. While challenges exist, ongoing advancements in technology and design ensure that CrewAI remains a cornerstone of innovation in automation and robotics.

12.2 Distributed Problem Solving

Distributed problem solving (DPS) is a critical aspect of multi-agent systems (MAS) like CrewAI, where multiple agents collaborate to address complex optimization problems that exceed the capabilities of a single agent or centralized approach. By dividing tasks, sharing information, and leveraging the collective intelligence of agents, DPS enables efficient, scalable, and robust solutions across a range of domains.

Optimization problems often involve finding the best solution among many possibilities, considering constraints and objectives. Distributed problem solving employs a multi-agent approach to tackle these challenges, particularly when problems are computationally intensive, geographically dispersed, or dynamic.

1. The Core Principles of Distributed Problem Solving

DPS involves the following core principles:

1. Task Decomposition:
    - Break down a complex problem into smaller, manageable subproblems.

- Example: In logistics, divide delivery tasks by regions.
2. Agent Collaboration:
    - Enable agents to communicate and coordinate their actions to solve subproblems effectively.
    - Example: Robots in a warehouse collaborate to optimize item retrieval.
3. Information Sharing:
    - Agents share relevant data to ensure alignment and consistency.
    - Example: Traffic management agents share road congestion data.
4. Solution Integration:
    - Combine individual solutions from agents into a cohesive global solution.
    - Example: In a manufacturing system, integrate sub-solutions for assembly, quality control, and packaging.

2. Applications of Distributed Problem Solving

1. Supply Chain Optimization:
    - Agents representing factories, warehouses, and distribution centers collaborate to minimize costs and delivery times.
2. Traffic and Transportation Management:
    - Traffic lights, autonomous vehicles, and navigation systems work together to reduce congestion and improve flow.
3. Energy Management:
    - Smart grid agents optimize energy distribution, balancing supply and demand dynamically.
4. Healthcare Resource Allocation:

- Agents coordinate the allocation of medical staff, equipment, and beds in hospitals to improve patient outcomes.
5. Telecommunications:
    - Agents optimize network routing and bandwidth allocation to ensure reliable communication.

3. Distributed Problem Solving Techniques

1. Distributed Constraint Satisfaction (DCSP):
    - Solve problems where agents must satisfy a set of constraints collaboratively.
    - Example: Scheduling tasks in a factory while avoiding conflicts.
2. Swarm Intelligence:
    - Mimic natural systems, such as ant colonies, to find optimal solutions through decentralized collaboration.
    - Example: Drones collaborate to map a disaster area efficiently.
3. Market-Based Algorithms:
    - Use auction or bidding mechanisms to allocate resources among agents.
    - Example: Allocate computational resources in a cloud environment based on agent bids.
4. Consensus Algorithms:
    - Enable agents to reach agreement on shared decisions.
    - Example: Distributed databases use consensus to ensure data consistency.

4. Step-by-Step Guide to Solving Optimization Problems with CrewAI

Below is a detailed implementation guide for solving a complex distributed optimization problem using CrewAI in a smart grid scenario.

Step 1: Define the Problem

Scenario: Optimize energy distribution in a smart grid.

1. Objective:
    - Minimize energy wastage and ensure equitable distribution.
2. Constraints:
    - Limitations on grid capacity.
    - Dynamic demand fluctuations.

Step 2: Decompose the Problem

1. Divide the grid into regions:
    - Assign an agent to each region.
2. Define subproblems for each agent:
    - Optimize energy distribution within its region.

Step 3: Enable Collaboration

1. Design Communication Protocols:
    - Agents share demand, supply, and load data.

Code Example:

python

```python
class EnergyAgent:
```

```python
    def __init__(self, region):
        self.region = region
        self.demand = 0
        self.supply = 0

    def share_data(self):
        return {"region": self.region, "demand": self.demand, "supply": self.supply}

    def receive_data(self, data):
        print(f"Received data from {data['region']}: Demand={data['demand']}, Supply={data['supply']}")
```

Step 4: Solve Subproblems

1. Implement Optimization Algorithms:
   - Use linear programming or heuristic methods to optimize regional distribution.

Code Example:

python

```python
from scipy.optimize import linprog

# Example optimization: Minimize energy cost
```

```python
c = [1, 2, 3]  # Costs
A = [[1, 1, 1], [2, 1, 0]]  # Constraints
b = [100, 150]  # Limits

result = linprog(c, A_eq=A, b_eq=b, bounds=(0, None))
print(f"Optimal solution: {result.x}")
```

Step 5: Integrate Solutions

1. Combine Regional Outputs:
    - Aggregate data from all agents to form a global solution.

Code Example:

python

```python
class GridCoordinator:
    def integrate_solutions(self, agent_solutions):
        total_demand = sum(solution['demand'] for solution in agent_solutions)
        total_supply = sum(solution['supply'] for solution in agent_solutions)
        print(f"Global Demand: {total_demand}, Global Supply: {total_supply}")
```

Step 6: Monitor and Adjust

1. Continuous Monitoring:
      - Track performance metrics like energy efficiency and grid stability.
   2. Dynamic Reoptimization:
      - Reallocate resources in response to changing demands or failures.

5. Advantages of Distributed Problem Solving with CrewAI

   1. Scalability:
      - Handles large, complex problems by dividing tasks among agents.
   2. Resilience:
      - Continues to operate even if some agents fail.
   3. Flexibility:
      - Adapts to dynamic environments and changing conditions.
   4. Efficiency:
      - Reduces computational overhead through parallel processing.
   5. Decentralization:
      - Eliminates bottlenecks associated with centralized systems.

6. Challenges and Solutions

   1. Challenge: Communication Overhead.
      - Solution: Use efficient messaging protocols and data compression techniques.
   2. Challenge: Coordination Complexity.
      - Solution: Implement robust coordination algorithms, such as leader election.
   3. Challenge: Data Privacy.

- Solution: Use federated learning or encrypted data sharing.
4. Challenge: Conflict Resolution.
    - Solution: Develop consensus mechanisms to align agent goals.

7. Case Study: Traffic Flow Optimization

Scenario:

- Agents represent intersections in a city, managing traffic lights to reduce congestion.

Steps:

1. Define Subproblems:
    - Each agent optimizes its intersection.
2. Enable Collaboration:
    - Agents share traffic data with neighboring intersections.
3. Solve Subproblems:
    - Use reinforcement learning to adjust light timings dynamically.
4. Integrate Solutions:
    - Ensure smooth traffic flow across the city.

Outcome:

- Reduced congestion and travel times by 30%.

Summary

Distributed problem solving leverages the power of CrewAI to address complex optimization problems in various domains, from energy management to traffic control. By decomposing tasks, enabling collaboration, and integrating solutions, DPS delivers efficient, scalable, and adaptive systems. While challenges exist, robust communication protocols, coordination algorithms, and monitoring systems ensure success in real-world applications.

12.3 AI-Powered Marketplaces and Trading Systems

The rise of artificial intelligence (AI) has significantly transformed marketplaces and trading systems in domains such as e-commerce and financial trading. AI-powered multi-agent systems like CrewAI play a pivotal role in these transformations by enabling intelligent decision-making, real-time adaptability, and enhanced user experiences. This section explores how AI and CrewAI are applied in e-commerce and financial trading, detailing use cases, benefits, and challenges.

AI-powered multi-agent systems facilitate the automation and optimization of complex tasks in e-commerce and financial trading. They handle massive amounts of data, enable seamless interactions, and adapt dynamically to changes in the market environment.

1. Applications in E-Commerce

AI-powered marketplaces are built on sophisticated systems where intelligent agents interact to enhance user experiences, optimize inventory, and drive sales. CrewAI agents play critical roles in personalizing recommendations, managing logistics, and ensuring efficient platform operations.

1.1 Personalized Recommendations

Role of CrewAI:

- Leverages AI algorithms to analyze user behavior, preferences, and past purchases.
- Provides dynamic, real-time product recommendations tailored to individual customers.

Example:

- A marketplace like Amazon uses recommendation agents to suggest complementary products (e.g., "customers who bought this also bought...").

Implementation:

- Use collaborative filtering, content-based filtering, or hybrid models to generate recommendations.

Code Example: Content-Based Recommendation:

python

```
from sklearn.metrics.pairwise import cosine_similarity
import pandas as pd

# Sample product data
products = pd.DataFrame({
    'Product': ['Laptop', 'Phone', 'Tablet'],
    'Features': ['electronics, portable', 'electronics, handheld', 'electronics, touchscreen']
})
```

```python
# Vectorize features
from sklearn.feature_extraction.text import TfidfVectorizer
vectorizer = TfidfVectorizer()
features_matrix = vectorizer.fit_transform(products['Features'])

# Compute similarity
similarity = cosine_similarity(features_matrix)
print("Similarity Matrix:\n", similarity)
```

1.2 Dynamic Pricing

Role of CrewAI:

- Implements dynamic pricing algorithms to adjust product prices based on demand, competition, and inventory levels.
- Agents collaborate to identify optimal pricing strategies.

Example:

- An online retail platform adjusts the prices of seasonal products like winter jackets based on weather forecasts and competitor pricing.

Benefits:

- Maximizes revenue and maintains competitive advantage.

1.3 Inventory Management

Role of CrewAI:

- Coordinates between warehouse agents, logistics agents, and sales agents to maintain optimal stock levels.
- Predicts demand using AI models and ensures timely restocking.

Example:

- A grocery delivery service uses CrewAI to manage perishable inventory, ensuring items are replenished based on consumption patterns.

1.4 Fraud Detection

Role of CrewAI:

- Identifies suspicious activities such as fake reviews, payment fraud, or counterfeit products.
- Collaborates with security agents to flag and mitigate risks.

Example:

- A payment system detects unusual transactions (e.g., multiple high-value orders in a short time) and alerts administrators.

Code Example: Fraud Detection Using Anomaly Detection:

python

```
from sklearn.ensemble import IsolationForest
```

```python
# Sample transaction data

data = [[100], [110], [120], [10_000], [130]]

model = IsolationForest(contamination=0.1)

predictions = model.fit_predict(data)

print("Anomalies Detected:", [d for d, p in zip(data, predictions) if p == -1])
```

2. Applications in Financial Trading

AI has revolutionized financial trading by enabling algorithms to process market data at high speeds, predict trends, and execute trades with precision. CrewAI amplifies these capabilities by introducing multi-agent collaboration for enhanced performance.

2.1 Algorithmic Trading

Role of CrewAI:

- Executes high-frequency trades using pre-defined algorithms.
- Analyzes market data to identify profitable trading opportunities in real time.

Example:

- A hedge fund uses trading agents to monitor stock prices, detect arbitrage opportunities, and execute trades within milliseconds.

Implementation:

- Use machine learning models like Long Short-Term Memory (LSTM) for price prediction and integrate with APIs for automated trading.

Code Example: LSTM for Price Prediction:

python

```
import numpy as np
import tensorflow as tf
from tensorflow.keras.models import Sequential
from tensorflow.keras.layers import LSTM, Dense

# Sample price data
data = np.array([[1], [2], [3], [4], [5], [6]])
X = data[:-1].reshape(1, 5, 1)
y = data[1:]

# Build LSTM model
model = Sequential([
    LSTM(10, activation='relu', input_shape=(5, 1)),
    Dense(1)
])
```

```python
model.compile(optimizer='adam', loss='mse')
model.fit(X, y, epochs=10)

# Predict next price
prediction = model.predict(X)
print("Next Price Prediction:", prediction)
```

2.2 Portfolio Optimization

Role of CrewAI:

- Allocates investments across various assets to maximize returns and minimize risks.
- Agents simulate different scenarios and suggest optimal portfolio configurations.

Example:

- A robo-advisor recommends a diversified portfolio based on the client's risk tolerance and market conditions.

Benefits:

- Reduces human bias and improves investment performance.

2.3 Market Sentiment Analysis

Role of CrewAI:

- Uses NLP models to analyze news, social media, and reports to gauge market sentiment.
- Provides actionable insights to trading agents.

Example:

- A trading system detects positive sentiment around a stock (e.g., Tesla) and recommends a buy order.

2.4 Risk Management

Role of CrewAI:

- Continuously monitors market fluctuations and adjusts trading strategies to mitigate risks.
- Implements stop-loss mechanisms to prevent excessive losses.

Example:

- A trading agent detects high volatility in cryptocurrency markets and shifts investments to safer assets.

3. Benefits of AI-Powered Marketplaces and Trading Systems

1. Efficiency:
    - Automates repetitive tasks, reducing human workload and errors.
2. Personalization:
    - Tailors services to individual users, enhancing satisfaction.
3. Scalability:
    - Handles massive datasets and complex transactions effortlessly.

4. Real-Time Decision Making:
    - Processes information and executes actions at lightning speeds.
5. Cost Reduction:
    - Minimizes operational costs through automation.

4. Challenges and Mitigation Strategies

1. Challenge: Data Privacy Concerns.
    - Solution: Use encryption and secure protocols for data handling.
2. Challenge: Algorithmic Bias.
    - Solution: Regularly audit models and datasets to ensure fairness.
3. Challenge: System Downtime.
    - Solution: Implement redundant systems and failover mechanisms.
4. Challenge: Regulatory Compliance.
    - Solution: Integrate compliance checks within the system.

5. Case Study: E-Commerce Platform Optimization

Scenario:

- An online retail platform uses CrewAI agents for dynamic pricing, inventory management, and fraud detection.

Implementation:

1. Pricing Agents adjust prices based on demand and competition.
2. Inventory Agents predict restocking needs using sales data.
3. Security Agents monitor transactions for anomalies.

Outcome:

- Increased sales by 20%.
- Reduced fraud-related losses by 15%.

6. Case Study: Multi-Agent Trading System

Scenario:

- A financial institution deploys CrewAI for high-frequency trading.

Implementation:

1. Market Analysis Agents process real-time data.
2. Risk Management Agents enforce stop-loss mechanisms.
3. Execution Agents place trades based on insights.

Outcome:

- Improved portfolio returns by 25%.
- Reduced trading risks during volatile markets.

Summary

AI-powered marketplaces and trading systems driven by CrewAI are reshaping industries by automating complex tasks, optimizing decisions, and enhancing user experiences. From personalized recommendations in e-commerce to algorithmic trading in financial markets, these systems demonstrate unparalleled efficiency and scalability. While challenges like data privacy and bias persist, robust strategies ensure their ethical and effective deployment.

12.4 Collaborative Research and Innovation Systems

Collaborative research and innovation systems are crucial for advancing knowledge and developing cutting-edge solutions across academia and industry. These systems rely on the collective efforts of multiple agents—human, computational, or robotic—to achieve shared objectives. CrewAI, as a multi-agent framework, plays a pivotal role in enabling intelligent collaboration, resource sharing, and efficient decision-making, transforming how research and innovation are conducted.

This section explores the application of collaborative systems in academia and industry, highlighting real-world examples and their impact on driving progress.

1. Collaborative Research in Academia

Academia has increasingly adopted collaborative systems to address complex challenges that require interdisciplinary expertise and large-scale coordination. CrewAI enhances these efforts by streamlining workflows, facilitating communication, and optimizing resource allocation.

1.1 Distributed Scientific Computing

Application:
Distributed computing systems enable researchers from different institutions to share computational resources and collaboratively solve large-scale problems.

Example:

- CERN: The European Organization for Nuclear Research uses distributed systems to process vast amounts of data from particle physics experiments.
- Role of CrewAI:
    - Coordinates tasks among computing nodes to ensure balanced resource utilization.
    - Manages data workflows to prioritize high-impact research.

Benefits:

- Accelerates data analysis and reduces computational costs.
- Facilitates global collaboration among researchers.

1.2 Collaborative Knowledge Graphs

Application:
Knowledge graphs aggregate and link data across disciplines, enabling researchers to identify connections and insights.

Example:

- Semantic Scholar: A research tool that uses knowledge graphs to connect academic papers, authors, and topics.
- Role of CrewAI:
    - Agents curate and update knowledge graphs based on new research.
    - NLP agents extract insights from unstructured documents.

Benefits:

- Enhances literature discovery for researchers.
- Identifies interdisciplinary trends and opportunities.

1.3 Autonomous Research Agents

Application:
Agents autonomously design experiments, analyze results, and suggest hypotheses.

Example:

- Molecular Discovery:
    - AI-driven agents in academic chemistry labs design and test compounds for drug discovery.
    - CrewAI enables agents to share findings, preventing redundant experiments.

Benefits:

- Speeds up the research cycle.
- Reduces resource wastage by optimizing experiment selection.

2. Collaborative Innovation in Industry

Industry leverages collaborative systems to foster innovation, improve operational efficiency, and gain a competitive edge. CrewAI enhances innovation processes by facilitating seamless interaction among teams, machines, and computational agents.

2.1 Open Innovation Platforms

Application:
Open innovation platforms connect companies, researchers, and individuals to collaboratively solve industry challenges.

Example:

- InnoCentive:
    - An online platform where companies post problems and solicit solutions from a global community of innovators.
    - Role of CrewAI:
        - Agents evaluate submissions based on predefined criteria.
        - Coordination agents manage communication between stakeholders.

Benefits:

- Expands access to diverse expertise.
- Reduces time-to-market for new ideas.

2.2 AI-Assisted Product Design

Application:
Collaborative systems assist in designing innovative products by integrating inputs from multiple teams and automating repetitive tasks.

Example:

- Automotive Industry:
    - AI systems help design energy-efficient vehicle components.
    - Role of CrewAI:
        - Design agents simulate component performance.
        - Coordination agents integrate insights from engineers and machine learning models.

Benefits:

- Reduces prototyping costs.

- Enhances product performance through data-driven design.

2.3 Supply Chain Optimization

Application:
Collaborative systems optimize supply chains by aligning production, logistics, and inventory management.

Example:

- Consumer Electronics:
    - Companies use multi-agent systems to coordinate supply chain activities.
    - Role of CrewAI:
        - Logistics agents monitor shipment status.
        - Inventory agents predict demand and adjust stock levels.

Benefits:

- Minimizes delays and operational costs.
- Enhances responsiveness to market demand.

2.4 Research-Driven Innovation Labs

Application:
Corporate R&D labs use collaborative systems to prototype and test new technologies.

Example:

- IBM Research:
    - Combines AI with robotics to explore quantum computing applications.
    - Role of CrewAI:

- Orchestrates simulation tasks across computing nodes.
- Facilitates collaboration among interdisciplinary teams.

Benefits:

- Accelerates technology development cycles.
- Promotes cross-functional innovation.

3. Enabling Technologies for Collaboration

CrewAI relies on several enabling technologies to power collaborative research and innovation systems:

1. Cloud Computing:
    - Provides scalable infrastructure for sharing resources and running simulations.
2. Blockchain:
    - Ensures secure and transparent sharing of research data and intellectual property.
3. NLP and Knowledge Representation:
    - Enables agents to process and summarize large volumes of textual data.
4. Federated Learning:
    - Allows agents to collaborate on training machine learning models without sharing raw data.

4. Case Studies

4.1 Case Study: Collaborative Climate Modeling

Scenario:
A global team of researchers models climate change scenarios to predict long-term impacts.

Role of CrewAI:

1. Task Assignment:
   - Agents distribute modeling tasks among high-performance computing nodes.
2. Data Integration:
   - Aggregates data from satellites, weather stations, and historical records.
3. Simulation Analysis:
   - Agents analyze simulation outputs and generate actionable insights.

Outcome:

- Improved accuracy in climate predictions.
- Faster turnaround for policy recommendations.

4.2 Case Study: Pharmaceutical Research Collaboration

Scenario:
A pharmaceutical company collaborates with universities to develop vaccines.

Role of CrewAI:

1. Data Management:
   - Agents aggregate and preprocess genomic data.
2. Experiment Automation:
   - Laboratory robots autonomously test compounds.
3. Collaboration:
   - Agents share progress updates among stakeholders.

Outcome:

- Accelerated vaccine development timelines.
- Reduced research costs.

5. Challenges and Solutions

    1. Challenge: Data Silos.
        - Solution: Implement federated systems for secure and collaborative data access.
    2. Challenge: Coordination Complexity.
        - Solution: Use CrewAI to automate task assignments and monitor progress.
    3. Challenge: Intellectual Property Concerns.
        - Solution: Leverage blockchain to track and secure IP ownership.
    4. Challenge: Scalability.
        - Solution: Use cloud-based architectures to accommodate growing demands.

Summary

Collaborative research and innovation systems powered by CrewAI are driving transformative changes in academia and industry. From distributed computing in scientific research to open innovation in product design, these systems enable stakeholders to tackle complex challenges efficiently. By leveraging enabling technologies and addressing coordination challenges, CrewAI enhances the impact and scalability of collaborative efforts.

12.5 Case Study: CrewAI in Smart City Management

The integration of CrewAI in smart city management has revolutionized how urban environments are monitored, optimized, and controlled. By enabling multiple intelligent agents to collaborate seamlessly, CrewAI has demonstrated its capability to address the complexities of modern cities, such as traffic congestion, energy management, public safety, and waste disposal.

This case study focuses on the successful deployment of CrewAI in a real-world smart city project, detailing its implementation, challenges, and the transformative outcomes it delivered.

Overview of the Smart City Project

City Name:

Urbania (fictionalized for illustration)

Objective:

To enhance the quality of urban life by implementing a smart city framework powered by CrewAI, addressing challenges like:

- Traffic congestion.
- Energy inefficiency.
- Waste management.
- Public safety.

Key Stakeholders:

- City government.
- Utility providers.
- Law enforcement.
- Citizens.

Implementation of CrewAI

1. Infrastructure Setup

    1. IoT Integration:
        - Sensors installed across the city to monitor traffic, energy usage, air quality, and waste levels.
        - Connected to CrewAI's central system for real-time data collection.
    2. Agent Deployment:
        - Traffic Agents: Deployed at intersections to manage signals dynamically.
        - Energy Agents: Monitor and optimize power distribution across residential and commercial areas.
        - Waste Management Agents: Track bin levels and coordinate collection schedules.
        - Safety Agents: Integrate with surveillance cameras to identify and respond to security threats.

2. Traffic Management

Challenge:
Urbania faced severe traffic congestion during peak hours, leading to delays, increased pollution, and commuter frustration.

Solution with CrewAI:

- Traffic Monitoring:
    - IoT-enabled cameras and sensors detected real-time traffic flow and congestion patterns.
- Dynamic Signal Control:
    - Traffic agents adjusted signal timings dynamically based on current traffic conditions.

- Collaborative Routing:
  - Agents communicated with navigation apps to suggest alternative routes.

Outcome:

- Reduced average commute time by 25%.
- Improved air quality due to reduced idling.

3. Energy Management

Challenge:
Frequent power outages due to inefficient energy distribution.

Solution with CrewAI:

- Load Balancing:
  - Energy agents analyzed consumption patterns and redirected power from low-demand areas to high-demand zones.
- Demand Forecasting:
  - Machine learning models predicted peak usage times, enabling preemptive adjustments.
- Integration with Renewable Sources:
  - Agents optimized the use of solar and wind energy by monitoring weather patterns.

Outcome:

- Decreased power outages by 40%.
- Reduced energy wastage by 20%.

4. Waste Management

Challenge:
Irregular waste collection schedules led to overflowing bins and sanitation issues.

Solution with CrewAI:

- Real-Time Monitoring:
    - Waste management agents used sensors to track bin fill levels.
- Optimized Collection Routes:
    - Dynamic routing minimized travel distance and fuel consumption.
- Collaboration:
    - Agents coordinated collection efforts to avoid duplicate pickups.

Outcome:

- Improved waste collection efficiency by 30%.
- Enhanced cleanliness ratings from citizens.

5. Public Safety

Challenge:
Rising incidents of theft and vandalism strained local law enforcement.

Solution with CrewAI:

- Surveillance Integration:
    - Safety agents analyzed live feeds from cameras to detect suspicious activities.
- Automated Alerts:
    - Alerts were sent to law enforcement for real-time intervention.
- Incident Analysis:

- Machine learning algorithms provided insights for crime pattern prediction.

Outcome:

- Decreased crime rates by 15% in monitored areas.
- Faster response times to incidents.

Challenges and Mitigation Strategies

1. Challenge: Data Privacy Concerns.
   - Solution: Implemented end-to-end encryption for data transmission and anonymized sensitive information.
2. Challenge: High Initial Costs.
   - Solution: Partnered with private organizations for funding and phased implementation to spread costs.
3. Challenge: System Scalability.
   - Solution: Used cloud computing to handle increasing data volumes and agent activities.
4. Challenge: Resistance to Adoption.
   - Solution: Conducted awareness campaigns to educate citizens on the benefits of smart city systems.

Outcomes of CrewAI Deployment

1. Improved Quality of Life:
   - Citizens reported greater satisfaction due to reduced commuting times, improved public safety, and cleaner surroundings.
2. Cost Savings:

- The city saved approximately 15% on operational costs through optimized energy and waste management.
3. Environmental Benefits:
    - Reduction in carbon emissions due to efficient traffic and energy systems.
4. Data-Driven Governance:
    - City administrators leveraged real-time insights to make informed decisions and respond proactively to issues.

Real-World Success Metrics

Metric	Before CrewAI	After CrewAI	Improvement
Average Commute Time	45 minutes	34 minutes	25%
Power Outage Frequency	10/month	6/month	40%
Waste Collection Efficiency	70%	91%	30%
Crime Rate (per 1000 residents)	15 incidents	12 incidents	15%

Operational Costs	$5M annually	$4.25M annually	15%

Key Takeaways

1. **Scalability:**
   - CrewAI demonstrated the ability to scale its operations as the city grew and citizen demands increased.
2. **Adaptability:**
   - The system adapted to dynamic conditions, such as traffic surges during events or seasonal energy demand fluctuations.
3. **Citizen Engagement:**
   - By integrating with mobile apps, CrewAI empowered citizens to report issues, track services, and provide feedback.
4. **Future-Ready:**
   - The city laid a foundation for further smart city innovations, such as autonomous vehicles and AI-driven healthcare systems.

The deployment of CrewAI in Urbania showcases the transformative potential of multi-agent systems in smart city management. By addressing key urban challenges through intelligent collaboration, real-time decision-making, and optimized resource use, CrewAI set a benchmark for future smart city projects worldwide. This success story highlights how AI-powered systems can enhance urban living, improve sustainability, and foster data-driven governance.

Chapter 13. Advanced Topics

13.1 Multi-Agent Systems in Cloud and Edge Environments

The integration of multi-agent systems (MAS) into cloud and edge environments has emerged as a powerful paradigm for managing complex, distributed tasks across diverse domains. Cloud-edge integration leverages the computational power of the cloud and the low-latency capabilities of edge devices to create scalable, responsive, and efficient systems. When applied to multi-agent systems, this hybrid approach enhances the ability of agents to collaborate, make decisions, and respond in real-time while leveraging the centralized resources of the cloud.

Overview of Cloud and Edge Integration

1. Cloud Computing:
    - Refers to centralized servers and infrastructure that provide high computational power, large storage capacity, and global accessibility.
    - Example: A centralized server hosting AI models for predictive analytics.
2. Edge Computing:
    - Places computing resources closer to the data source or user, reducing latency and bandwidth usage.
    - Example: Smart cameras processing video feeds locally for real-time object detection.
3. Cloud-Edge Integration:
    - Combines the centralized power of the cloud with the decentralized responsiveness of edge devices.

- Example: A smart home system where local devices (edge) handle immediate actions, while the cloud provides long-term data analysis and updates.

Benefits of Cloud-Edge Integration in Multi-Agent Systems

1. Scalability

Description:

- Cloud resources enable the deployment and management of large-scale MAS by providing virtually unlimited computational and storage capabilities.

Use Case:

- In a global logistics system, cloud servers manage large-scale data such as inventory levels and delivery routes, while edge agents at warehouses and delivery vehicles handle local tasks.

Benefits:

- Supports the deployment of thousands of agents without performance degradation.
- Facilitates easy expansion as the number of agents grows.

2. Low Latency and Real-Time Decision-Making

Description:

- Edge computing reduces latency by processing data locally, allowing agents to make real-time decisions.

Use Case:

- Autonomous vehicles use edge computing for obstacle detection and immediate navigation, while the cloud processes global traffic patterns.

Benefits:

- Improves responsiveness in time-sensitive scenarios.
- Enhances user experience through real-time interaction.

3. Efficient Resource Utilization

Description:

- Combines the processing power of the cloud for heavy tasks with edge devices for localized actions, optimizing resource use.

Use Case:

- A smart city system where cloud servers analyze large-scale traffic data, while edge agents at intersections control signals based on immediate conditions.

Benefits:

- Reduces bandwidth costs by limiting data transfer to the cloud.
- Prevents overloading of edge devices with complex computations.

4. Fault Tolerance and Redundancy

Description:

- Distributing tasks between cloud and edge agents enhances system reliability by reducing single points of failure.

Use Case:

- In disaster response, drones equipped with edge computing can function independently if cloud connectivity is lost.

Benefits:

- Ensures continued operation even during network disruptions.
- Improves system resilience in unpredictable environments.

5. Enhanced Security and Privacy

Description:

- Sensitive data can be processed locally at the edge, reducing exposure to potential security breaches during transmission to the cloud.

Use Case:

- A healthcare system where patient data is anonymized and processed locally before being shared with the cloud for analysis.

Benefits:

- Protects sensitive data while leveraging cloud analytics.
- Complies with data privacy regulations like GDPR.

Challenges of Cloud-Edge Integration in Multi-Agent Systems

1. Connectivity Dependency

Description:

- Cloud-edge systems rely on consistent network connectivity, which can be a limitation in remote or resource-constrained environments.

Impact:

- Agents may experience delays or fail to perform tasks if the connection to the cloud is disrupted.

Mitigation Strategies:

- Use hybrid architectures where critical tasks are handled locally by edge agents during connectivity loss.
- Implement adaptive caching and synchronization mechanisms.

2. Heterogeneity of Devices

Description:

- Edge devices often have varying computational capabilities, operating systems, and connectivity options, complicating system integration.

Impact:

- Inconsistent performance and increased complexity in agent communication.

Mitigation Strategies:

- Standardize communication protocols across devices.
- Use lightweight frameworks optimized for edge devices.

3. Security and Data Integrity

Description:

- Edge devices, being geographically distributed, are more susceptible to physical and cyber-attacks.

Impact:

- Risk of compromised data integrity or unauthorized access.

Mitigation Strategies:

- Implement encryption for data at rest and in transit.
- Use secure boot mechanisms and tamper-resistant hardware for edge devices.

4. Latency-Sensitive Decision Distribution

Description:

- Determining which tasks should be processed at the cloud versus the edge can be challenging, especially for latency-sensitive decisions.

Impact:

- Suboptimal task allocation can lead to inefficiencies or delays.

Mitigation Strategies:

- Use AI-based orchestration to dynamically assign tasks based on current network and device conditions.

- Employ edge analytics for pre-processing before sending data to the cloud.

5. Cost Considerations

Description:

- While edge computing reduces latency, the hardware and maintenance costs of deploying and managing edge devices can be high.

Impact:

- Increased upfront investment and operational expenses.

Mitigation Strategies:

- Use shared edge infrastructure in collaborative settings.
- Optimize workload distribution to balance cloud and edge costs.

Use Cases in Cloud-Edge MAS Integration

1. Autonomous Fleet Management

Scenario:

- Managing a fleet of delivery drones.

Role of Cloud:

- Analyzes large-scale traffic and weather data to plan optimal routes.

Role of Edge:

- Drones process local sensory data to avoid obstacles and deliver packages.

Outcome:

- Improved delivery efficiency with minimal delays.

2. Industrial IoT Systems

Scenario:

- Smart factories with interconnected machines.

Role of Cloud:

- Monitors overall production performance and predicts maintenance needs using AI.

Role of Edge:

- Machines detect and resolve local issues like temperature anomalies.

Outcome:

- Enhanced productivity and reduced downtime.

3. Smart Healthcare Systems

Scenario:

- Remote patient monitoring.

Role of Cloud:

- Aggregates and analyzes patient data for long-term health insights.

Role of Edge:

- Wearable devices monitor vitals and alert caregivers to critical conditions.

Outcome:

- Faster response to emergencies and improved health outcomes.

Future of Cloud-Edge Integration in MAS

1. AI-Driven Orchestration:
   - Intelligent algorithms will further optimize task allocation between cloud and edge.
2. Edge AI Advancements:
   - Increased computational power in edge devices will reduce reliance on the cloud.
3. 5G Connectivity:
   - Enhanced network speeds and reliability will address connectivity challenges.
4. Decentralized Architectures:
   - Blockchain and federated learning will enable more secure and autonomous edge systems.

Summary

Cloud-edge integration in multi-agent systems unlocks unparalleled opportunities for scalability, real-time responsiveness, and resource optimization. While challenges such as connectivity, heterogeneity, and security must be addressed, the benefits far outweigh the drawbacks, particularly in scenarios requiring fast, distributed decision-making. By leveraging the strengths of both cloud and edge computing, CrewAI can power advanced, intelligent systems for applications ranging from autonomous vehicles to smart cities.

13.2 Integrating IoT with CrewAI for Smart Systems

Integrating the Internet of Things (IoT) with CrewAI enables the creation of intelligent, interconnected smart systems where agents communicate with sensors, devices, and other components to make data-driven decisions. IoT enhances CrewAI's multi-agent capabilities by providing real-time data and actionable insights, while CrewAI empowers IoT systems to execute complex tasks collaboratively, manage resources efficiently, and adapt dynamically to changes.

This section explains how IoT devices and sensors connect with CrewAI agents to build robust smart systems, with examples and use cases across various domains.

Overview of IoT and CrewAI Integration

1. IoT (Internet of Things):
    - A network of physical devices, sensors, and actuators that collect and exchange data over the internet.
    - Examples: Smart thermostats, security cameras, and industrial machinery.
2. CrewAI:
    - A multi-agent framework that enables agents to communicate, collaborate, and make decisions in distributed environments.
3. Integration Goals:
    - Data Collection: Sensors gather real-time data from the environment.

- Processing and Decision-Making: CrewAI agents analyze the data and make decisions.
- Action Execution: Devices and actuators perform actions based on agent instructions.

How Sensors and Devices Connect with Agents

Integrating IoT devices with CrewAI involves several layers of interaction:

1. Sensor Layer: Data Collection

   1. Role:
      - Sensors collect data such as temperature, motion, humidity, and pressure.
   2. Connectivity:
      - Devices communicate through protocols like MQTT, CoAP, or HTTP.
   3. Example:
      - A smart thermostat collects temperature data and sends it to a CrewAI agent for analysis.

2. Communication Layer: Data Transmission

   1. Role:
      - Transfers data between IoT devices and CrewAI agents.
   2. Protocols:
      - MQTT (Message Queuing Telemetry Transport): Lightweight protocol ideal for IoT communication.
      - HTTP/REST APIs: Standard protocol for web-based communication.

- WebSockets: Real-time, bi-directional communication.
3. Example:
    - A security camera uses MQTT to transmit motion detection data to a CrewAI surveillance agent.

3. Processing Layer: Agent Decision-Making

1. Role:
    - CrewAI agents process data, apply machine learning models, and make decisions.
2. Functions:
    - Data Filtering: Remove noise and irrelevant data.
    - Event Detection: Identify actionable events, such as detecting anomalies.
    - Task Allocation: Assign tasks to appropriate agents or devices.
3. Example:
    - An energy management agent detects high electricity usage and adjusts device settings to conserve energy.

4. Action Layer: Device Control

1. Role:
    - Agents instruct actuators or devices to perform actions.
2. Execution:
    - Commands are sent back to IoT devices using protocols like MQTT or Zigbee.
3. Example:
    - A sprinkler system receives instructions from an irrigation agent to water specific zones.

Step-by-Step Guide to Connecting IoT Devices with CrewAI

Step 1: Set Up IoT Devices

1. Choose Sensors:
    - Select sensors based on system requirements (e.g., temperature sensors for smart homes, motion sensors for security).
2. Install and Configure:
    - Deploy sensors in the target environment and configure them to collect data.

Example:

- A warehouse installs RFID sensors to track inventory.

Step 2: Establish Communication Protocols

1. Select a Protocol:
    - Use MQTT for lightweight, real-time communication or REST APIs for standardized web-based interaction.
2. Set Up a Broker:
    - Use an MQTT broker (e.g., Mosquitto) to manage communication between IoT devices and CrewAI agents.

Example Code: Setting Up MQTT Communication:

python

```python
import paho.mqtt.client as mqtt
```

```python
# Define MQTT callbacks
def on_connect(client, userdata, flags, rc):
    print("Connected with result code", rc)
    client.subscribe("sensor/temperature")

def on_message(client, userdata, msg):
    print(f"Received message: {msg.payload.decode()} from topic: {msg.topic}")

# Initialize MQTT client
client = mqtt.Client()
client.on_connect = on_connect
client.on_message = on_message

# Connect to broker
client.connect("mqtt-broker-address", 1883, 60)
client.loop_forever()
```

Step 3: Connect Devices to CrewAI

1. Data Ingestion:

- Configure CrewAI agents to receive data from IoT devices via the chosen protocol.
2. Agent Processing:
    - Agents process incoming data and decide actions.

Example Code: Data Processing by CrewAI Agent:

python

```python
class TemperatureAgent:
    def process_data(self, temperature):
        if temperature > 25:
            print("Activating cooling system")
        else:
            print("Temperature is normal")

# Example usage
agent = TemperatureAgent()
agent.process_data(28)  # Simulate data input
```

Step 4: Implement Actuators for Actions

1. Integrate Devices:
    - Link actuators (e.g., motors, valves) to CrewAI agents.
2. Send Commands:
    - Agents send instructions to actuators to execute tasks.

Example Code: Sending Commands to an Actuator:

python

```python
class SprinklerAgent:
    def control_sprinkler(self, action):
        if action == "ON":
            print("Sprinkler activated")
        elif action == "OFF":
            print("Sprinkler deactivated")

# Example usage
agent = SprinklerAgent()
agent.control_sprinkler("ON")
```

Use Cases for IoT-CrewAI Integration

1. Smart Homes

- Sensors: Temperature, humidity, motion.
- Agents: Climate control, security, energy management.
- Actions:
    - Adjust thermostats to maintain comfort.
    - Activate alarms when motion is detected.

2. Industrial Automation

- Sensors: Vibration, pressure, proximity.
- Agents: Predictive maintenance, quality control.
- Actions:
    - Schedule equipment maintenance based on sensor data.
    - Stop production lines when anomalies are detected.

3. Smart Cities

- Sensors: Traffic flow, air quality, waste levels.
- Agents: Traffic management, waste collection, pollution monitoring.
- Actions:
    - Dynamically adjust traffic lights.
    - Dispatch waste collection trucks to full bins.

4. Healthcare Systems

- Sensors: Heart rate, blood pressure, glucose levels.
- Agents: Health monitoring, emergency response.
- Actions:
    - Alert caregivers to abnormal readings.
    - Administer automated insulin doses.

Challenges and Mitigation Strategies

1. Challenge: Data Privacy and Security.
    - Solution: Encrypt data and use secure communication protocols.
2. Challenge: Device Interoperability.
    - Solution: Use standardized protocols like MQTT or Zigbee.

3. Challenge: High Latency.
   - Solution: Process critical data at the edge to reduce delays.
4. Challenge: Scalability.
   - Solution: Deploy cloud-based CrewAI systems to manage large-scale IoT networks.

Summary

Integrating IoT devices with CrewAI enables the creation of intelligent, adaptive, and efficient smart systems. By leveraging sensors for data collection, CrewAI agents for decision-making, and actuators for execution, these systems excel in a wide range of applications, from smart homes to industrial automation. While challenges like security and interoperability exist, careful planning and robust technologies ensure successful implementation.

13.3 AI + Multi-Agent Systems Synergies

The integration of artificial intelligence (AI) with multi-agent systems (MAS) represents a transformative synergy that is reshaping industries and advancing the capabilities of autonomous systems. By combining the decision-making power of AI with the collaborative and distributed nature of MAS, organizations can tackle complex problems, optimize operations, and unlock innovative applications across diverse domains.

This section explores emerging trends and innovations at the intersection of AI and MAS, providing insights into how these synergies are driving the future of technology.

Emerging Trends in AI + Multi-Agent Systems

1. Reinforcement Learning in Multi-Agent Environments

Overview: Reinforcement learning (RL) enables agents to learn optimal strategies through trial and error in dynamic environments. In MAS, RL is applied to train multiple agents to collaborate or compete.

Applications:

1. Traffic Management:
    - Agents learn to optimize traffic light timings, reducing congestion.
2. Robotics:
    - Swarms of robots learn to collaborate on tasks like search and rescue.

Innovation:

- Multi-Agent Deep Reinforcement Learning (MADRL):
    - Combines deep learning with RL to enable agents to handle high-dimensional data, such as images and sensor inputs.

Example: In a warehouse, robotic agents use MADRL to learn optimal paths for item retrieval, minimizing energy consumption and time.

2. Explainable AI in Multi-Agent Systems

Overview: As MAS become more complex, understanding the decisions made by agents is critical for debugging, trust, and compliance. Explainable AI (XAI) provides insights into the reasoning behind agent actions.

Applications:

1. Healthcare:
   - Agents assisting in diagnosis explain their recommendations to doctors.
2. Finance:
   - Trading agents provide rationales for investment decisions.

Innovation:

- Graph-Based Explanations:
  - Uses knowledge graphs to illustrate how agents arrive at decisions.
- Human-Agent Interaction:
  - Combines XAI with natural language processing to make explanations user-friendly.

Example: In an autonomous vehicle system, XAI explains why the vehicle chose a specific route, considering traffic and weather conditions.

3. Federated Learning in Multi-Agent Systems

Overview: Federated learning enables agents to collaboratively train machine learning models without sharing raw data. This preserves privacy while allowing agents to learn from distributed datasets.

Applications:

1. Healthcare:
   - Hospitals use federated learning to train diagnostic models without sharing sensitive patient data.
2. IoT Networks:
   - Smart devices collaboratively improve energy management algorithms.

Innovation:

- Hierarchical Federated Learning:
    - Implements multi-level training, where local agents train on-device models that are aggregated at regional or global levels.

Example: A fleet of autonomous drones collaboratively learns to optimize flight paths while ensuring data security.

4. Cognitive Architectures for MAS

Overview: Cognitive architectures simulate human-like reasoning and decision-making in MAS, enabling agents to handle complex tasks that require logic, memory, and adaptability.

Applications:

1. Customer Service:
    - Chatbots and virtual assistants simulate empathetic and logical conversations.
2. Game AI:
    - Non-player characters (NPCs) in video games exhibit realistic behaviors.

Innovation:

- Hybrid Cognitive Systems:
    - Combine symbolic reasoning (logic-based) with neural networks to enhance decision-making.
- Memory-Augmented Agents:
    - Agents use memory modules to recall past interactions and adapt future actions accordingly.

Example: A customer support chatbot remembers a user's previous issues and provides personalized assistance.

5. Blockchain for Decentralized Multi-Agent Systems

Overview: Blockchain ensures secure and transparent communication between agents in decentralized MAS, preventing data tampering and enabling trustless interactions.

Applications:

1. Supply Chain:
    - Agents in logistics systems track and verify the provenance of goods.
2. Energy Trading:
    - Agents facilitate peer-to-peer energy transactions in smart grids.

Innovation:

- Smart Contracts:
    - Automate transactions and enforce agreements between agents.
- Tokenized Incentives:
    - Reward agents for completing tasks or contributing resources.

Example: In a decentralized marketplace, agents representing buyers and sellers use blockchain to verify transactions.

6. Adaptive Learning in MAS

Overview: Adaptive learning allows agents to continuously update their knowledge and strategies based on real-time feedback and changing environments.

Applications:

1. Smart Cities:
   - Agents dynamically adjust energy distribution based on demand fluctuations.
2. Disaster Management:
   - Agents adapt rescue strategies as new information emerges.

Innovation:

- Meta-Learning:
  - Agents learn how to learn, enabling faster adaptation to novel tasks.
- Self-Healing Systems:
  - Agents detect and resolve issues autonomously, such as network disruptions.

Example: A fleet of delivery robots adapts to unexpected roadblocks by recalculating routes in real-time.

Innovations Driving AI + Multi-Agent Systems

1. Multi-Agent Generative AI

Overview: Generative AI models like GPT and DALL-E are integrated into MAS to enable creative problem-solving and dynamic content generation.

Applications:

1. Content Creation:
   - Agents collaborate to produce marketing campaigns or educational materials.
2. Simulations:
   - Agents generate realistic virtual environments for training or gaming.

2. Hierarchical Agent Architectures

Overview: Hierarchical architectures organize agents into levels based on responsibilities, enabling efficient task management in large systems.

Applications:

1. Logistics:
    - High-level agents plan global delivery routes, while low-level agents handle local operations.
2. Autonomous Vehicles:
    - Regional agents manage traffic flow, while vehicle-level agents handle navigation.

3. Multi-Agent Collaboration Frameworks

Overview: Frameworks like OpenAI's Multi-Agent Gym provide standardized environments for training and testing MAS.

Applications:

1. Education:
    - Researchers use frameworks to experiment with MAS behaviors.
2. Enterprise:
    - Organizations simulate workflows before deploying MAS in production.

Challenges and Mitigation Strategies

1. Communication Overhead

- Challenge:
    - Frequent communication between agents can cause delays and reduce efficiency.
- Solution:
    - Use hierarchical or event-driven communication protocols to minimize unnecessary exchanges.

2. Scalability

- Challenge:
    - Adding more agents increases complexity.
- Solution:
    - Deploy cloud-based infrastructures and implement load-balancing techniques.

3. Coordination Conflicts

- Challenge:
    - Conflicts arise when agents have overlapping goals or resource requirements.
- Solution:
    - Use negotiation algorithms or consensus mechanisms to resolve conflicts.

Future Directions

1. Convergence of AI and Quantum Computing:
    - Quantum agents capable of solving computationally intractable problems.
2. Human-Agent Collaboration:
    - Seamless integration of human input into MAS workflows.

3. Ethical MAS:
    - Agents trained to prioritize fairness, accountability, and transparency.

Summary

The synergies between AI and multi-agent systems are unlocking new possibilities across industries, from real-time traffic management to advanced healthcare systems. Innovations like reinforcement learning, blockchain integration, and generative AI are pushing the boundaries of what MAS can achieve. While challenges remain, ongoing research and development promise to make these systems more scalable, adaptable, and impactful in solving real-world problems.

13.4 Concept-to-Code: Emerging Research in Multi-Agent Systems

Emerging research in multi-agent systems (MAS) focuses on leveraging cutting-edge technologies to solve complex problems in dynamic and distributed environments. This section explores a practical implementation inspired by recent advancements, highlighting the use of Multi-Agent Reinforcement Learning (MARL) in disaster response systems. This example combines state-of-the-art algorithms, communication protocols, and real-world scenarios to demonstrate how MAS can address challenges in an innovative and effective manner.

Overview of the Problem

Scenario:

A natural disaster has struck an urban area, causing widespread damage and displacing people. Autonomous drones are deployed to assist in search-and-rescue operations. These drones must:

1. Locate survivors.
2. Deliver medical supplies.
3. Coordinate with other drones to avoid duplication of efforts.

Challenges:

- Dynamic Environment: The disaster area is constantly changing, with new obstacles and shifting priorities.
- Limited Resources: Drones have constrained battery life and payload capacity.
- Coordination: Drones must communicate and collaborate to optimize their efforts.

Solution: Multi-Agent Reinforcement Learning (MARL)

Multi-Agent Reinforcement Learning is a branch of AI where multiple agents learn to cooperate or compete in an environment by maximizing cumulative rewards. This approach is ideal for dynamic, multi-objective problems like disaster response.

1. System Architecture

Key Components:

1. Agents:
    - Autonomous drones equipped with sensors for mapping, object detection, and communication.
2. Environment:

- A simulated disaster zone represented as a grid with obstacles, survivors, and supply drop points.
3. Rewards:
    - Positive rewards for locating survivors and delivering supplies.
    - Negative rewards for collisions or running out of battery.

2. MARL Algorithm

Algorithm Used: Proximal Policy Optimization (PPO)

- PPO is a state-of-the-art reinforcement learning algorithm that balances exploration and exploitation, making it well-suited for multi-agent environments.

Agent Training:

1. Each drone acts independently but shares critical information with other agents.
2. Drones are trained to learn:
    - Efficient navigation.
    - Optimal resource allocation.
    - Collaborative behaviors.

Step-by-Step Implementation

Step 1: Setting Up the Environment

Tools:

- Gym: For environment simulation.
- Stable-Baselines3: For RL algorithms.
- Python: For coding and integration.

Code Example: Environment Initialization:

python

```python
import gym
from gym import spaces
import numpy as np


class DisasterZoneEnv(gym.Env):
    def __init__(self, grid_size=10, n_agents=3):
        super().__init__()
        self.grid_size = grid_size
        self.n_agents = n_agents
        self.state = None
        self.action_space = spaces.Discrete(4)  # 0: Up, 1: Down, 2: Left, 3: Right
        self.observation_space = spaces.Box(
            low=0, high=1, shape=(grid_size, grid_size, n_agents), dtype=np.float32
        )
        self.reset()

    def reset(self):
```

```python
        self.state = np.zeros((self.grid_size, self.grid_size, self.n_agents))

    for agent in range(self.n_agents):
        x, y = np.random.randint(0, self.grid_size, size=2)
        self.state[x, y, agent] = 1

    return self.state


def step(self, actions):
    rewards = []
    for agent, action in enumerate(actions):
        x, y = np.where(self.state[:, :, agent] == 1)
        x, y = x[0], y[0]
        self.state[x, y, agent] = 0
        if action == 0: x = max(x - 1, 0)  # Up
        if action == 1: x = min(x + 1, self.grid_size - 1)  # Down
        if action == 2: y = max(y - 1, 0)  # Left
        if action == 3: y = min(y + 1, self.grid_size - 1)  # Right
        self.state[x, y, agent] = 1
        rewards.append(1 if np.random.random() > 0.8 else -1)  # Example reward logic
```

```
        return self.state, rewards, False, {}
```

```
env = DisasterZoneEnv()
print(env.reset())
```

Step 2: Training Agents with PPO

Training Pipeline:

1. Use Stable-Baselines3 for PPO implementation.
2. Train agents in the simulated disaster zone.
3. Adjust rewards and penalties to encourage collaboration.

Code Example: PPO Training:

python

```python
from stable_baselines3 import PPO
from stable_baselines3.common.env_util import make_vec_env


# Create a vectorized environment
env = make_vec_env(lambda: DisasterZoneEnv(grid_size=10, n_agents=3), n_envs=1)


# Define the PPO model
model = PPO("MlpPolicy", env, verbose=1)
```

```python
# Train the model
model.learn(total_timesteps=20000)

# Save the model
model.save("disaster_response_ppo")
```

Step 3: Simulation and Evaluation

Simulating Agent Behavior:

- Load the trained model and simulate agent behavior in different scenarios.

Code Example: Simulation:

python

```python
# Load the trained model
model = PPO.load("disaster_response_ppo")

# Run a simulation
state = env.reset()
done = False
while not done:
    actions, _ = model.predict(state)
```

```
state, rewards, done, _ = env.step(actions)

print("Rewards:", rewards)
```

Evaluation Metrics:

1. Task Completion Rate:
   - Percentage of survivors located and supplies delivered.
2. Resource Efficiency:
   - Average energy consumption per task.
3. Collision Rate:
   - Frequency of drones colliding with obstacles or each other.

Key Innovations in the Implementation

1. Dynamic Task Allocation:
   - Agents dynamically adjust priorities based on real-time conditions, such as focusing on high-priority zones.
2. Decentralized Communication:
   - Agents communicate through a peer-to-peer protocol, reducing dependence on a central controller.
3. Adaptive Learning:
   - Agents adapt their strategies to changing environments, such as avoiding newly detected obstacles.

Benefits of the System

1. Scalability:
   - The system can manage hundreds of agents, making it suitable for large-scale disaster scenarios.
2. Resilience:
   - The decentralized architecture ensures continued operation even if some agents fail.
3. Real-Time Responsiveness:
   - Agents respond to dynamic changes in the environment, improving mission success rates.
4. Resource Optimization:
   - Efficient use of limited resources, such as drone battery life and payload capacity.

Challenges and Future Directions

Challenges:

1. Communication Overhead:
   - High-frequency communication between agents can increase latency.
2. Complex Reward Design:
   - Balancing rewards to encourage both individual efficiency and collaboration is challenging.

Future Directions:

1. Integration with IoT:
   - Connect agents with IoT devices for enhanced situational awareness.
2. Explainable AI:
   - Incorporate explainability features to improve trust and debugging.
3. Real-World Deployment:
   - Transition from simulations to real-world environments with hardware integration.

This cutting-edge implementation of Multi-Agent Reinforcement Learning for disaster response demonstrates the potential of AI-driven MAS to address complex, real-world problems. By combining innovative algorithms, robust communication protocols, and adaptive decision-making, CrewAI showcases its capability to revolutionize how autonomous systems operate in dynamic environments. With further advancements, such systems can redefine disaster management, smart cities, and beyond.

Chapter 14: Hands-On Projects

This chapter provides step-by-step guidance on implementing hands-on projects using CrewAI to explore various applications of multi-agent systems. These projects cover collaborative fleets, customer support automation, logistics optimization, competitive and cooperative agent behaviors, and integration with external APIs. Each project emphasizes practical implementation, clear explanations, and professional workflows.

14.1 Project 1: Building a Collaborative AI Fleet

Objective:

Design a multi-agent system where a fleet of autonomous drones collaborates to deliver packages efficiently within a city.

Steps:

1. Setup:
   - Install Python libraries such as gym, stable-baselines3, and matplotlib for visualization.
2. Define Environment:
   - Create a grid-based city map with delivery points and obstacles.
   - Each drone is an agent with attributes like battery life, location, and payload capacity.

Code Example:
python

```
class DeliveryEnv(gym.Env):
    def __init__(self, grid_size=10, n_drones=3):
```

```python
self.grid_size = grid_size

self.n_drones = n_drones

self.state = None

self.action_space = spaces.Discrete(4)  # 0: Up, 1: Down, 2: Left, 3: Right

self.observation_space = spaces.Box(
    low=0, high=1, shape=(grid_size, grid_size, n_drones), dtype=np.float32
)

self.reset()
```

3. Agent Collaboration:
    - Implement communication between drones to avoid overlapping tasks.
    - Use reinforcement learning to optimize delivery routes.
4. Simulation:
    - Visualize drone movements and delivery progress using matplotlib.
5. Evaluation:
    - Measure delivery time, energy consumption, and task completion rate.

14.2 Project 2: Workflow Automation for a Customer Support System

Objective:

Automate a customer support system where AI agents handle queries, escalate complex issues, and provide follow-ups.

Steps:

1. Define Roles:
   - Agents have specific roles: Query Handler, Escalation Manager, and Follow-Up Specialist.
2. Data Integration:
   - Connect the system to a mock customer database for storing tickets.
3. Workflow Implementation:
   - Query Handler:
     - Responds to common queries using a pretrained NLP model (e.g., GPT).
   - Escalation Manager:
     - Routes complex issues to human agents.
   - Follow-Up Specialist:
     - Sends reminders or updates to customers.

Code Example:
python

```python
from transformers import pipeline

class QueryHandler:
    def __init__(self):
        self.model = pipeline("question-answering", model="distilbert-base-uncased")

    def handle_query(self, query, context):
```

        return self.model(question=query, context=context)["answer"]

Example usage

handler = QueryHandler()

print(handler.handle_query("What is your return policy?", "Our return policy lasts 30 days."))

4. Test Scenarios:
    - Simulate customer interactions to evaluate response accuracy and escalation logic.

14.3 Project 3: Real-Time Task Allocation in Logistics

Objective:

Develop a multi-agent system to allocate tasks dynamically among warehouse robots.

Steps:

1. Environment Setup:
    - Represent the warehouse as a grid with robots, storage areas, and delivery points.
2. Agent Roles:
    - Picker Robots: Retrieve items from shelves.
    - Sorter Robots: Organize items for delivery.
    - Loader Robots: Load packages onto trucks.
3. Task Allocation Logic:

- Use a task queue and priority system to assign tasks based on robot availability and proximity.
4. Optimization:
    - Implement task reassignment for idle robots and prioritize urgent deliveries.

Code Example:
python

```python
class TaskAllocator:
    def __init__(self):
        self.tasks = []

    def add_task(self, task):
        self.tasks.append(task)

    def assign_task(self, robot):
        if self.tasks:
            return self.tasks.pop(0)
        return "No tasks available"

allocator = TaskAllocator()
allocator.add_task("Pick item A")
print(allocator.assign_task("Robot 1"))
```

5. Evaluation:
   - Analyze system performance in terms of task completion rate and idle time.

14.4 Project 4: Simulating Competitive and Cooperative Agent Behaviors

Objective:

Simulate competitive and cooperative behaviors in a resource-sharing environment.

Steps:

1. Scenario:
   - Agents compete for limited resources while cooperating to maximize group rewards.
2. Environment:
   - A grid world with resources scattered randomly.
   - Agents can collect resources individually or share with others for higher rewards.
3. Behavior Design:
   - Competitive: Agents prioritize individual gain.
   - Cooperative: Agents share resources for collective benefits.
4. Reward Mechanism:
   - Higher rewards for cooperation, lower for competition.
5. Simulation:
   - Run simulations to observe agent strategies under different conditions.

Code Example:
python

```python
class ResourceSharingEnv(gym.Env):
    def __init__(self):
        self.resources = np.random.randint(0, 2, (10, 10))
        self.agents = [{"position": (0, 0), "score": 0} for _ in range(3)]

    def step(self, actions):
        for agent, action in zip(self.agents, actions):
            if action == "collect":
                x, y = agent["position"]
                if self.resources[x, y] > 0:
                    agent["score"] += self.resources[x, y]
                    self.resources[x, y] = 0
```

6. Insights:
    - Compare cooperative vs. competitive strategies and their impact on group performance.

14.5 Project 5: Integrating AI Agents with External APIs

Objective:

Integrate CrewAI agents with external APIs for real-time data processing and decision-making.

Steps:

1. API Selection:
   - Choose APIs relevant to the project, such as weather, traffic, or financial data.
2. Agent Design:
   - Create agents to fetch data, analyze it, and take appropriate actions.
3. Integration:
   - Use Python libraries like requests to interact with APIs.

Code Example:
python

```python
import requests


class WeatherAgent:
    def get_weather(self, location):
        api_key = "your_api_key"
        url = f"http://api.openweathermap.org/data/2.5/weather?q={location}&appid={api_key}"
        response = requests.get(url)
```

```python
        if response.status_code == 200:
            return response.json()["weather"][0]["description"]
        return "Failed to fetch weather"

# Example usage
agent = WeatherAgent()
print(agent.get_weather("New York"))
```

4. Use Case:
    - A logistics system uses weather data to reroute deliveries during adverse conditions.
5. Evaluation:
    - Test the system under various real-world scenarios and assess its adaptability.

These hands-on projects illustrate the practical implementation of multi-agent systems in diverse applications. By following the step-by-step guides, you can gain a deeper understanding of how CrewAI can be applied to solve real-world challenges in collaboration, automation, optimization, simulation, and integration. Each project emphasizes scalability, efficiency, and innovation, providing a strong foundation for further exploration and development in MAS.

Chapter 15: Developer Challenges

This chapter provides a structured set of challenges designed to help developers of all levels—beginner, intermediate, and advanced—practice and master the concepts of multi-agent systems (MAS) using CrewAI. The challenges range from fundamental exercises to real-world problem-solving scenarios, culminating in detailed solutions and explanations to solidify understanding.

15.1 Beginner Challenges

Objective:

Introduce basic concepts of multi-agent systems, agent communication, and task management.

Challenge 1: Create a Basic Agent

- Description: Write a Python class to represent an agent with attributes such as name, position, and a simple ability to move.
- Requirements:
    - The agent should have methods to move up, down, left, and right within a grid.
    - Print the agent's position after each move.

Example Starter Code:

python

```python
class Agent:
    def __init__(self, name, position=(0, 0)):
```

```
        self.name = name

        self.position = position


    def move(self, direction):

        x, y = self.position

        if direction == "up":

            self.position = (x, y + 1)

        elif direction == "down":

            self.position = (x, y - 1)

        elif direction == "left":

            self.position = (x - 1, y)

        elif direction == "right":

            self.position = (x + 1, y)

        print(f"{self.name} moved to {self.position}")
```

Challenge 2: Implement Simple Agent Communication

- Description: Implement a messaging system where agents can send and receive messages.
- Requirements:
    - Create a method for an agent to send a message to another agent.
    - Display the received messages.

Example Scenario:

- Agent A sends "Hello" to Agent B.
- Agent B replies with "Hi, Agent A."

Challenge 3: Create an Agent Grid

- Description: Build a 5x5 grid environment where agents can navigate without exceeding boundaries.
- Requirements:
    - Restrict agent movements to remain within the grid.
    - Allow multiple agents to occupy the grid.

15.2 Intermediate Challenges

Objective:

Develop skills in collaboration, resource allocation, and conflict resolution.

Challenge 1: Collaborative Task Allocation

- Description: Implement a system where agents collaboratively complete tasks from a shared pool.
- Requirements:
    - Each task should have a difficulty level and a specific agent assigned to it based on capabilities.
    - Agents should avoid duplicating efforts.

Challenge 2: Resource Sharing

- Description: Simulate agents sharing a finite resource (e.g., energy or bandwidth).
- Requirements:
    - Implement rules for resource allocation.
    - Introduce penalties for overuse or conflicts.

Example:

- Agents in a network share bandwidth. Each agent requests bandwidth, and the system allocates it fairly.

Challenge 3: Build a Multi-Agent Simulation

- Description: Create a simulation where agents search for and collect resources in a grid environment.
- Requirements:
    - Include obstacles and limited visibility for agents.
    - Introduce a reward system for successful resource collection.

15.3 Advanced Challenges

Objective:

Master complex behaviors such as adaptive learning, dynamic collaboration, and optimization.

Challenge 1: Adaptive Learning

- Description: Implement reinforcement learning for agents to learn optimal paths in a dynamic environment.
- Requirements:

- Train agents to adapt to changes such as moving obstacles or shifting goals.

Challenge 2: Decentralized Coordination

- Description: Develop a system where agents coordinate tasks without a central controller.
- Requirements:
    - Implement peer-to-peer communication and consensus mechanisms.
    - Introduce scenarios requiring dynamic task reallocation.

Challenge 3: Implement Competitive Behaviors

- Description: Create a system where agents compete for limited resources.
- Requirements:
    - Balance agent strategies to encourage both competition and occasional cooperation.

Example Scenario:

- Agents compete for access to a charging station, but must cooperate to avoid a system-wide outage.

15.4 Real-World Problem-Solving Scenarios

Objective:

Apply concepts to practical, real-world problems.

Scenario 1: Smart Traffic Management

- Problem: Design a system where agents (traffic lights) optimize traffic flow in a city.
- Requirements:
    - Minimize congestion and reduce travel time.
    - Adapt to dynamic traffic patterns.

Scenario 2: Emergency Response System

- Problem: Develop a multi-agent system where drones coordinate to locate and assist victims in a disaster zone.
- Requirements:
    - Ensure coverage of the entire area without overlap.
    - Optimize resource allocation (e.g., battery life).

Scenario 3: Warehouse Automation

- Problem: Create a system where robots collaborate to pick, sort, and pack items in a warehouse.
- Requirements:
    - Avoid collisions and idle time.
    - Prioritize urgent orders.

15.5 Solutions and Explanations

This section provides detailed solutions to each challenge and scenario, with clear explanations to help developers understand the underlying concepts and logic.

Solution Example: Collaborative Task Allocation

Code:

python

```python
class TaskAllocator:
    def __init__(self):
        self.tasks = {"Task1": "Agent1", "Task2": "Agent2", "Task3": "Agent1"}

    def assign_tasks(self):
        for task, agent in self.tasks.items():
            print(f"{task} is assigned to {agent}")

allocator = TaskAllocator()
allocator.assign_tasks()
```

Explanation:

- Tasks are stored in a dictionary, mapping each task to the most suitable agent.
- The system ensures each task is assigned to one agent, avoiding duplication.

Solution Example: Emergency Response System

Code:

python

```python
class Drone:
    def __init__(self, id, battery):
        self.id = id
        self.battery = battery
        self.position = (0, 0)

    def move_to(self, position):
        self.position = position
        self.battery -= 1
        print(f"Drone {self.id} moved to {self.position}. Battery: {self.battery}")

# Example usage
drone1 = Drone("D1", 100)
drone1.move_to((5, 5))
```

Explanation:

- Each drone tracks its position and battery life.

- Movement reduces battery, simulating real-world constraints.

This chapter bridges theoretical concepts and practical applications, guiding developers through challenges of varying complexity. By solving these problems and analyzing the provided solutions, developers will deepen their understanding of multi-agent systems, building the skills needed to tackle real-world projects with confidence.

Chapter 1. Introduction

- **1.1 What is CrewAI?**
    - 1.1.1 Overview of CrewAI as a framework for multi-agent systems.
    - 1.1.2 Key features and capabilities of CrewAI.
- **1.2 Why Multi-Agent Systems?**
    - 1.2.1 Challenges of traditional AI systems.
    - 1.2.2 Benefits of decentralized decision-making.
- **1.3 The Role of CrewAI in Advanced AI Workflows**
    - 1.3.1 Practical applications in automation, optimization, and collaboration.

- ○ 1.3.2 Real-world examples of CrewAI's impact.
- **1.4 Key Benefits of Multi-Agent Systems**
  - ○ 1.4.1 Flexibility, scalability, and fault tolerance.
  - ○ 1.4.2 Improved decision-making through collaboration.
- **1.5 Overview of the Book**
  - ○ 1.5.1 How the book is structured.
  - ○ 1.5.2 Tips for getting the most out of this guide.

Chapter 2. Setting Up Your Development Environment

- **2.1 Required Tools and Technologies**
  - ○ 2.1.1 Overview of programming languages, libraries, and frameworks.
  - ○ 2.1.2 Hardware and software requirements.
- **2.2 Installing and Configuring CrewAI**
  - ○ 2.2.1 Step-by-step installation instructions for CrewAI.
  - ○ 2.2.2 Troubleshooting common installation errors.
- **2.3 Environment Setup Validation**
  - ○ 2.3.1 Testing the setup to ensure functionality.
  - ○ 2.3.2 Sample scripts for validation.
- **2.4 Troubleshooting Common Issues**
  - ○ 2.4.1 Common errors and how to resolve them.

Chapter 3. What Are Agents in Multi-Agent Systems?

- **3.1 Defining Agents and Their Characteristics**
  - ○ 3.1.1 Core features: autonomy, communication, and adaptability.
  - ○ 3.1.2 Types of agents: reactive, proactive, and hybrid.
- **3.2 Core Principles of Multi-Agent Design**

- 3.2.1 Key concepts: modularity, scalability, and resilience.
- **3.3 Applications of Multi-Agent Systems in Real Life**
    - 3.3.1 Examples in robotics, logistics, and smart systems.
- **3.4 Concept-to-Code: Creating a Simple Agent**
    - 3.4.1 Hands-on example of building a basic agent.

Chapter 4. CrewAI Architecture

- **4.1 Overview of CrewAI's Modular Design**
    - 4.1.1 Key components: agents, communication layer, and decision-making logic.
- **4.2 Communication Protocols in CrewAI**
    - 4.2.1 Types of protocols: peer-to-peer, client-server.
    - 4.2.2 Implementing communication pipelines.
- **4.3 Orchestration and Decision-Making in Multi-Agent Systems**
    - 4.3.1 Centralized vs. decentralized orchestration.
    - 4.3.2 Role of decision-making algorithms.
- **4.4 Concept-to-Code: Building Agent Communication Pipelines**
    - 4.4.1 Practical example of inter-agent communication.

Chapter 5. Designing and Building Agents

- **5.1 Structuring Agent Behavior**
    - 5.1.1 Designing agent roles and responsibilities.
- **5.2 Creating Specialized Agents for Specific Tasks**
    - 5.2.1 Examples of task-specific agents in real-world scenarios.

- **5.3 Agent-to-Agent Communication: Protocols and Patterns**
  - 5.3.1 Messaging patterns and implementation techniques.
- **5.4 Handling Errors and Failures in Agent Interactions**
  - 5.4.1 Strategies for error recovery and conflict resolution.
- **5.5 Concept-to-Code: Building a Functional Agent System**
  - 5.5.1 Step-by-step guide to creating a multi-agent system.

Chapter 6. Collaboration and Coordination

- **6.1 Strategies for Agent Collaboration**
  - 6.1.1 Collaborative planning and task sharing.
- **6.2 Centralized vs. Decentralized Coordination**
  - 6.2.1 Trade-offs and use cases.
- **6.3 Conflict Resolution and Consensus Mechanisms**
  - 6.3.1 Techniques to ensure smooth collaboration.
- **6.4 Algorithms for Distributed Decision-Making**
  - 6.4.1 Overview of common algorithms and their applications.
- **6.5 Concept-to-Code: Collaborative Task Allocation**
  - 6.5.1 Hands-on example of building collaborative agents.

Chapter 7. Building Advanced AI Workflows with CrewAI

- **7.1 Workflow Automation with Multi-Agent Systems**
  - 7.1.1 Automating complex tasks using CrewAI.

- **7.2 Leveraging Machine Learning in Multi-Agent Workflows**
  - 7.2.1 Integrating ML models for intelligent decision-making.
- **7.3 Real-Time Communication and Data Sharing in Workflows**
  - 7.3.1 Techniques for maintaining synchronization and consistency.
- **7.4 Project: Multi-Agent Workflow for a Logistics System**
  - 7.4.1 Step-by-step implementation guide.

Chapter 8. Scaling Multi-Agent Systems

- **8.1 Challenges in Scaling Multi-Agent Systems**
  - 8.1.1 Resource allocation and communication overhead.
- **8.2 Distributed Deployment Strategies**
  - 8.2.1 Techniques for deploying agents across multiple nodes.
- **8.3 Load Balancing and Dynamic Agent Allocation**
  - 8.3.1 Strategies for optimizing performance.
- **8.4 Optimizing Performance and Resource Utilization**
  - 8.4.1 Practical tips for improving efficiency.
- **8.5 Concept-to-Code: Scaling a Fleet of Agents**
  - 8.5.1 Real-world implementation example.

Chapter 9. Debugging and Monitoring Multi-Agent Systems

- **9.1 Tools and Techniques for Debugging CrewAI Applications**

- 9.1.1 Debugging agents, workflows, and communication.
- **9.2 Setting Up Real-Time Monitoring and Logging**
  - 9.2.1 Tools for tracking agent behavior and performance.
- **9.3 Ensuring System Stability and Reliability**
  - 9.3.1 Identifying and mitigating system bottlenecks.
- **9.4 Example: Debugging a Faulty Agent Interaction**
  - 9.4.1 Practical troubleshooting walkthrough.

Chapter 10. Security and Ethical Considerations

- **10.1 Security Challenges in Multi-Agent Systems**
  - 10.1.1 Potential vulnerabilities and threat mitigation.
- **10.2 Securing Communication Between Agents**
  - 10.2.1 Encryption and secure protocols.
- **10.3 Designing Resilient Systems to Handle Attacks**
  - 10.3.1 Techniques for building robust systems.
- **10.4 Ethical Design of Agent Behaviors**
  - 10.4.1 Considerations for transparency and accountability.
- **10.5 Mitigating Risks of Unintended Outcomes**
  - 10.5.1 Avoiding errors in decision-making and agent actions.

Chapter 11. Integrating Machine Learning with CrewAI

- **11.1 Using Machine Learning for Agent Optimization**
  - 11.1.1 Training agents to improve performance.
- **11.2 Reinforcement Learning in Multi-Agent Systems**

- 11.2.1 Teaching agents to adapt through trial and error.
- **11.3 Combining CrewAI with Pretrained Models**
  - 11.3.1 Integration with NLP models, computer vision, and more.
- **11.4 Project: Reinforcement Learning in Multi-Agent Environments**
  - 11.4.1 End-to-end implementation guide.

Chapter 12. Real-World Applications and Case Studies

- **12.1 Automation and Robotics**
  - 12.1.1 Examples of CrewAI in industrial and household robots.
- **12.2 Distributed Problem Solving**
  - 12.2.1 Solving complex optimization problems.
- **12.3 AI-Powered Marketplaces and Trading Systems**
  - 12.3.1 Applications in e-commerce and financial trading.
- **12.4 Collaborative Research and Innovation Systems**
  - 12.4.1 Examples from academia and industry.
- **12.5 Case Study: CrewAI in Smart City Management**
  - 12.5.1 Real-world success story.

Chapter 13. Advanced Topics

- **13.1 Multi-Agent Systems in Cloud and Edge Environments**
  - 13.1.1 Benefits and challenges of cloud-edge integration.
- **13.2 Integrating IoT with CrewAI for Smart Systems**

- - 13.2.1 Connecting sensors and devices with agents.
- **13.3 AI + Multi-Agent Systems Synergies**
  - 13.3.1 Emerging trends and innovations.
- **13.4 Concept-to-Code: Emerging Research in Multi-Agent Systems**
  - 13.4.1 Cutting-edge implementation example.

Chapter 14. Hands-On Projects

- **14.1 Project 1**: Building a Collaborative AI Fleet
- **14.2 Project 2**: Workflow Automation for a Customer Support System
- **14.3 Project 3**: Real-Time Task Allocation in Logistics
- **14.4 Project 4**: Simulating Competitive and Cooperative Agent Behaviors
- **14.5 Project 5**: Integrating AI Agents with External APIs

---

Chapter 15. Developer Challenges

- **15.1 Beginner Challenges**
- **15.2 Intermediate Challenges**
- **15.3 Advanced Challenges**
- 15.4 Real-World Problem-Solving Scenarios
- 15.5 Solutions and Explanations

Chapter 16. Conclusion

- **16.1 Summary of Key Learnings**
  - 16.1.1 Recap of major concepts and techniques.
- **16.2 Future of CrewAI and Multi-Agent Systems**
  - 16.2.1 Trends and opportunities for developers.
- **16.3 Resources for Further Learning**

- 16.3.1 Books, courses, and tools for continued exploration.

Appendix

- **A.1 Glossary of Terms**
- **A.2 Quick Reference: CrewAI Functions and APIs**
- **A.3 Categorized Resources**
    - A.3.1 Code repositories, tools, and learning materials.

Index

- Comprehensive Index of Terms and Concepts

This is now a **practical, detailed, and developer-friendly table of contents**, ensuring thorough coverage of CrewAI and multi-agent systems. Let me know where you'd like to begin drafting!

Conclusion

Summary of Key Learnings

The journey through this book has provided a comprehensive understanding of multi-agent systems (MAS) and their application in real-world scenarios using CrewAI. In this concluding chapter, we revisit the major concepts, techniques, and insights covered, offering a clear and structured summary to reinforce your understanding and prepare you for practical implementation.

1. Understanding Multi-Agent Systems

- Definition: Multi-agent systems consist of multiple autonomous agents that interact within an environment to achieve individual or collective goals.
- Core Characteristics:
    - Autonomy: Agents operate independently.
    - Communication: Agents share information and coordinate actions.
    - Adaptability: Agents respond to changes in the environment dynamically.
- Types of Agents:
    - Reactive Agents: Respond to immediate stimuli without long-term planning.
    - Proactive Agents: Pursue goals based on pre-defined strategies.
    - Hybrid Agents: Combine reactive and proactive behaviors.

2. CrewAI Architecture

- Modular Design:
    - Key components include agents, the communication layer, and decision-making logic.
- Scalability and Flexibility:

- Supports various deployment scenarios, from small-scale systems to complex networks.
- Communication Protocols:
  - Enables seamless agent interactions using peer-to-peer, client-server, and hybrid models.
- Decision-Making Algorithms:
  - Centralized and decentralized orchestration models for task allocation and resource optimization.

3. Designing and Building Agents

- Agent Behavior:
  - Structuring roles and responsibilities for specific tasks, ensuring clarity and efficiency.
- Specialized Agents:
  - Custom-designed agents for tasks such as data analysis, logistics, or security.
- Agent-to-Agent Communication:
  - Protocols and messaging patterns for smooth interaction.
- Error Handling:
  - Techniques for resolving conflicts and recovering from failures.

4. Collaboration and Coordination

- Collaboration Strategies:
  - Planning and task sharing for cooperative behaviors.
- Centralized vs. Decentralized Coordination:
  - Exploring trade-offs and use cases for each model.
- Conflict Resolution:
  - Consensus mechanisms and negotiation techniques to ensure smooth collaboration.

5. Advanced Concepts in Multi-Agent Systems

- Integration with IoT:

- Connecting sensors and devices to agents for real-time data processing and decision-making.
- Cloud and Edge Computing:
  - Benefits and challenges of integrating MAS into cloud-edge environments for scalability and responsiveness.
- Machine Learning Integration:
  - Using AI to optimize agent behaviors, including reinforcement learning and federated learning.

6. Hands-On Applications and Projects

- Collaborative AI Fleet:
  - Building a system where agents coordinate to optimize delivery routes.
- Workflow Automation:
  - Automating customer support systems with specialized agents.
- Logistics Optimization:
  - Implementing task allocation systems in warehouse environments.
- Competitive and Cooperative Simulations:
  - Analyzing agent strategies in resource-sharing scenarios.
- Integration with External APIs:
  - Connecting agents to real-world data sources for informed decision-making.

7. Challenges and Solutions

- Beginner to Advanced Challenges:
  - Exercises that build foundational skills and progress to solving real-world problems.
- Troubleshooting Techniques:
  - Debugging agent interactions, resolving communication issues, and optimizing performance.
- Practical Scenarios:

- Case studies in traffic management, emergency response, and warehouse automation.

8. Ethical and Security Considerations

- Ethical Design:
  - Ensuring transparency, accountability, and fairness in agent behaviors.
- Data Privacy:
  - Securing sensitive information through encryption and federated systems.
- Risk Mitigation:
  - Preventing unintended outcomes through robust system design.

9. Real-World Applications and Impact

- Smart Cities:
  - Applications in traffic control, waste management, and public safety.
- Automation and Robotics:
  - Enhancing efficiency in industries like manufacturing and logistics.
- Healthcare and Emergency Response:
  - Improving patient care and disaster management through coordinated agent systems.

Key Takeaways

1. Comprehensive Understanding of MAS:
   - From foundational concepts to advanced applications, this book has covered the breadth of multi-agent systems.
2. Practical Skills:
   - Hands-on projects and challenges have equipped you with the tools to build and deploy MAS using CrewAI.

3. Strategic Thinking:
     ○ Insights into collaboration, coordination, and decision-making will guide you in designing efficient, scalable systems.
4. Future-Ready Knowledge:
     ○ Discussions on emerging trends, such as integration with IoT and machine learning, position you at the forefront of MAS innovation.

Moving Forward

As you conclude this book, you are now equipped to:

- Design and Deploy: Build multi-agent systems for real-world applications.
- Innovate and Experiment: Explore new use cases and test novel agent behaviors.
- Collaborate and Contribute: Share your learnings and contribute to the growing field of multi-agent systems.

Future of CrewAI and Multi-Agent Systems

As technology evolves, the potential of CrewAI and multi-agent systems (MAS) to transform industries continues to grow. Developers have a unique opportunity to leverage emerging trends, tools, and techniques to build innovative, efficient, and scalable solutions. This section explores the future of CrewAI and MAS, highlighting key trends and opportunities for developers looking to contribute to and benefit from this rapidly advancing field.

Key Trends in the Future of Multi-Agent Systems

1. Integration with Emerging Technologies

Trend: MAS are increasingly being integrated with cutting-edge technologies such as blockchain, IoT, and machine learning.

Opportunities:

- IoT Integration:
    - Develop smart systems where agents interact with IoT devices for real-time data collection and decision-making.
    - Example: Smart cities leveraging agents for traffic management and pollution control.
- Blockchain:
    - Implement decentralized MAS where blockchain ensures secure communication and transparency.
    - Example: Supply chains using agents to verify product provenance and enforce smart contracts.
- Machine Learning:
    - Use reinforcement learning to improve agent behaviors dynamically in complex environments.
    - Example: Training agents for adaptive decision-making in financial trading systems.

2. Decentralized and Distributed Systems

Trend: Decentralization is becoming a critical feature of MAS, ensuring scalability, fault tolerance, and resilience.

Opportunities:

- Build distributed systems that operate without reliance on central controllers, suitable for large-scale deployments.
- Example: Decentralized energy grids where agents manage energy production, distribution, and consumption collaboratively.

3. Real-Time Systems

Trend: Real-time decision-making and responsiveness are essential for MAS applications in dynamic environments.

Opportunities:

- Develop systems for industries requiring instant decisions, such as autonomous vehicles or disaster response.
- Example: Agents managing real-time communication between drones in a rescue operation.

4. Ethical AI and Explainability

Trend: The demand for ethical AI systems that are transparent and explainable is rising.

Opportunities:

- Design MAS that prioritize fairness, accountability, and ethical decision-making.
- Develop tools to explain agent behaviors, increasing user trust and system reliability.
- Example: Healthcare agents providing clear rationales for diagnosis and treatment recommendations.

5. Multi-Agent Collaboration Frameworks

Trend: Frameworks like CrewAI are evolving to simplify the design, testing, and deployment of MAS.

Opportunities:

- Contribute to open-source MAS frameworks by adding new features, improving scalability, or enhancing usability.
- Example: Extending CrewAI to support advanced orchestration techniques or integration with cloud-native tools.

6. Advanced Simulation and Virtual Environments

Trend: Simulation environments are becoming essential for testing MAS in safe, controlled settings.

Opportunities:

- Build high-fidelity simulations for training agents in complex scenarios.
- Example: Virtual environments where agents learn to cooperate in disaster recovery missions before real-world deployment.

7. Cross-Disciplinary Applications

Trend: MAS are expanding into new domains, including education, entertainment, and social systems.

Opportunities:

- Explore non-traditional applications such as educational platforms where agents act as personalized tutors.
- Develop gaming systems with NPCs (non-player characters) that exhibit realistic behaviors.
- Example: Multi-agent simulations teaching collaborative problem-solving in schools.

Opportunities for Developers

1. Developing Scalable MAS

Developers can focus on building MAS that scale across millions of devices and users. The challenges include managing communication overhead, maintaining low latency, and ensuring robust coordination.

- **Tools to Use:**
    - CrewAI for agent design.
    - Cloud platforms (e.g., AWS, Azure) for scalable deployments.
- Example: Building MAS for global e-commerce platforms to optimize inventory and logistics.

2. Creating Interoperable Systems

The ability to integrate MAS with existing systems is crucial. Developers can create APIs, middleware, or plugins to enhance interoperability.

- Tools to Use:
    - RESTful APIs for communication.
    - Protocols like MQTT or WebSockets for real-time data exchange.
- Example: An agent-based system that integrates with IoT devices for home automation.

3. Enhancing Security and Privacy

With the growing reliance on MAS, ensuring secure communication and protecting sensitive data are top priorities.

- Focus Areas:
    - Implement encryption techniques for agent communication.
    - Use federated learning to train agents collaboratively without sharing raw data.
- Example: A healthcare system where agents manage patient data securely while collaborating on diagnostic models.

4. Optimizing Agent Collaboration

Improving how agents collaborate and coordinate is a key area for developers.

- Techniques to Explore:
    - Reinforcement learning for collaborative behaviors.
    - Consensus algorithms for decision-making in decentralized systems.
- Example: Agents in autonomous fleets that dynamically coordinate to optimize delivery routes.

5. Contributing to Research and Open Source

Developers can engage with the broader MAS community by contributing to research or open-source projects.

- Opportunities:
    - Participate in hackathons or research collaborations.
    - Contribute to projects like CrewAI by developing new modules or improving documentation.
- Example: Adding a module to CrewAI for real-time resource allocation in logistics.

The Path Ahead

1. Expanding Developer Roles

The future of MAS requires developers who can think beyond traditional software engineering:

- AI Engineers:
    - Develop algorithms that empower agents to learn and adapt.
- System Architects:
    - Design robust, scalable architectures for MAS deployments.
- Ethics Consultants:
    - Ensure that MAS align with ethical standards and user expectations.

2. Driving Innovation

Developers can drive innovation in MAS by:

- Exploring underutilized domains like environmental monitoring and education.

- Using CrewAI to prototype new systems quickly and efficiently.

3. Shaping Future Industries

MAS will be pivotal in transforming industries such as:

- Healthcare:
    - Personalized medicine and real-time patient monitoring.
- Finance:
    - Automated trading systems and fraud detection.
- Energy:
    - Smart grids and renewable energy management.

The future of CrewAI and multi-agent systems is filled with opportunities for developers to innovate, solve complex problems, and shape the industries of tomorrow. By staying informed about emerging trends, mastering the latest tools, and embracing cross-disciplinary applications, developers can unlock the full potential of MAS. The journey ahead is as exciting as it is challenging, and the contributions of forward-thinking developers will undoubtedly pave the way for groundbreaking advancements.

Resources for Further Learning

The world of multi-agent systems (MAS) and CrewAI is vast, and staying updated requires continuous learning. Whether you're a beginner, intermediate developer, or advanced practitioner, exploring additional resources will deepen your understanding, broaden your skills, and keep you informed about the latest developments in the field. This section provides a curated list of books, courses, tools, and platforms for further learning.

1. Books

Books offer in-depth knowledge and theoretical foundations, often accompanied by practical examples. Below are highly recommended titles for learning about MAS, artificial intelligence, and related fields.

1.1 Multi-Agent Systems and Artificial Intelligence

1. "An Introduction to Multi-Agent Systems" by Michael Wooldridge
    - Overview: A comprehensive introduction to the theory and practice of multi-agent systems.
    - Key Topics:
        - Agent architectures.
        - Cooperation and competition.
        - Communication protocols.
    - Why It's Useful: Ideal for understanding the foundational principles of MAS.
2. "Artificial Intelligence: A Modern Approach" by Stuart Russell and Peter Norvig
    - Overview: Covers the breadth of AI, including concepts relevant to MAS.
    - Key Topics:
        - Search algorithms.
        - Decision-making.
        - Machine learning.
    - Why It's Useful: Provides theoretical insights and practical algorithms.
3. "Multiagent Systems: Algorithmic, Game-Theoretic, and Logical Foundations" by Yoav Shoham and Kevin Leyton-Brown
    - Overview: Focuses on algorithms and game theory in MAS.
    - Key Topics:
        - Distributed problem-solving.
        - Strategic interactions.
        - Cooperative and competitive behaviors.

- Why It's Useful: Ideal for developers interested in the mathematical foundations of MAS.

1.2 Specialized Topics

1. "Reinforcement Learning: An Introduction" by Richard S. Sutton and Andrew G. Barto
   - Overview: A definitive guide to reinforcement learning, a critical component of MAS.
   - Key Topics:
     - Q-learning.
     - Policy gradients.
     - Multi-agent reinforcement learning.
   - Why It's Useful: Essential for understanding how agents learn through trial and error.
2. "IoT and Edge Computing for Architects" by Perry Lea
   - Overview: Explores IoT and edge computing integration, crucial for MAS in smart systems.
   - Key Topics:
     - Sensor networks.
     - Real-time processing.
     - Scalable architectures.
   - Why It's Useful: Helps integrate IoT devices with MAS.

2. Online Courses

Courses provide structured learning paths with practical exercises, allowing you to build hands-on experience.

2.1 Beginner-Friendly Courses

1. "Introduction to Artificial Intelligence" by Stanford University (Coursera)
   - Instructor: Andrew Ng and Peter Norvig.
   - Focus: Core AI concepts, including agents, search algorithms, and game theory.

- Platform: Coursera.
- Why It's Useful: Establishes a strong AI foundation with applications to MAS.
2. "AI for Everyone" by Andrew Ng (Coursera)
    - Focus: Non-technical overview of AI and its applications.
    - Why It's Useful: Great for beginners looking to understand AI's role in MAS.

2.2 Intermediate to Advanced Courses

1. "Multi-Agent Reinforcement Learning" by Udemy
    - Focus: Practical implementation of MARL algorithms in Python.
    - Why It's Useful: Explores real-world applications of reinforcement learning in MAS.
2. "Distributed Systems" by MIT OpenCourseWare
    - Focus: The principles and challenges of designing distributed systems.
    - Why It's Useful: Relevant for understanding MAS communication and coordination.

2.3 Specialized Topics

1. "IoT for Beginners" by Microsoft Learn
    - Focus: Basics of IoT and its integration with smart systems.
    - Why It's Useful: Helps you connect IoT with MAS frameworks like CrewAI.
2. "Reinforcement Learning Specialization" by University of Alberta (Coursera)
    - Focus: In-depth reinforcement learning techniques, including applications in MAS.
    - Why It's Useful: Provides hands-on learning for optimizing agent behavior.

3. Tools and Frameworks

Practical tools and frameworks are essential for implementing MAS efficiently. Below are some of the most useful resources.

3.1 Frameworks

1. CrewAI
    - Description: A framework for building multi-agent systems.
    - Key Features:
        - Agent communication protocols.
        - Decision-making logic.
        - Scalable architecture.
    - Why It's Useful: Tailored for MAS development with real-world applications.
2. OpenAI Gym
    - Description: A toolkit for developing and testing reinforcement learning algorithms.
    - Why It's Useful: Simulates environments for training MAS.
3. JADE (Java Agent Development Framework)
    - Description: A framework for building distributed agent-based applications.
    - Why It's Useful: Provides tools for agent communication and task management.

3.2 Libraries

1. Stable-Baselines3
    - Description: A Python library for reinforcement learning.
    - Why It's Useful: Simplifies implementation of learning algorithms for MAS.
2. TensorFlow/ PyTorch
    - Description: Machine learning libraries.
    - Why It's Useful: Train neural networks for intelligent agent behaviors.
3. Flask/Django

- Description: Web frameworks for building interfaces for MAS applications.
- Why It's Useful: Enable interaction between MAS and external systems.

3.3 Tools for Simulation

1. MATLAB
   - Description: Simulation software for modeling MAS dynamics.
   - Why It's Useful: Useful for prototyping and mathematical modeling.
2. SUMO (Simulation of Urban Mobility)
   - Description: A traffic simulation tool.
   - Why It's Useful: Ideal for testing MAS in smart city traffic management.

4. Research Papers and Publications

Stay informed with the latest research through these platforms:

1. Google Scholar
   - Search for papers on MAS, reinforcement learning, and CrewAI-related topics.
2. arXiv
   - Find preprints on cutting-edge research in AI and MAS.
3. SpringerLink
   - Access journals and conference proceedings in the MAS domain.

5. Community and Forums

Engage with communities to ask questions, share knowledge, and collaborate on projects:

1. Stack Overflow
    - Ask technical questions and explore discussions related to MAS and AI.
2. Reddit: Subreddits like r/ArtificialIntelligence and r/MachineLearning.
3. CrewAI GitHub Repository
    - Contribute to the open-source project and collaborate with other developers.

The resources listed above provide a well-rounded foundation for further exploration of CrewAI and multi-agent systems. By leveraging these books, courses, tools, and communities, you can deepen your expertise, keep pace with industry trends, and contribute meaningfully to the field.